Antonyms in Mind a

Antonymy in Mind and Brain presents a multi-method empirical investigation of opposition with a particular focus on the processing of opposite pairs and their representation in the mental lexicon. Building on recent cognitive accounts of antonymy which highlight the fundamentally conceptual nature of antonymy, this book

- outlines previous literature to draw out criteria for good opposites and establish the state of the art on the question whether the strong connection of certain opposite pairs is primarily of a conceptual or lexical nature.
- presents a detailed cross-linguistic empirical study combining corpus data, speaker judgements and behavioural experiments for a wide range of central (e.g. *big:little*) and peripheral (e.g. *buy:sell; wife:husband*) opposite pairs to establish the contribution of individual factors.
- proposes a model of the representation of opposite pairs in the mental lexicon and illustrates how the processing consequences of such a model account for the patterns observed in the data.

The approach taken in this book highlights the importance of using a number of different methods to investigate complex phenomena such as antonymy. Such an approach forms the empirical foundation for a dynamic psycholinguistic model of opposition based on the conventionalisation and entrenchment of the conceptual and lexical relationship of antonyms.

Sandra Kotzor is a Senior Researcher in the Language and Brain Laboratory at the University of Oxford and Senior Lecturer in English Linguistics and Applied Linguistics at Oxford Brookes University.

Routledge Focus on Linguistics

Lexical Innovation in World Englishes
Cross-fertilization and Evolving Paradigms
Patrizia Anesa

The Pluricentricity Debate
On Austrian German and other Germanic Standard Varieties
Stefan Dollinger

Formalism and Functionalism in Linguistics
The Engineer and the Collector
Margaret Thomas

Understanding Abstract Concepts across Modes in Multimodal Discourse
A Cognitive Linguistic Approach
Elżbieta Górska

Multimodal Theory and Methodology
For the Analysis of (Inter)action and Identity
Sigrid Norris

Linguistic Description in English for Academic Purposes
Helen Basturkmen

Antonyms in Mind and Brain
Evidence from English and German
Sandra Kotzor

For more information about this series, please visit: https://www.routledge.com/
Routledge-Focus-on-Linguistics/book-series/RFL

Antonyms in Mind and Brain

Evidence from English
and German

Sandra Kotzor

Routledge
Taylor & Francis Group

LONDON AND NEW YORK

First published 2022
by Routledge
2 Park Square, Milton Park, Abingdon, Oxon OX14 4RN

and by Routledge
605 Third Avenue, New York, NY 10158

*Routledge is an imprint of the Taylor & Francis Group, an
informa business*

British Library Cataloguing-in-Publication Data
A catalogue record for this book is available from the British
Library

Library of Congress Cataloguing-in-Publication Data
Names: Kotzor, Sandra, 1980- author.
Title: Antonyms in mind and brain : evidence from English and
German / Sandra Kotzor.
Description: Abingdon, Oxon ; New York, NY : Routledge, 2022. |
Series: Routledge focus on linguistics | Includes bibliographical
references and index. |
Summary: "Antonyms in Mind and Brain: Evidence from
English and German presents a multi-method approach to the
investigation of lexical opposition using the language pair
English-German"-- Provided by publisher.
Identifiers: LCCN 2021035109 | ISBN 9780367461126
(hardback) | ISBN 9781032149592 (paperback) | ISBN
9781003026969 (ebook)
Subjects: LCSH: English language--Synonyms and antonyms. |
German language--Synonyms and antonyms. | English
language--Grammar, Comparative--German. | German
language--Grammar, Comparative--English.
Classification: LCC PE1591 .K68 2021 | DDC 428.1--dc23
LC record available at https://lccn.loc.gov/2021035109

ISBN: 978-0-367-46112-6 (hbk)
ISBN: 978-1-032-14959-2 (pbk)
ISBN: 978-1-003-02696-9 (ebk)

DOI: 10.4324/9781003026969

Typeset in Times New Roman
by MPS Limited, Dehradun

To my family

Contents

List of figures	xii
List of tables	xiv
List of abbreviations	xvi
Acknowledgements	xvii

PART I
Theoretical foundations   1

1 Introduction   3

  1.1 Background and aims 3
  1.2 Focus 5
  1.3 Structure of the book 7

2 Previous perspectives on antonymy   9

  2.1 What is lexical opposition? 10
  2.2 A Structuralist account of opposition 11
    2.2.1 Classifications of opposition: Lyons (1977) and Cruse (1986) 12
    2.2.2 Criteria for 'good' opposites 15
  2.3 Opposites in discourse: corpus perspectives 16
    2.3.1 Syntactic frames and co-occurrence patterns 17
    2.3.2 Semantic range and match of non-propositional meaning 18
    2.3.3 Textual functions 19
    2.3.4 Antonym order 20

2.3.5   *Key contributions of corpus research 21*
2.4   *Opposites in the mind: a lexical or conceptual relation? 21*
2.4.1   *A cognitive-pragmatic approach 23*
2.4.2   *Cognitive proposals 24*
2.5   *Opposites in the brain: psycholinguistic and neurolinguistic evidence 26*
2.5.1   *Psycholinguistic investigations 26*
2.5.2   *Neurolinguistic evidence 28*
2.5.3   *Key findings of cognitive and psycholinguistic antonym research 28*
2.6   *Towards a psycholinguistic model of antonymy – criteria for good antonyms 29*

PART II
Empirical investigation   33

3   Antonymic and associative strength: evidence from English and German   **35**

3.1   *Antonym selection 35*
3.1.1   *Type of antonymic relation 36*
3.1.2   *Morphological relatedness 39*
3.1.3   *Word class 39*
3.1.4   *Control items 40*
3.2   *Corpus data: measuring frequency of co-occurrence 40*
3.2.1   *Corpora 40*
3.2.2   *Analysis procedure 41*
3.3   *Assessing antonymic strength: a judgement task 41*
3.3.1   *Task and procedure 42*
3.3.2   *Participants 42*
3.4   *From best to worst: a judgement task analysis 42*
3.4.1   *Associative strength as a predictor for antonymic strength 43*
3.4.2   *Morphological relatedness 45*

3.4.3   *Gradable opposites: the role of symmetry*
         and conceptual distance 49
3.4.4   *Semantic range and semantic*
         generality 53
3.4.5   *Antonym order 55*
3.4.6   *Antonym type 58*
         3.4.6.1   *Verbal converses 59*
         3.4.6.2   *Nominal converses 61*
3.4.7   *Extending purity of opposition: the effect*
         of conceptual category structure 63
3.5   *Conclusions 67*

4   Processing opposite pairs: an antonym-decision task   70

4.1   *Rationale and design 71*
      4.1.1   *Task design 73*
      4.1.2   *Stimuli 73*
      4.1.3   *Participants 74*
      4.1.4   *Data cleaning and analysis procedure 74*
4.2   *Overview of results 74*
      4.2.1   *Antonymic strength*
               (judgement task scores) 75
      4.2.2   *Associative strength: frequency of*
               co-occurrence 78
      4.2.3   *Antonym sequence 81*
      4.2.4   *Symmetry of distribution 83*
      4.2.5   *Morphological relatedness 84*
      4.2.6   *Word class 85*
      4.2.7   *Antonym type 86*
4.3   *Conclusions 89*

5   Case studies   93

5.1   *Case study I: borrow:lend and rent:let – a*
      cross-linguistic comparison 93
5.2   *Case study II: a matter of size 96*
5.3   *Case study III: complementaries: pairs clustered*
      around male:female 104

PART III
Theoretical implications   115

6   **Antonyms in mind and brain: towards a psycholinguistic**
     model of opposition   117

    6.1   *Antonym canonicity: what makes an opposite pair*
        canonical? 117
        6.1.1   *Minimal and sufficient difference 118*
        6.1.2   *Morphological relatedness 119*
        6.1.3   *Purity and salience of opposition 121*
        6.1.4   *Symmetry 122*
        6.1.5   *Semantic range and generality 123*
        6.1.6   *Associative strength: a result of frequent*
              co-occurrence 124
    6.2   *Opposites in the mind: cognitive construal and*
        entrenchment of opposition 126
        6.2.1   *Antonymy as a prototype category 126*
        6.2.2   *The conceptual construal of opposites 127*
              6.2.2.1   *Complexity of category*
                       structure 128
              6.2.2.2   *Salience and context*
                       effects 130
              6.2.2.3   *Conceptual entrenchment 131*
    6.3   *Antonymy in the brain: a psycholinguistic model*
        of representation and processing 133
        6.3.1   *Lexical entries and the mental*
              lexicon 133
        6.3.2   *Looking up or working out? 137*
        6.3.3   *A psycholinguistic model of*
              opposition 139

7   **Conclusions**   148

    7.1   *What is antonymy? 148*
    7.2   *Methodological considerations 150*
    7.3   *Further implications 152*

Appendix 1	154
Appendix 2	160
Appendix 3	165
Appendix 4	170
Bibliography	172
Index	181

Figures

2.1 Classifications of opposition (Lyons, 1977 and Cruse, 1986)   13

2.2 Syntactic frames commonly containing (non-)canonical opposites (adapted from Jones, 2002; Jones et al., 2012; Davies, 2012)   18

3.1 Antonym judgements (QR) and co-occurrence data (FoC) for English (left) and German (right) TEMPERATURE pairs   46

3.2 Antonym judgements (QR) and co-occurrence data (FoC) for English (left) and German (right) for verbal converses   47

3.3 Antonym judgements (QR) and co-occurrence data (FoC) for English (left) and German (right) for nominal converses   64

4.1 RT (in ms) by judgement rating for English and German   77

4.2 RT (in ms) by frequency of co-occurrence   79

4.3 RT (in ms) for English pairs with a difference > 50 ms between sequences   82

4.4 RT (in ms) by morphological relatedness for English and German   85

4.5 RT (in ms) by word class for English and German   86

4.6 RT (in ms) by antonym type for English and German   87

4.7 Comparison of RT (in ms) and co-occurrence (left) and judgement scores (right) for English converse pairs   88

5.1 Antonymic relationships between *big*, *large*, *small* and *little*   97

5.2 Comparison of RT (in ms) for pairs on the SIZE continuum in English and German   99

5.3 Judgements scores and co-occurrence rates for pairs on the SIZE continuum in English (left) and German (right)   101
5.4 Comparison of RT (in ms) and co-occurrence (left) and judgement ratings (right) for English SIZE adjectives   102
5.5 RT (in ms) for GENDER pairs in English and German   106
5.6 GOE-rating and FoC for pairs based on male:female in English (left) and German (right)   108
5.7 Comparison of RT (in ms), co-occurrence rates and judgement ratings of GENDER pairs for English (top) and German (bottom)   113
6.1 Levels of lexical representation in the mental lexicon (based on Bock & Levelt, 1994; Levelt et al., 1999)   135
6.2 *Representations for* big:little *and* big:small   140
6.3 *Representations for* giant:dwarf   142
6.4 *Representations for* mother:father   143

Tables

2.1 Main classes of binary opposition in Lyons 1977 and
Cruse 1986   14

2.2 Criteria for good antonyms   31

3.1 *English and German sample stimuli* (whole-page table
in separate file)   37

3.2 Ten highest and lowest scoring pairs in the judgement
task in English and German (shaded pairs are present
in both languages)   44

3.3 Cross-linguistic differences in morphological relatedness   50

3.4 Pairs on the TEMPERATURE scale ordered by English
GOE-rating scores   51

3.5 Pairs with discrepancies greater than 0.5 in the
English and German judgement task   56

3.6 Verbal converses (ordered by English overall
GOE-rating)   60

3.7 Comparison of verbal converses and canonical
antonyms by FoC   61

3.8 Nominal converses (ordered by English overall
GOE-rating)   62

3.9 Attribute listing results for GIANT and DWARF   66

3.10 Attribute listing results for RIESE and ZWERG   66

4.1 Summary of behavioural results for individual factors   76

4.2 RT by judgement ratings and antonym type
(*denotes statistical significance)   77

4.3 RT for antonym types by frequency of co-occurrence
for English and German   80

4.4 RT for pairs by antonymic strength and frequency of
co-occurrence for English and German   81

5.1 Data for pairs on the SIZE continuum (ordered by
English judgement score)   98

5.2 Opposite pairs based on *male:female* (ordered by
    English GOE-rating)   105
5.3 Attribute listing results for father, Vater, mother,
    Mutter   110
5.4 Attribute listing results for woman, Frau, man, Mann   111
A.1 English and German word pairs included in the
    judgement task   154
A.2 Frequencies, t-scores and judgement ratings for all
    English pairs   160
A.3 Frequencies, t-scores and judgement ratings for all
    German pairs   165
A.4 Target stimuli for the antonym decision task   170

List of Abbreviations

BNC   British National Corpus
FoC   frequency of co-occurrence
GOE   goodness of exemplar
LDCE   Longman Dictionary of Contemporary English
OED   Oxford English Dictionary
OALD   Oxford Advanced Learners' Dictionary
RT   reaction time

Acknowledgements

There are a great many people who have contributed to this book either directly or indirectly but any shortcomings are, of course, my own responsibility. As the empirical study is based on my PhD dissertation, I would first like to thank my supervisors, Aditi and David, and examiners, Mary and Frans, for their support, encouragement and constructive comments, not only during the course of writing my dissertation but far beyond that. They, and many other colleagues subsequently, have nurtured my intellectual curiosity and given me a great number of opportunities to develop my thinking, knowledge and skills.

Many colleagues, whose roles as sounding boards for various aspects of this book have been absolutely invaluable, also deserve a mention here. I would like to express my gratitude to Aditi for her unwavering support over the last decade, Linda, Allison and Isabella for listening to me while I tried to disentangle my thoughts regarding the theoretical implications of my work and invariably providing constructive feedback, Rachele for our goal-setting and writing meetings and Steven for his patience and attention to detail in proofreading the manuscript. My thanks also go to the team at Routledge who supported and encouraged me at every stage.

Finally, my family and friends (linguists and non-linguists alike) have motivated me and believed in me, often more than I did myself, and they were all instrumental in the completion of this book, whether they realise it or not. They provided encouragement or distraction and without them this would have been a very different journey.

Part I
Theoretical foundations

1 Introduction

1.1 Background and aims

The notion that human thought, and the way we see the world, is determined by binary concepts is not a recent one; it has been shared by many, and there are countless examples which lend support to this view – not just in language.[1] The mere fact that Richard Wilbur chose to write a whole series of children's poems on opposites (Wilbur, 2000, 2004) highlights the fact that binary opposition forms part of our 'education' (in the widest sense) and provides a structuring mechanism to make sense of the world.

In academic discourse, binary concepts, such as *dichotomy*, are key terms in Western economics, sociology, mathematics, philosophy, logic and many other fields which deal with a wide range of different topics. Opposition has been a key component of logic since the 4th century BC, and Aristotle's square of opposition[2] is the foundation for much research in the field.

From a linguistic perspective, much work has centred on binarity, negation (cf. Zimmer, 1964; Horn, 1989; Kjellmer, 2005) and opposition (cf. Ogden, 1967; Clark, 1972[3]; Lehrer & Lehrer, 1982; Lehrer, 1985) in fields such as formal semantics, syntax and lexical semantics as well as in computational linguistics and language acquisition. Lakoff and Johnson (1980), for example, provided support for the idea that opposition is a fundamental cognitive structuring principle by illustrating the construction of a number of conceptual metaphors with an inherently binary structure which underlie many of the metaphorical expressions we use in everyday language (e.g. *Things are finally looking up.* vs. *I'm feeling down*).

This book examines the word pairs that we use to express opposed concepts from a cognitive and psycholinguistic perspective on the basis of a cross-linguistic empirical study of opposite pairs in English and

DOI: 10.4324/9781003026969-1

German. The main aim is the proposal of a model of the representation and processing of opposition which is based on empirical evidence and can account for the factors which have been identified as influential in the creation and entrenchment of opposite pairs. In order to achieve this, two additional questions have to be considered: the validity of a categorical division of opposites into canonical and non-canonical pairs and the long-standing question whether the relation of opposition holds between concepts or between the words encoding these concepts.

Despite the large amount of research in the field of opposition, several questions have only recently received renewed interest and remain controversial. Firstly, ever since the early empirical investigations into opposition, there has been a debate about whether antonymy[4] is a lexical relation between words or a semantic one between the concepts encoded by said lexemes (cf. among others Gross et al., 1989; Miller & Fellbaum, 1991; Cruse, 1992; Charles et al., 1994; Murphy, 2003; Paradis et al., 2009; Jones et al., 2012). Is antonymy simply based on the contrastive association of certain words which becomes conventionalised in our mental lexicon, or are the meanings of these words, and their oppositeness, the guiding factor in the association process? Croft and Cruse (2004, p. 164) start their chapter on opposition by reminding the reader that 'like all sense relations, oppositeness is a matter of construal, and is subject to cognitive, conventional and contextual constraints.' Thus, if, as many recent proposals suggest, different types of constraints are at work in antonym construal,[5] how can the respective contributions of conceptual and lexical effects be assessed? There is still much discussion on this issue and the choice of a multi-method approach used in the present research aims to address this question more fully, in particular through a cross-linguistic comparison between English and German opposite pairs.

Another key question, which has yet to be answered comprehensively, is which factors have the greatest influence on antonymic strength. Several criteria have been proposed, such as word class, purity of opposition and symmetry, and there have been several studies examining the contribution made by each of these factors. Many earlier studies focused on canonical adjectival antonyms while, more recently, others have taken into account a wider range of antonymic relationships (among others Jones, 2002; Paradis et al., 2009; Jones et al., 2012; Davies, 2012; van de Weijer et al., 2014; Kostić, 2015b) but there is often still a distinction made between canonical and non-canonical opposition with the underlying assumption that there are fundamental differences between these two categories.

The contribution of the current research is not only the inclusion of a large number of opposites which are not generally considered part of the central core of antonyms but also the use of different empirical measures to gather several sets of data in two languages, which are then compared and contrasted to reveal discrepancies and similarities. These serve as starting points for further investigation of the role of conceptual and lexical factors in the generation, conventionalisation and entrenchment of antonym pairs in the mental lexicon. Within the cognitive and psycholinguistic approach taken here, this allows for the integration of these factors into one coherent model which can be applied to all types of opposites and provide explanations for their relative strength of opposition.

1.2 Focus

The notion of opposites is interpreted more broadly in this book than in most previous research, in order to encompass pairs at the boundaries of the category of lexical opposition, because it is very frequently the case that an analysis of the differences between peripheral and central cases of a phenomenon leads to valuable insights as to what makes the central members particularly good representatives (e.g. prototype categories – Taylor, 1989, 1990; Vandeloise, 1990; Cruse, 1990, 1994; Ungerer & Schmid, 2006). Therefore, the range of opposite pairs in the study includes pairs from different word classes as well as a large number of non-canonical pairs (e.g. *excellent:atrocious, work: play, king:queen, buy:sell*). Some of these pairs are deliberately modified to be weaker than related canonical pairs (e.g. *freezing:hot* vs. *cold:hot*) in order to allow for systematic investigation of the factors which influence speaker judgements of the strength of an antonymic relation (e.g. symmetrical distribution on a scale in the example here).

Furthermore, the present research makes use of several distinct empirical methods to investigate antonymy: corpus studies, judgement tasks, attribute listing and behavioural experiments. The results of these different empirical techniques are brought together, and it is the comparison of data in this comprehensive data set that enables a detailed analysis of the discrepancies. These differences, as well as broader patterns observed in the data, are of crucial importance in informing the fundamental questions this research is aiming to address. The selection of word pairs combined with the multi-method approach remains relatively rare in antonym studies (with the exception of work such as Paradis et al., 2009 or Jones et al., 2012) and allows for conclusions which are not only able to advance the study of antonymic relations in lexical semantics and psycholinguistics but also contribute to the evaluation of the methods used in antonym research.

This book addresses three overarching questions which are to a certain degree interdependent: the answer to the first question determines the scope of the second and both have an impact on the treatment of the third.

1. Is antonymy a relation between concepts or between the lexemes which encode these concepts? How are antonyms processed and stored in the mental lexicon?
2. Is antonymy a gradient phenomenon or is there a clear distinction between canonical and non-canonical opposites?
3. What factors determine the antonymic strength of an opposite pair on a canonicity continuum or, if the data supports a categorical division between canonical and non-canonical opposition, how are word pairs assigned to one category or the other?

Many scholars (among others Cruse, 1986; Lyons, 1977; Gross & Miller, 1990; Mettinger, 1994; Muehleisen, 1997; Jones, 2002; Murphy, 2003)[6] propose the division of opposites into two clearly defined subgroups: a category of 'canonical' opposites and one of 'non-canonical' pairs. However, it is never firmly established which features determine membership of the former category, and whether a pair automatically falls into the latter if it does not meet a certain set of criteria. Questions (2) and (3) are both related to this previous theoretical standpoint. Recent approaches, which are based on a broader range of empirical data, show growing support for a continuum approach to antonymy. However, the question of what criteria influence the 'goodness' of any given opposite pair remains, and many still propose a central core of canonical opposites (e.g. Paradis et al., 2009). Evaluation of the factors which allow for an accurate prediction of the antonymic strength of any opposite pair is a key component of this study.

Question (1) centres on the focal point of a long-standing debate spanning at least two decades, with one camp advocating a conceptual approach and claiming that the lexical relatedness and high associative strength of conceptually opposed word pairs is a result of this opposition and the other claiming that the strong associative bond between the two lexemes, which is entrenched through frequent co-occurrence, is the source of their high degree of opposition. Both sides have provided evidence which supports their arguments, but this evidence is rarely comprehensive and often includes only very central phenomena of opposition. This book will thus bring together the different strands of research, including recent corpus and psycholinguistic research, and evaluate the theoretical proposals with the support of evidence from three distinct methodological perspectives using a wide range of English and German opposite pairs.

1.3 Structure of the book

This book is divided into three main sections: theoretical foundations (Part I), empirical evidence (Part II) and an evaluation of the implications of the experimental evidence and proposal of a cognitive-psycholinguistic model of antonymy in the mental lexicon (Part III). Chapter 2 introduces the phenomenon of lexical opposition, addresses definitional issues and introduces theoretical classifications of opposition. It then brings together current perspectives on lexical opposition with a focus on recent work from corpus and cognitive perspectives to provide the foundation for the empirical investigation and determine a set of criteria for 'good' opposition which forms the foundation for the data analysis presented in Part II.

The data collected during this study (Part II) is presented in three parts. The first, Chapter 3, introduces the rationale behind the selection of German and English antonym pairs used in the empirical investigation, and presents measures of associative strength in the form of corpus data as well as the results of cognitive judgement tasks such as goodness-of-exemplar ratings and attribute listing tasks. These results establish the degree of antonymic and associative strength of the antonym pairs in the study.

Chapter 4 focuses on the results of the behavioural experiments and builds on the analysis presented in Chapter 3. In both chapters, the factors affecting antonymic strength introduced in Chapter 2 are evaluated in the light of the data. This allows for the investigation of correspondences and discrepancies in different data types, which provides support for the effect individual criteria have on lexical opposition. Certain factors, such as purity of opposition, are reframed from a cognitive perspective and the structure of the conceptual categories of each member of the antonym pair is considered as an important factor in determining antonymic strength.

The last chapter in Part II (Chapter 5) contains three detailed case studies, each focused on a different set of opposite pairs: gradable pairs on the SIZE scale, converses and a cluster of complementary pairs around *male:female*. While the first two empirical chapters focused on analyses, these case studies allow for a more detailed, qualitative approach. Each case study revisits a discrepancy in the previously presented data sets which allow for the probing of the relative contributions of conceptual and lexical factors to antonymic strength.

Part III relates the empirical findings to the theoretical perspectives introduced in Part I and returns to the overarching questions this study set out to answer. In Chapter 6, the factors affecting antonymic strength are re-evaluated and their contribution to the antonymic relationship is summarised on the basis of the empirical findings. Lexical opposition is considered as a cognitive prototype category, with its members distributed on a continuum of opposition and each pair's place dependent on conceptual, contextual and cultural factors. The question of the relative contribution of conceptual and lexical factors is addressed and a model of the representation and processing of opposite pairs is proposed, defining antonymy as a fundamentally cognitive relation which can be lexically entrenched by frequent association. Chapter 7 provides a summary of the questions asked and answered as well as an evaluation of the methodological approach used in this study and sets out possible ways to further advance our understanding of antonymy in mind and brain.

Notes

1 Needham (1987, blurb) calls opposition 'an elementary and necessary mode of thought' and a 'constant feature of the human mind' while Saussure (1916) considers opposition one of the basic tenets of structuralism.
2 See Kneale and Kneale (1962) for a discussion of Aristotle's square of opposition.
3 The developmental angle has been investigated in several studies aside from Clark 1972 (e.g. Nelson, 1977; Jones & Murphy, 2005; Murphy & Jones, 2008).
4 Antonymy is used here as a synonym of opposition, rather than in its more specific sense referring only to gradable adjectival opposite pairs (see section 2.1).
5 Meaning in cognitive linguistics is not fixed but constructed which is generally referred to as *construal* (Ungerer & Schmid, 2006).
6 This is not to say that all these scholars support the 'lexical categorical model' (Gross & Miller 1990), but they have worked with the assumption that there are two groups of opposites which are, at least to some extent, definable.

2 Previous perspectives on antonymy

As indicated in the introduction, not all opposites are created equal. Theoretical accounts of opposition from different perspectives, e.g. structuralist (e.g. Lyons, 1977; Cruse, 1986) and cognitive (Cruse & Togia, 1995; Murphy, 2003; Paradis, 2005), have proposed a number of categories of opposites based on their logical, conceptual and pragmatic perspectives. These subcategories show different behaviours in language use and conceptual construal, but it has not been firmly established what role they play in the perceived degree of opposition and the representation and processing of opposites in the mind and brain. In this chapter, we will first provide a definition of antonymy and briefly introduce structuralist classifications of antonymy, as much of this terminology is still widely used and the effect of their underlying logical properties on canonicity is evaluated in Part II.

This is followed by an overview of previous theoretical and empirical research on opposition from a number of different perspectives. Corpus-linguistic (e.g. Mettinger, 1994; Jones, 2002; Kostić, 2015b; Hsu, 2015; Hassanein, 2018), cognitive (e.g. Murphy, 2003; Paradis, 2005; Jones et al., 2012, Paradis et al., 2015) and psycholinguistic (e.g. Paradis et al., 2009; Willners & Paradis, 2010; van de Weijer et al., 2012, 2014) accounts will be outlined in order to determine the essential properties of canonical opposition and establish a set of criteria which can be tested empirically. A second key function of this overview is to determine the current state of the art regarding the question whether antonymy is a relation between lexical items or between concepts. These current positions are then developed into a model of the storage and processing of opposites supported by the data presented in Part II of this book.

DOI: 10.4324/9781003026969-2

2.1 What is lexical opposition?

The concept of opposition has a long history and several terms are used for the same, or very similar, phenomena. The English words *opposition* and *opposite* are both in regular use from the 14th century onwards, and although both have been used in narrower senses within specialist terminology, they are very firmly part of speakers' everyday vocabulary.

Antonym, however, is a more specific term and a comparatively recent addition coined in 1867 (Preface 6) by C. J. Smith as a counterpart to *synonym*. In linguistics, the use of the term *antonymy* is heavily influenced by the categorisations of opposition proposed by Lyons 1977 and Cruse 1986 (cf. also Cruse, 1976), who use *antonymy* to refer solely to gradable adjectival pairs of opposites (e.g. *hot:cold* [1] or *long:short*). Recently, however, the term has been applied more broadly to include other phenomena of opposition. This is also the definition of the term *antonymy* adopted here: a concept which subsumes all phenomena of lexical opposition which are perceived as such by the average native speaker of a language.

The concept of lexical opposition and the fact that there are certain words which have opposites and others which do not are familiar concepts. If a layperson was asked to provide the opposite of *happy*, they would almost certainly respond very quickly with either *unhappy* or *sad*, and if asked for the opposite of *long,* the response would be *short*. No complex explanations are needed of what constitutes an opposite – it seems to be a rapid intuitive decision (Chaffin & Herrmann, 1984). However, the question *What is the opposite of* **work**? is more difficult to answer, and the responses would likely be more varied: for example, *fun, free time, play* or *relaxation*. Speakers find it relatively easy to determine the degree of opposition between two concepts or words and are able to make clear distinctions between what they consider 'good' and 'bad' opposite pairs.[2] There are many cases where this decision depends strongly on the context in which these concepts are presented (e.g. Murphy, 2003; Croft & Cruse, 2004). Take, for instance, *dry:sweet*, which is a very opposite pair when used in the context of choosing wine or sherry but not an ideal pairing when talking about food. While there are many word pairs which satisfy the criterion of being in some way conceptually opposed (*bow:curtsey* for example – one (stereo) typically performed by a man, the other by a woman), only a fairly small number are extremely closely related and are the kind of pairings for which, when people are asked, their answer can be predicted with reasonable certainty.

Opposites are also extremely frequent in everyday speech and are often used as a rhetorical tool, for emphasis and to create or underscore a contrast (e.g. *we take care of everyone, the young and the old*). Opposition is an emergent lexical relation and children are introduced to it very early. We tend to divide things into *good* and *bad*, *allowed* and *forbidden*, *right* and *wrong* to simplify complex situations with which we are confronted in everyday life. It has been shown that children use opposites as frequently as adults and in a variety of functions (cf. Clark, 1972; Jones & Murphy, 2005; Jones, 2007; Murphy & Jones, 2008) from very early on in their linguistic development. This prevalence of opposites, and the ease with which we accept them as a natural part of our linguistic repertoire as well as a tool which aids us in compartmentalising our experiences, suggests that the concept of binary opposition functions as a fundamental cognitive structuring principle (Croft & Cruse, 2004).

In addition, there is evidence that lexemes which encode opposing concepts are closely related to each other in the mental lexicon. This evidence comes from two investigative strands: psycholinguistic experiments such as elicitation, word association and lexical decision tasks and the analysis of speech errors. The study of mistakes made in natural speech provides insights into how utterances are constructed and at which points this production can go wrong (cf. among others Fromkin, 1973; Cutler, 1981). Replacing one member of an antonym pair with another is a common selection error and utterances such as *Go and have a cold shower!* (instead of *hot*) or *Well, she's not very young* (instead of *old*) occur fairly frequently. This suggests a close link between the two items in the lexicon. The contribution made by psycholinguistic experiments, for example word association (among many others Deese, 1964/1965), elicitation (Paradis et al., 2009; Willners & Paradis, 2010) and lexical decision tasks (Gross et al., 1989, Charles et al., 1994; Sabourin & Libben, 2000; van de Weijer et al., 2014), are outlined alongside evidence from corpus studies and judgement tasks after the introduction of theoretical classifications of opposition.

2.2 A Structuralist account of opposition

The most thoroughly studied type of antonym is the gradable, adjectival antonym (*good:bad*; *hot:cold*), as opposite pairs of this type display the most overtly interesting linguistic characteristics (such as markedness and polarity) with regard to their behaviour in, for example, question formation, comparatives and superlatives. Furthermore, adjectives are considered the prototypical lexical category for antonymic relations due to their conceptual simplicity (Jones et al., 2012) and many of the studies introduced here focus their attention solely on adjectival opposite pairs. However, there are also numerous well-established nominal and verbal antonym pairs which are not derived from, or related to, an adjectival pair. Hence a comprehensive discussion of antonymy has to take into account that, despite being most prominent and prototypical among adjectives, the phenomenon also occurs in all other open word classes and also, very strongly, among certain prepositions (cf. Cruse, 1986).

2.2.1 Classifications of opposition: Lyons (1977) and Cruse (1986)

The best-known structuralist classifications of opposition are those by Lyons (1977) and Cruse (1986). Although their introspective approaches have been criticised as subjective and not empirically substantiated (e.g. Jones, 2002, p. 20), they have nevertheless provided many linguists with a foundation for their own investigations of antonymy. Furthermore, the proposed categories (cf. Figure 2.1) have given important insights into the linguistic behaviour of antonyms. Both scholars have also made attempts at describing the features of the canonical antonym and provided some of the fundamental criteria of good antonymy (cf. Section 2.1.2).

Lyons (1977: 275), who bases his work on antonymy on the categories proposed by Sapir (1944), states that the 'most common opposites in English tend to be morphologically unrelated' but that they are outnumbered by morphologically related pairs. He claims that morphologically unrelated antonyms show the dichotomy central to opposition best as the lexical items have nothing at all in common (e.g. *good:bad, high:low*).

Lyons' initial distinction was drawn between binary and non-binary contrasts but, while all categories are illustrated in Figure 2.1, only binary contrasts and their subsequent subdivision by Cruse (1986) will be introduced here. Lyons' classification of binary contrast consists of five categories while Cruse (1986) divides this into three types, and in both classifications only one of these categories is labelled 'antonymy' (see Table 2.1).[3] Cruse (1986) subsumes Lyons' categories of orthogonal and antipodal opposition under directional opposition as both are fundamentally directional in nature, very specific and only include a small number of items. However, Cruse then divides directional opposition into four sub-types: directions (e.g. *up:down*), antipodals (e.g. *top:bottom*), counterparts (e.g. *ridge: groove*) and reversives (e.g. *rise:fall; tie:untie*).

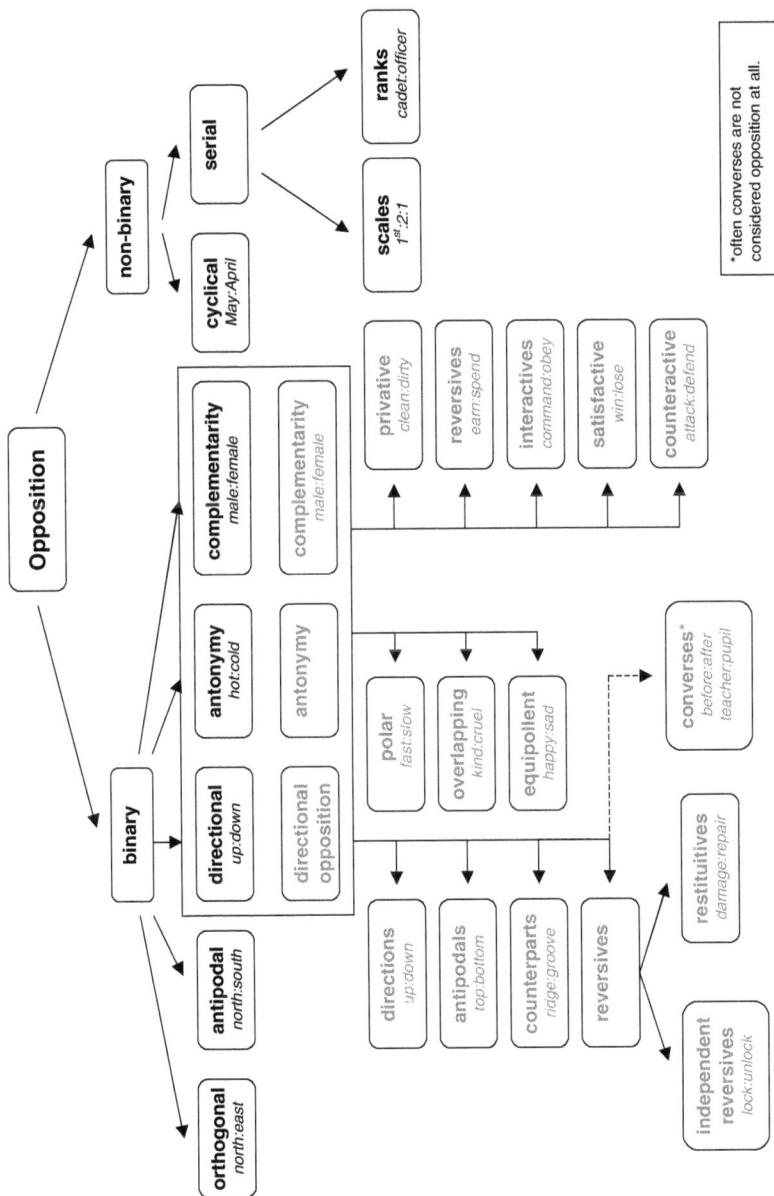

Figure 2.1 Classifications of opposition (Lyons, 1977; Cruse, 1986).

Table 2.1 Main classes of binary opposition in Lyons 1977 and Cruse 1986

Lyons 1977	Cruse 1986
Orthogonal opposition	Directional opposition
Antipodal opposition	
Directional opposition	
Antonymy	
Complementarity	

In addition to directional opposition, there are three further sub-categories which are relevant here: antonyms, complementaries and converses (which are not always considered part of opposition). Antonymy proper only includes fully gradable adjectives which denote a certain degree of a variable property (Cruse, 1986). The more strongly intensified these adjectives are, the further apart on a scale they move (*hot:cold – extremely hot:extremely cold*). Antonyms do not strictly bisect a domain; as illustrated in (2.1) and (2.2), something can be neither hot nor cold (*tertium datur*; Lyons 1977). This middle region, however, is usually not lexicalised (with some exceptions: e.g. *tepid, warm*).

2.1   *The tea was hot.* = *The tea was not cold.*
2.2   *The tea was not cold.* ≠ *The tea was hot.*

In the second category, that of complementarity, the two terms bisect a domain between them and cover it completely. There is, at least logically, no third possibility (*tertium non datur*; Lyons 1977), for example, *married:unmarried, true:false* or *dead:alive*. The negation of one member of the pair implies the affirmation of the other (see Examples 2.3 and 2.4) and Cruse (1986) calls this the conceptually simplest type of opposition.

2.3   *The budgie was dead.* = *The budgie was not alive.*
2.4   *The budgie was alive.* = *The budgie was not dead.*

Complementary pairs are usually adjectives or verbs (and derived nominal pairs, e.g. *success:failure*) but some also have gradable uses (e.g. *Which shirt is cleaner?* or *I feel very alive today.*)
    Converses (e.g. *buy:sell, parent:child*), also called relational opposition, are sometimes excluded from theoretical classifications of opposition proper (e.g. Lyons 1977; Cruse 1986). While all converses are based on a spatial notion, they are not restricted to the spatial domain

(e.g. *below:above*) but can be extended by analogical or metaphorical processes (*before:after*). Lexical converses often express a relationship between two entities (e.g. *father:son, teacher:pupil, husband:wife*) or an event or interaction from two different perspectives (e.g. *come:go, borrow:lend*). Converses are an important type of opposition in this investigation as they include a large number of verbal and nominal opposite pairs and thus allow for an investigation of criteria beyond the adjectival pairs that have traditionally been examined. The empirical part of this book (Part II) includes representatives from all central categories of opposition in the investigation and examines the effect of type of opposition on speaker judgements and the processing of pairs with different logical properties.

2.2.2 Criteria for 'good' opposites

The theoretical accounts above provide the starting point for a catalogue of criteria for good opposites. The first criterion which is considered essential for opposition is that of binarity. For good opposites, this opposition must be not just binary but inherently binary, as almost all pairs of co-hyponyms (e.g. *cat:dog*) can be construed in a binary way with the appropriate contextual support. In addition, the property of gradability has been shown to affect linguistic patterns such as combination with quantifying adjectives as well as cognitive construal (Cruse & Togia, 1995). It is, however, not yet clear whether this distinction affects the degree of perceived opposition and/or the representation and processing of opposition.

Cruse also proposes three further conceptual and distributional criteria which he considers crucial for 'good' opposition (Cruse, 1986, p. 262): ease of cognitive construal, purity of opposition and matching non-propositional meaning. Each of these is illustrated briefly below. The first criterion contains two important factors in antonym judgement:

a   ease of construal of a uni-dimensional scale and
b   symmetrical distribution on this scale

The positive effect of a readily available scale on the degree of antonymy can be seen in many of the most canonical adjectival opposite pairs: *big:little* (SIZE), *fast:slow* (SPEED), and *hot:cold* (TEMPERATURE). Cases where establishing this salient scale is more difficult, for example *work:play, town:country*, or *dry:sweet,* often require greater contextual support because they do not have an inherent scale along which the members of the pair differ.

The second criterion in (b) proposes that the best opposites are distributed symmetrically and are equidistant from the mid-point of the scale (cf. also Lehrer & Lehrer, 1982). However, if we apply these criteria to the TEMPERATURE scale, pairs such as *boiling:freezing, hot:-cold, warm:cool* are all symmetrical and equidistant from the midpoint of the scale. Among those examples, *hot:cold* is arguably the best pair despite the fact that all follow the criteria proposed so far. Thus, further criteria are needed to successfully distinguish these three pairs.

The second factor Cruse (1986) proposes is purity of opposition. There are opposites whose meaning is largely determined by the underlying opposition, which are therefore more basic than others. For instance, Cruse claims that '[...] *father* and *mother* are weaker opposites than *man* and *woman*, which, in turn, are weaker than *male* and *female*' (Cruse, 1986, p. 262). Greater complexity, with the resulting loss of salience of the opposing property, is considered detrimental to the recognition and judgement of the antonymic relation (see also Paradis, 2005; Jones et al., 2012).

The third additional criterion introduced by Cruse (1986) is the requirement for a close match in non-propositional meaning. Essentially, the two lexemes concerned should share a similar range of application and similar collocational restrictions. Effects of register, connotations and collocational range all play a part in the match or mismatch of non-propositional meaning. Cruse uses the example of *tubby* and *emaciated* which, while conceptually opposed, are not a good opposite pair as they are used in clearly distinct registers and have very different connotations.

Beyond the early, purely theoretical work on opposition, antonymy has been researched widely from a number of different perspectives and this empirical research has generated a number of models of the phenomenon. To establish the current positions in the field, seminal and more recent research from three fields, corpus-linguistic, cognitive and psycholinguistic, is outlined in the following sections. This survey will result in a catalogue of criteria for antonymic strength and an understanding of the positions regarding the nature of the antonymic relationship. This provides the foundation for the design, analysis and discussion of the data in Part II and the psycholinguistic model of opposition proposed in Part III.

2.3 Opposites in discourse: corpus perspectives

The main focus of corpus studies of antonyms is examining their use in text (and, more recently, speech; Jones 2006, 2007), the patterns of usage and functions antonymy fulfils in discourse and what this may reveal about the nature of the relation of antonymy. After a number of early corpus investigations in the 1990s (e.g. Justeson & Katz, 1991; Mettinger, 1994; Fellbaum, 1995), antonymy has received renewed interest from corpus linguists more recently (e.g. Jones, 2002; Jones & Murphy, 2005; Jones, 2007; Paradis et al., 2007; Kostić, 2015b), and a number of cross-linguistic studies (e.g. Paradis et al., 2009 and Willners & Paradis, 2010) and work on languages other than English (e.g. Muehleisen & Isono, 2009 for Japanese; Lobanova et al., 2010 for Dutch; Willners & Paradis, 2010 for Swedish; Kostić, 2011, 2015b for Serbian; Storjohann, 2015 for German; Hsu 2015, 2017 for Chinese; Hassanein, 2018 for Classical Arabic) have contributed rich data to this growing body of research. Corpus studies have provided evidence for co-occurrence patterns of antonyms, textual functions, canonicity and the sequencing of opposition as well as making an important contribution to the debate regarding the lexical or conceptual nature of the relation of opposition.

2.3.1 *Syntactic frames and co-occurrence patterns*

Early corpus studies established the co-occurrence patterns of opposites in text (e.g. Justeson & Katz, 1991, 1992; Mettinger, 1994; Fellbaum, 1995) in certain syntagmatic or contextual frames with characteristics that would pre-dispose them to the contrastive use of antonyms (e.g. *X or Y*). They found that adjectival opposites not only co-occurred in texts at a higher than chance rate but that these occurrences were tied to specific, often contrastive, syntactic frames. Fellbaum (1995) extended the work on adjectives to nouns and verbs, which she, and others since, also found to co-occur in the same sentence but in different structures from adjectival pairs. Jones (2002) provided a thorough investigation of 56 English opposite pairs which serves as the foundation for much of the current research into antonym co-occurrence.

Beyond the identification of co-occurrence patterns, Paradis et al. (2007), for instance, conducted a large-scale corpus study of ten adjectives and their opposites (as determined in elicitation experiments; Paradis et al., 2009) to determine the co-occurrence patterns of antonyms within certain syntactic frames (see Figure 2.2 for examples). Their aim was twofold: to assess whether this method could be used as an antonym-detection tool (i.e. if a lexeme is put in the X slot, the Y slot should be filled with an antonymically related word) and whether the co-occurrence rates can be used as measures of antonymic strength.

X and Y (alike)	from X to Y	more X than Y
between X and Y	X versus Y	X instead of Y
both X and Y	whether X or Y	X not Y
(either) X or Y	X rather than Y	not X but Y

Figure 2.2 Syntactic frames commonly containing (non-)canonical opposites (adapted from Jones, 2002; Jones et al., 2012; Davies, 2012).

If the above examples were used in a corpus search with *hot* in the X position, *cold* should head the list of results generated for Y. While most results in this study were largely consistent with the elicitation task results reported by Paradis et al. (2007), some of the results for Y in certain frames were not antonyms of the lexeme in the X position (2007, p. 9); for example, *boring* triggered *dull* as well as antonymically related adjectives such as *interesting* or *exciting*. Co-ordinating constructions like *either X or Y* and *both X and Y* thus seem to be able to be used with more than one meaning or discourse function. As the number of studies have increased both in English and other languages, additional frames have been proposed for both canonical opposition and non-canonical pairs (Izutsu, 2008; Davies, 2012). Paradis et al. (2007) equate co-occurrence in a larger number of syntactic frames with increased antonymic strength. Thus, those pairs which show the greatest breadth of co-occurrence across the possible syntactic frames are likely to be the most canonical.

Simple co-occurrence data merely reflects associative strength and also reflects collocations, unique binominals and other frequently co-occurring items which are not antonymically related. Co-occurrence in these (inherently) contrastive syntactic frames, however, favours opposites and thus the investigation of the behaviour of opposites in certain contexts is a more reliable measure of antonymy than co-occurrence data. However, automatic extraction studies, such as Lobanova et al. (2010), also result in a large number of non-antonymic pairs which occur in the same frames at greater-than-chance rates. Thus, as proposed in conceptual models of antonymy (Jones et al., 2012), co-occurrence in these frames can only be considered a contributing, rather than a determining factor of antonymic strength or canonicity.

2.3.2 Semantic range and match of non-propositional meaning

Building on Cruse's (1986) notion of matching non-propositional meaning (as well as work by Lehrer and Lehrer (1982) on distribution and Lyons (1995) on collocational restrictions), Muehleisen (1997) conducted a study which combines corpus data and the use of learners' dictionaries with texts from English literature to determine the semantic range of certain adjectival opposite pairs. Her underlying assumption is that 'good opposites also describe the same kinds of things' (Muehleisen, 1997, p. 113). The patterns found in her data support the intuition that better antonyms should have a larger overlapping range than more peripheral pairs. Thus, her findings led her to introduce the term *semantic range* as a factor in antonym canonicity.

This notion of semantic range is very similar to Jones' (2002) breadth of co-occurrence and Jones et al.'s (2012) semantic generality and will be used here to encompass these concepts. In terms of antonym canonicity, those items which both share the greatest amount of semantic range (including connotational meaning) and have the broadest range of applicability (are very general in their use) make the best antonym pairs (Muehleisen, 1997). Thus, for example, *dry:wet* is a better pair than *humid:arid* due to its greater applicability in a variety of contexts and both are better pairs than, for instance, *dry:humid* or *wet:parched*, for which the range of the individual pairs is not well matched. Muehleisen (1997) also considers higher frequency of co-occurrence a result of a larger overlap in semantic range, rather than the lexical co-occurrence being the driving factor in greater shared applicability.

2.3.3 Textual functions

In his seminal corpus study of English opposites, Jones (2002) identified eight distinct textual functions of antonymy based on certain syntactic frames. Two types, ancillary and co-ordinated antonymy, emerge as the two most prominent functions in Jones' study of English opposite pairs and this dominance is also attested in similar studies in a number of different languages such as Swedish (Murphy et al., 2009), German (Storjohann, 2015), Chinese (Hsu, 2017) and Arabic (Hassanein, 2018). In ancillary antonymy, the antonym pair functions as a lexical signal of a nearby contrast which is not necessarily entrenched in the lexemes used to express the contrast (e.g. *It is meeting **public** need not **private** greed*). This results in a sentence with two contrast relations, in which the antonymous contrast underlines the contrast of what Jones calls the 'B-Pair' (*need-greed* in the example above). In coordinated antonymy, however, the antonymous pairs indicate the inclusiveness or exhaustiveness of a scale and are usually conjoined by *and* or *or* (*the rich as well as the poor, both high and low incomes*).

The fact that antonyms fulfil different discourse functions which can either highlight or hide their 'oppositeness' is an important point to bear in mind with regard to antonymic strength. The frequent contrastive use of two members of an antonym pair can strengthen both the conceptual entrenchment and the associative connection between the two lexemes.

2.3.4 Antonym order

Another feature of opposite pairs which has been raised by corpus research (e.g. Jones, 2002; Murphy, 2006; Kostić, 2015a; Wu, 2017) is the order or sequence in which the two members of an antonym pair occur. Jones (2002) was one of the first to explicitly investigate this distribution and found that most pairs (42/56) favour a particular sequence (e.g. *good:bad* vs. *bad:good*). The criteria proposed to underlie this preference are morphology (base:derived, e.g. *healthy:unhealthy*), positivity (positive:negative, e.g. *true:false*), magnitude (more:less), chronology (earlier:later, e.g. *begin:end)*, gender (male:female), phonology (tendency to separate identical/similar syllables), idiomaticity (frequent use in a certain combination), frequency (more frequent:less frequent) and markedness (unmarked:marked).

Kostić's (2015a) investigation of Serbian opposite pairs subsumes many of the factors proposed by Jones (2002) under markedness, and she adds two additional factors not covered by markedness: temporal or visual-spatial ordering and gender. She proposes that markedness as a basic principle can explain most sequencing orders. Wu (2017), however, argues that markedness, in the sense used by Kostić (2015a; based on Waugh, 1982), is too general a concept and that many of the same factors which contribute to markedness also contribute to sequencing preferences. Based on Kostić's (2015a) suggestion that markedness is an effect of the cognitive figure-ground distinction (with the unmarked member the ground and the marked member the figure), Wu (2017) proposes a cognitive account of antonym ordering with iconicity as the principle underlying antonym sequence. Both Kostić and Wu argue for an approach based on conceptual, and in Kostić's case, pragmatic factors.

While there is no one comprehensive explanation for all sequencing effects or for the fact that not all antonym pairs have a preferred sequence, this is an important criterion to consider in a model of lexical representation. It is also a methodological consideration when designing psycholinguistic experiments, as the order of presentation may affect the reciprocal strength of the links between the lexical items (e.g. *good* may elicit or activate *bad* more easily than the reverse) due to the frequency of use of this pair in that particular order, which results in an asymmetry in the strength of their connection.

2.3.5 Key contributions of corpus research

Key factors regarding the behaviour of antonyms are frequency and breadth of co-occurrence and sequencing. Canonical antonyms co-occur significantly more frequently and in a broader range of syntactic frames than non-canonical pairs. This high incidence of co-occurrence is generally seen as a result of a strong conceptual opposition and broad semantic range rather than its cause. However, there have also been proposals which see the basis of antonymy on the lexical level and propose canonical antonyms as a structuring mechanism of the mental lexicon. These contrasting perspectives, and the debate they have generated, will form the starting point for the following overview of research on the representation and storage of opposites in the brain.

2.4 Opposites in the mind: a lexical or conceptual relation?

There has been a long-standing debate in the field of antonym studies about the nature of the relation of antonymy. Some argue that it is a purely lexical relation and that opposites can be divided into direct and indirect opposites in a categorical fashion (e.g. Miller, 1998; Charles & Miller, 1989). There are many, however, who consider this view overly simplistic and argue for a conceptual account of antonymy (e.g. Paradis et al., 2009; Jones et al., 2012) as a gradable prototype category with better and worse examples (e.g. Herrmann et al., 1986; Murphy & Andrew, 1993; Croft & Cruse, 2004; Jones et al., 2012). Most recent work, however, still attributes special status to a certain number of highly canonical pairs (e.g. Jones et al., 2012; van de Weijer et al., 2014) – a proposal which may have consequences for lexical representation and processing. Lexical and conceptual approaches will be outlined briefly below to draw out the main arguments and determine the empirical evidence necessary to lead to a better understanding of the nature of opposition and its representation in the lexicon.

An early psycholinguistic model of the organisation of the English lexicon, *WordNet* (Gross et al., 1989; Gross & Miller, 1990), was proposed based on earlier knowledge and assumptions about the way lexical and semantic information is stored in our minds, and proposed antonymy as a possible structuring principle of the adjectival lexicon (as also proposed by Deese (1965) on the basis of early word association experiments). The creators of *WordNet* take the stance that 'antonymy is a lexical relation between word forms, not a semantic relation between word meanings' (Miller, 1990, p. 242) and propose a system that relies on a clear distinction between semantic and lexical relations. This approach (e.g. Gross et al., 1988, 1989; Charles & Miller, 1989; Gross & Miller, 1990; Miller, 1990) is based on the observation that near-synonyms of antonymous lexemes, while semantically opposed, are generally not considered a canonical antonym pair. *Ascend*, for example, is considered a synonym of *rise* but *ascend:fall* is not considered a particularly good antonym pair and neither is *rise:descend*. The canonical pairs here are, of course, *rise:fall* and *ascend:descend*. Therefore, the relation established here is not one between the semantic meaning of the words, as the direct and indirect pairs are synonymous, but between the word forms themselves.

In this proposal, the principal connecting devices are direct antonym pairs which are linked in the mental lexicon, whereas indirect pairs which are conceptually but not lexically opposed are considered to be linked via the corresponding direct pair. Thus, the processing of indirect (non-canonical) antonyms, such as *soggy:parched* or *humid:arid*, would be mediated by the direct antonym pair *wet:dry*, which is connected on the lexical level. This explains the slower recognition speeds of indirect relations found in several experimental studies (e.g. Herrmann et al., 1979; Gross et al., 1989) which have been shown to be modulated by conceptual distance (Charles et al., 1994). This approach, while supported by some empirical evidence, does not account for the flexibility with which opposites are used, especially in context, as has been demonstrated amply in the previous section on corpus linguistic studies.

There have since been several challenges to this categorical division between direct and indirect opposites and the lexical basis of direct opposition. As early as 1986, Herrmann and colleagues proposed antonym canonicity as a scalar property rather than a categorical one. They conducted an antonym judgement task which resulted in a distribution of judgements along a five-point scale. They propose that judgements are influenced by conceptual criteria similar to those suggested by Cruse (1986). Murphy and Andrew (1993) also consider antonymy a relation between opposed concepts and attribute no special status to direct antonyms as far as the type of relation is concerned. Stylistic, connotational and morphological factors are included in their explanation of differences in the degree of opposition. Their experimental research required informants to provide antonym responses either in isolation or in a noun phrase and measured the degree of agreement between the two contexts. For example, when provided with the lexeme *fresh* in three contexts – *fresh shirt*, *fresh idea* and *fresh fish* – the antonyms provided did not match. The replies given were, for example, *dirty shirt*, *old idea* and *frozen fish* (cf. Murphy & Andrew, 1993; p. 306). This shows that even those pairs considered canonical are strongly context-dependent, which firmly points towards a conceptual basis and representation of opposition. Two further, more recent accounts of opposition which emphasise the importance of the conceptual opposition are outlined in the following sections. The model proposed by Jones and colleagues (2012) constitutes the most comprehensive cognitive model of antonymy to date.

2.4.1 A cognitive-pragmatic approach

In a pragmatic approach, Murphy (2003) considers opposites (and other semantic relations) in order to determine their status in the human mind and to model the processes involved in determining semantic relations (Murphy, 2003, pp. 4f.). She proposes the relational contrast principle (Murphy, 2003, p. 44) which functions on the basis of minimal difference and states that parings among semantic relations of all kinds (e.g. synonymy, antonymy, meronymy etc.) are minimally different, albeit in different ways. For antonymy, this relational principle is extended into RC-LC (Relation by Contrast – Lexical Contrast) which is seen as a relation between word-concepts. This means that opposites share all relevant features but one, but Murphy does not base this directly on semantic meaning as this broader principle also includes non-canonical contextual examples and allows for different 'ideal' pairings in different contexts (e.g. *smooth/bumpy* journey, *smooth/rough* paper, *smooth/lumpy* cake; Murphy, 2003, p. 174).

Unlike the structuralist accounts, rather than focusing on stable denotational meaning, this approach highlights the salience of particular aspects of meaning in certain contexts. Lexical factors, such as phonological or morphological properties, are also considered to contribute to the perceived strength of the antonymous relation. Thus, even words which are not overtly semantically related can be construed as opposites in context and the category of opposites includes more and less stable (or canonical) pairs which need varying degrees of contextual support in order to function as antonyms. Thus, Murphy (2003) considers fine-grained classifications of opposition, such as those introduced above, irrelevant for a conceptual approach. Instead she advocates a general definition which can account for all opposites as well as ad hoc construals in context and the prototype effects displayed by this category. The key criteria for opposites emerging from this account are those of minimal difference and, at the same time, the largest possible degree of similarity of contextual properties in any given context.

2.4.2 Cognitive proposals

There have been a small number of proposals which model antonymy within cognitive linguistic theory. Starting from a structuralist foundation, Cruse and Togia (1995) proposed a model of gradable adjectival antonyms based on the cognitive principles of schema (Lakoff, 1987), domain and construal (Langacker, 2008),[4] which was then extended further in Cruse (2000) and Croft and Cruse (2004). They consider schematic domains, such as SCALE and ANTONYMY in interaction with content domains (e.g. MERIT or TEMPERATURE), resulting in the construal of the content domain in terms of a greater or lesser degree of its core property (e.g. something having a higher or lower temperature). This cognitive account was extended to included non-gradable opposites (Paradis, 2005) which are not based on a scalar dimension but which are BOUNDED (i.e. a domain is split along a boundary with each member of an opposite pair occupying one side, e.g. *dead:alive*). In line with other cognitive approaches, Paradis advocates a conceptual evaluation as the basis of opposition, where the oppositeness is one between construals of meaning rather than between lexical items encoding those concepts (cf. also Croft & Cruse, 2004).

This cognitive approach is further developed, supported by a range of empirical work, by Jones et al. (2012) within the framework of Lexical Meanings as Ontologies and Construals (LOC) introduced by Paradis (2005). In their cognitive construal account, Jones et al. propose a model of antonymy as a conceptually based relation which is flexible and dynamic. Their aims are twofold: to explain the construal of two lexical items in any given occurrence and to account for the evidence that some opposite pairs are 'better' than others (Jones et al., 2012, p. 129).

With regard to the first aim, they propose antonymy as a dynamic phenomenon based on the cognitive notions of ontologies (conceptual structures which can be lexicalised; e.g. concrete objects, events, abstract notions) and construals (cognitive processes which are used to construct meaning in language use).[5] In the construal of any antonym pair, whether it is a highly conventionalised (e.g. *good:bad*) or a more contextually dependent pair (e.g. *dark:milk* with regard to chocolate), the two members of a pair always bisect a domain. This results in a BOUNDED configuration for all lexical items used as binary opposites even if they are, out of context, UNBOUNDED (i.e. scalar; *hot:cold*) or not usually considered opposites at all (see Jones et al., 2012, p. 135). If the domain is a more complex one where multiple dimensions are present, then the success of the antonymic construal is dependent on the salience of the opposing dimension which can be foregrounded by the context. Thus, in language use, pairs of words are either construed antonymically or they are not, which results in a categorical distinction with all pairs construed as opposites considered equivalent.

The second part of the proposal considers antonymy as a prototype category, with members ranging from highly canonical (conventionalised) pairs at its core to peripheral ones at the boundary. Adjectives are generally perceived as some of the most canonical examples, and this is explained in terms of conceptual category structure (e.g. Paradis, 2005). Regardless of their word class, the best opposite pairs are conceptually simple and often inherently binary (either in the SCALE or BOUNDARY configuration depending on gradability, e.g. *hot:cold* or *dead:alive*). Adjectives, spatial expressions (e.g. *up:down*), abstract nouns (*absence:-presence*) and common verbal opposites (*accept:reject*) are all conceptually relatively simple and often refer to bounded events or actions (Jones et al., 2012). This conceptual simplicity, which is similar to Cruse's (1986) purity of opposition, is crucial as it facilitates binary construal. In addition to being conceptually predisposed for antonymic construal, canonical opposites are, according to Jones et al. (2012), also very strongly associated and individually frequent, as well as co-occurring frequently due to being widely applicable. They emphasise very strongly, however, that the frequent co-occurrence and resulting conventionalisation of a pair are the effect of strong conceptual opposition rather than its cause.

These investigations foreground the conceptual nature of antonymy based on cognitive construal rather than an association of certain lexemes and provide the following crucial conceptual criteria which further develop the factors proposed by Cruse 1986: ease and salience of binary construal and 'semantic generality' (Jones et al., 2012, p. 141), which corresponds to Cruse's match of non-propositional meaning. Frequent co-occurrence is not considered a key property as it is simply an effect of the conceptual relation and the overlap of semantic applicability of the two members of a pair. These factors emerged as the most significant in a body of empirical work from different methodological perspectives. An overview of this research is the focus of the following section.

2.5 Opposites in the brain: psycholinguistic and neurolinguistic evidence

In the last decade, the representation and processing of antonymy, and sense relations in general, have become of interest to psycholinguists and neurolinguists in the context of the study of the structure of the mental lexicon. Over the last decades, our understanding of how language is represented in the brain, and more specifically how words and relationships between them are stored and computed in processing, has improved vastly. However, there are many questions which still remain unanswered. Two which are relevant here are, firstly, what information is stored in the lexicon (e.g. meaning, phonological form, orthographic form) and how is this knowledge structured? Secondly, how is this information used during language comprehension and production? While there is now convincing evidence for the conceptual basis of opposition, such as that informing the models presented above, little research has been conducted on the storage and processing of opposite pairs from a psycholinguistic or neurolinguistic perspective which goes beyond the lexical account provided by the WordNet group. Some recent multi-method studies have included psycholinguistic experiments and there is also some neurolinguistic evidence, which is summarised below and forms the foundations for the present research and the psycholinguistic model of opposition proposed in Chapter 6.

2.5.1 *Psycholinguistic investigations*

Recent work has taken an approach similar to that adopted in this book, combining different methods to obtain a better understanding of the precise nature of antonymy. Paradis et al. (2009) and Willners and Paradis (2010),[6] for instance, use a combination of corpus-driven and psycholinguistic methods to investigate antonym canonicity in English and Swedish. Their aims are similar to those of the present research. They investigate whether antonymy is a lexical relation, with representations of opposite pairs stored or linked in the mental lexicon, or a conceptual relation, where opposite pairs are computed 'online' in any given situation. Paradis et al. (2009) furthermore tackle the question whether lexical entrenchment is the consequence of a strong conceptual relation or whether the conceptual relation is strengthened by frequent co-occurrence of the two members of an antonym pair. The main hypothesis put forward is that there is a small core of very strongly entrenched opposite pairs with a much larger proportion distributed along a continuum of canonicity (Paradis et al., 2009, p. 381). This hypothesis seems to be confirmed by the data collected despite the fact that the different methods used do not always result in entirely compatible patterns. Both studies employed corpus methods, an offline elicitation task and an online judgement task.

It seems clear that the elicitation task used by Paradis et al. (2009, p. 414) and Willners and Paradis (2010) shows that antonymy is indeed a gradient phenomenon which manifests in the category-internal prototypicality structure of lexical opposition, with the exception of a small set of highly canonical opposites. Both psycholinguistic tasks (elicitation and judgement tasks) employed in the two studies show a significant difference between those central antonyms and more peripheral antonymic pairs (Paradis et al., 2009, p. 414; Willners & Paradis, 2010, p. 38). In their online judgement task, Willners & Paradis (2010) also controlled for antonym sequence and predicted differences for certain pairs based on markedness accounts (see Section 2.3.4) but, interestingly, these were not borne out by the data.

In order to determine the role played by frequent co-occurrence in psycholinguistic experiments, van de Weijer et al. (2012) conducted a visual lexical decision task with adjectival word pairs which were either antonymically related (e.g. *horizontal:vertical*) or semantically unrelated (*little:nice*) and exhibited either high or low frequency of co-occurrence. The words were presented in isolation and primes either directly preceded targets (with a 1500 ms inter-stimulus interval) or were separated by one or two intervening items. Their results show no facilitation effect for unrelated words at all (regardless of co-occurrence rates) and no difference in the response times between high and low frequency opposites which reliably resulted in priming. Based on these findings, van de Weijer et al. claim that the facilitation observed in antonyms is not a result of lexical association (entrenched by frequent co-occurrence) and conclude that conceptual or semantic relation is more important and that antonymy is essentially conceptual in nature. However, considering the time course of word processing, there may well be a lexical-associative element which was not captured in their task, as the lag time between primes and targets was relatively long and automatic associative effects on the basis of form occur very early in processing (Cutler, 2012).

2.5.2 Neurolinguistic evidence

Neurolinguistic studies remain particularly rare. One such study (Jeon et al., 2009) investigated the processing of synonyms and antonyms contrastively using functional magnetic resonance imaging (fMRI) techniques in combination with a behavioural elicitation task. Jeon et al. (2009) advocate a conceptual feature-matching process and explain the spatial difference in the processing of synonymy and antonymy which can be seen in the fMRI data as a result of 'reversing the semantic meaning in one dimension and finding opposite features in case of antonyms' (Jeon et al., 2009, p. 453). The similarities in activation are, according to Jeon et al. (2009, p. 455), due to the activation of the bundle of shared semantic features of the two concepts, whether antonymous or synonymous.

In what is, so far, the only electrophysiological study on antonym canonicity, van de Weijer et al. (2014) used event-related potentials (ERPs) in an EEG study on antonym canonicity in Swedish adjectives. They compared the processing of canonical antonyms (*black:white*), non-canonical antonyms (*white:dark*) and unrelated word pairs (*dark:small*) in two experiments: pairs were presented in isolation in one, and following a contextually related noun in the other (e.g. GLASS; *full:empty*). Participants had to decide whether the pairs presented were opposites or not. The second word of a pair was presented after either 200 ms or 800 ms to determine possible effects of controlled processing (van de Weijer et al., 2014, p. 2). Both experiments showed that the N400 component, an indicator of facilitation of access (e.g. Kutas & Federmeier, 2011), was significantly reduced for canonical opposites in comparison with non-canonical and unrelated pairs but non-canonical opposites only showed a facilitation effect in the second experiment where a context was provided. The authors conclude that non-canonical pairs depend on context to facilitate access to the semantic domain in which the antonymic relation is construed. The study does not make any claims regarding the underlying reasons for the greater amount of facilitation obtained by the canonical pairs, and the authors propose a number of factors for their conventionalised pairings.

2.5.3 Key findings of cognitive and psycholinguistic antonym research

The cognitive and psycholinguistic research on antonymy presented in this section provides support for the conceptual criteria put forward in early theoretical accounts and, in many cases, has resulted in a further development of these criteria. The symmetric distribution of opposites on an easily identifiable scale and the complexity of the conceptual category (as originally proposed by Cruse 1986) have been found to strongly affect antonym judgements as well as their co-occurrence patterns (e.g. Jones et al., 2012). The importance of minimal difference and the salience of the opposition were highlighted along with context effects which even played a role in highly canonical pairs (Murphy, 2003). Semantic range or semantic generality (Jones et al., 2012) has also been shown to have a strong effect, but frequency of co-occurrence, which was considered an important factor in early psycholinguistic models of antonymy (e.g. Gross et al., 1989; Charles & Miller, 1989), is mostly considered a consequence of strong conceptual opposition rather than its cause.

Antonymy is seen as a fundamentally conceptual relation, with opposite pairs distributed along a continuum of canonicity largely dependent on their inherent conceptual properties with the possible exception of some highly canonical pairs (see among many others Paradis et al., 2009; Jones et al., 2012). A number of (interrelated) factors have been proposed which affect the perceived strength of opposition between two members of an antonym pair. There are now detailed cognitive models of the conceptual construal of opposition which explain many of the effects observed in empirical research. What has not yet been addressed, however, is the representation and processing of opposite pairs and how the criteria for good opposition and the patterns of data they create can be integrated into a psycholinguistic model of antonymy. The empirical studies presented in Part II will be used to inform such a proposal, which accounts for all previously proposed factors and aims to provide a unified mode which can account for the processing patterns of all opposite pairs. Before the data is presented, the criteria determining antonym canonicity resulting from the research presented above are summarised as they form the basis of the design and analysis of the empirical work.

2.6 Towards a psycholinguistic model of antonymy – criteria for good antonyms

All research on opposites divides opposition into good and bad (or better and worse), 'canonical' and 'peripheral' or 'systemic' and 'non-systemic' antonyms. In some accounts, the distinction is largely based on speaker intuition while others take empirical results such as word association experiments, judgement tasks, corpus data or reaction time experiments as the basis for this division. While, as just outlined above, the field of antonym studies has moved away from the notion of a strict binary distinction between canonical and non-canonical opposites (e.g. Herrmann et al., 1986; Mettinger, 1994; Davies, 2012; Jones et al., 2012), many studies still attribute special status to a select number of core pairs which elicit specific data patterns (e.g. Murphy, 2003; Paradis et al., 2009; van de Weijer et al., 2014).

It has proven difficult to disentangle the factors which determine an opposite pair's place on the canonicity continuum, and while both lexical and conceptual factors have been put forward, recent proposals have shifted towards a conceptual basis of antonymy and often consider co-occurrence phenomena as a consequence of a strong underlying conceptual opposition which is based on a number of factors (Jones et al., 2012). This view also provides comprehensive explanations for the ad hoc construction of contextually based antonymic relations, which must be the result of online cognitive construal because they have no conventionalised lexical basis.

However, as antonymy is a relation based on minimal difference, any difference – lexical or conceptual – weakens this opposition (e.g. Murphy & Andrew, 1993). The best antonyms will generally only differ in one respect, which will usually be a salient conceptual one. Differences in the encoding of opposing concepts may also play a role in the perception of this salient difference and have a contributory effect. This applies to factors such as morphological relatedness as, early on, Lyons (1977) observed that the best opposites are morphologically unrelated. In terms of processing, morphologically related items have caused much debate regarding their representation in the lexicon and many proposals argue that derived lexemes (e.g. *unhappy*) are not represented in a separate lexical entry but are separated into their constituent parts and are computed via the root (*happy*) and the prefix (*un-*). Thus, both items in a morphologically related opposite pair would essentially be represented by the same entry in the lexicon. Another aspect which may be more crucial in a psycholinguistic account is the lexical association between two members of a pair which has become conventionalised and entrenched through frequent co-occurrence, as such relations can show strong facilitatory effects which point towards a link on the lexical level of representation.

To generate a dataset that is as comprehensive as possible in terms of the factors which can be evaluated, the choice and design of opposite pairs in this study was guided by the factors proposed by the body of work introduced in this chapter. Table 2.2 provides a summary of these criteria.

Table 2.2 Criteria for good antonyms

Criterion	Previous evidence
Frequency/breadth of co-occurrence	• Canonical opposites co-occur extremely frequently in a wide range of contexts/syntactic frames (e.g. Jones, 2002)
Morphological relatedness	• Not extensively studied • Unrelated pairs generally more canonical than related pairs
Sequencing	• Some pairs show strong sequencing preferences (Jones, 2002; Kostić, 2015a, Wu, 2017) • Sequencing can be determined by both conceptual and lexical (e.g. phonological) factors • No effect found in previous psycholinguistic studies (e.g. Willners & Paradis, 2010)
Semantic range/semantic generality	• Greater overlap of semantic range increases canonicity (e.g. Muehleisen, 1997, Murphy, 2003) • Canonical pairs are less restricted in their use (Jones et al., 2012)
Conceptual category structure	• Canonical opposites have simpler conceptual structures (Paradis, 2005; Jones et al., 2012) • Strongly related to word class and accounts for primacy of adjectival pairs
Binary construal/salience of opposite dimension	• All oppositions are binary (Jones et al., 2012) • Canonical opposites are inherently binary along a conceptually salient dimension (Cruse, 1986)
Symmetry	• Canonical pairs are usually symmetrically distributed on a salient scale (e.g. Cruse, 1986, Jones et al., 2012)
Antonym type	• Early studies considered gradable antonyms the most canonical (e.g. Lyons, 1977; Cruse, 1986) • Cognitive accounts make no distinction between scalar and bounded opposition • Differences have not been investigated in psycholinguistic studies

The present study takes the possibility of a difference in the processing and representation of canonical and non-canonical opposites as a working hypothesis, as some previous research highlights a lexical-associative contribution in certain cases of antonymy. In order to address the question(s) whether there is a categorical distinction between canonical and non-canonical opposites, and if so, which criteria determine which category a pair belongs to, the data presented in Part II has been designed to directly investigate the effect of the criteria summarised above and assess their influence on both antonym judgements on a conceptual level and the conclusions which can be drawn for the representation of the antonymic relationship in the mental lexicon.

Notes

1 The format *lexeme:lexeme* will be used for all opposite pairs in this book.
2 There is no value judgement associated with the use of *good* or *bad* for opposite pairs; these terms are widely used in research and here are considered synonymous with *canonical* and *non-canonical/peripheral*.
3 Both accounts provide very detailed categorisations of opposition which are not discussed in full here but can be found in the original texts and also in Mettinger (1994) and Croft and Cruse (2004).
4 These three concepts are only explained insofar as they are directly relevant to an understanding of the theoretical approach proposed here. For a detailed account of all three see Ungerer and Schmid (2006).
5 For a more detailed account of their model, see Jones et al. (2012), Chapter 7.
6 Their research is summarised and extended in Jones et al. (2012), which provides an excellent overview of antonymy in English.

Part II
Empirical Investigation

3 Antonymic and associative strength: evidence from English and German

As other recent work has shown, several different measures are necessary to assess the nature of the relationship between the two members of an antonym pair and identify the factors which affect the strength of this relation. In this study, three main methods are used to collect a data set which allows for robust conclusions regarding the nature of antonymy and its possible storage and processing in the mental lexicon. Firstly, co-occurrence data from corpora is used to assess the lexical-associative strength of the two members of an antonym pair, a measure which is very strongly influenced by how often the two items are used together, especially in certain sentential frames (e.g. Jones, 2002; 2.3.1). The second set of data comes from an antonym judgement task to assess perceived antonymic strength (or antonym canonicity) and the third from an antonym decision task where participants' reaction times are measured (Chapter 4). This chapter introduces the stimulus selection and methods of data collection before presenting an analysis of the results of the English and German data gathered using corpora and judgement ratings. The different data sets are then compared to determine the correlation between associative strength and antonymic strength and to assess the effect of the individual factors proposed in previous research on perceived antonymic strength, which were used to guide the choice of antonym pairs used as stimuli.

3.1 Antonym selection

The 210 opposite pairs in this study were carefully selected according to the lexical and conceptual criteria proposed to influence antonym canonicity (see Table 2.1). Rather than including only canonical pairs, or canonical pairs with indirect counterparts (e.g. *wet:dry* and *soggy:parched*), less conventional pairings (*tea:coffee, landline:mobile* or

DOI: 10.4324/9781003026969-3

credit:debit) which conform to certain criteria and antonym types such as converses (*buy:sell*) are also included. Certain pairs are designed to cluster around a canonical gradable or non-gradable pair to allow for the investigation of criteria such as symmetry (e.g. *big:little* vs. *big:tiny*), conceptual distance (*lukewarm:tepid* vs. *hot:cold*) and complexity of category structure (e.g. *male:female* vs. *mother:father*). Table 3.1 illustrates the types of opposites included and a full list for both languages can be found in Appendix 1. The German data set is based on the English pairs using direct translations wherever possible. However, 38 pairs had to be replaced as there were no suitable translation equivalents; replacements were chosen to match the salient features of the English pairs they were replacing. Thus, the German questionnaire contains almost exactly the same distribution of opposite pairs as the English questionnaire (see Table 3.1).

3.1.1 Type of antonymic relation

Antonym type, according to the structuralist classifications introduced in Section 2.2.1, was an important factor in choosing antonym pairs for this study, as it is not clear whether these classifications, including properties such as gradability, do in fact influence judgements of antonymy. Thus, pairs beyond the traditional 'best' examples of binary, gradable, adjectival opposite pairs (e.g. *cold:hot*), such as nominal and verbal converses, were also included. All pairs were chosen for particular properties, e.g. very strong predicted antonymic or associative strength, the systematic violation of criteria for 'good' antonymy or cross-linguistic differences.

In addition to canonical gradable opposites (e.g. *good:bad*), the stimuli also include non-canonical gradable pairs, with many constructed around a central, canonical pair to form a word field of related pairs. It is not always easy to distinguish between gradable and non-gradable antonym pairs since certain pairs have an absolute and a gradable member and some, such as *clean:dirty*, seem to be borderline gradable (e.g. Cruse, 1986, p. 203). As this is mostly a formal distinction, all pairs containing an absolute member are included in the category of non-gradable opposition for analysis purposes.

The set of stimuli also contains a number of verbal and nominal converse pairs (e.g. *student:teacher*) and reversatives (e.g. *pack:unpack/einpacken:auspacken*). These pairs were chosen to determine whether the more complex conceptual structure and relationship (Paradis, 2005) between the members of these pairs are detrimental to their antonymic strength. They also provide diversity in terms of word class.

Table 3.1 English and German sample stimuli (whole-page table in separate file)

Language	English			German[*]		
Type	n	Canonical examples	Further examples	n	Canonical examples	Further examples
Gradable pairs (antonyms)	69	dark:light old:new good:bad hot:cold big:little	dark:pale old:young excellent::atrocious; bad:excellent warm:cool; boiling::freezing; hot:cool† tiny:huge; large:small, small:huge	66	dunkel:hell alt:neu gut:schlecht heiß:kalt groß:klein	dunkel:blass alt:jung exzellent:miserabel; exzellent:schlecht warm:kühl; kochend:eisig; heiß:kühl winzig:riesig; klein:riesig
Non-gradable pairs (complementaries)	58	right:wrong male:female	right:incorrect; wrong:suitable father:mother, king:queen, bull:cow	60	richtig:falsch männlich:weiblich	richtig:inkorrekt; falsch:passend Vater:Mutter; König:Königin; Bulle:Kuh
Converses	19	life:death buy:sell come:go doctor:patient	keep:sell; rent:let flee:chase; escape:hunt	18	Leben:Tod kaufen:verkaufen kommen:gehen Arzt:Patient	behalten:verkaufen; mieten:vermieten fliehen:jagen; ausbrechen:jagen

(Continued)

Table 3.1 (Continued)

Language	English			German*		
Type	n	Canonical examples	Further examples	n	Canonical examples	Further examples
Directional opposites	3	pack:unpack dress:undress damage:repair	tenant:landlord; employer:employee	3	einpacken:auspacken anziehen:ausziehen beschädigen:reparieren	Mieter:Vermieter; Arbeitgeber: Arbeitnehmer
Spatial opposites	10	in:out up:down over:under	next to:opposite far:near together:apart	8	hinein:hinaus hoch:runter über:unter	neben:gegenüber weit:nah zusammen:alleine
Morphologically related pairs	23	unhealthy: healthy unhappy:happy	healthy:sick – healthy:unhealthy happy:sad – happy:unhappy	28	ungesund:gesund unglücklich:glücklich	gesund:krank; gesund:ungesund glücklich:traurig; glücklich:unglücklich
Non-antonym pairs	43		sad:unhappy; book:page; blue:orange	42	traurig:unglücklich;	Buch:Seite; blau:orange

Note
* There are no glosses here as all pairs are in the same position as their English equivalents.

The category of spatial opposites is small as these items form a closed-class system. These pairs were included to determine whether spatial opposites, which are generally considered excellent examples of opposition, are similarly 'good' examples in both languages.

3.1.2 Morphological relatedness

To determine the effect of morphological relatedness on antonymic strength, which is particularly relevant for a psycholinguistic model of antonymy as, in the psycholinguistic approach taken here, regular morphologically related items are represented by the same lexical entry (e.g. Baayen et al., 1997), both morphologically related and unrelated pairs are included in the stimulus set. The number of unrelated pairs is much larger (187 vs. 23 for English and 182 vs. 28 for German) as the other factors to be evaluated are more evident in unrelated pairs and as these are likely to be more broadly distributed along the canonicity continuum.

The morphologically related pairs cover all common negative prefixes (*un-, in-, dis-*) and some pairs are composed of one item with a negative prefix and a morphologically unrelated conceptual opposite (e.g. *exact:imprecise*; German *exakt:unpräzise*). In both the German and English questionnaire, the morphologically related pairs are expected to be rated relatively highly in the judgement task due to their overt antonymic relationship.

3.1.3 Word class

As it has been established that the best examples of antonymy are adjectives, the questionnaire shows a clear bias towards adjectival pairs (E: 63.94%; G: 65.24%). However, due to the inclusion of converses, there is also a comparatively large number of nouns (E: 22.12%; G: 23.33%) and verbs (E: 11.54%; G: 11.43%), including a number of verb-noun conversion pairs in English (e.g. *escape:hunt*). Prepositions were also included (E: 4.33%; G: 5.23%) along with single additional pairs (e.g. adverbs or quantifiers: E: 2.4%; G: 1.43%).

Members of a pair always belong to the same word class, and in English, zero-derived pairs were either classed according to frequency (if both members could be part of two lexical categories) or the unambiguous member of the pair was used to guide classification, as participants would be more likely to interpret the other item as belonging to the same lexical category. The inclusion of different lexical categories is necessary to assess the effect of the complexity of conceptual structure attested in previous literature (e.g. Paradis, 2005; Jones et al., 2012) and an attribute listing task using a subset of stimuli is used to further examine this hypothesis (Section 3.4.7).

3.1.4 Control items

To ensure a balance of scores across the whole rating scale in the judgement task and to determine whether informants had understood the task correctly, a number of control items were included (English: 43; German: 42). All items display some measure of associative strength resulting from relatedness or frequency of co-occurrence: meronyms (*book-page, hand-finger*), synonyms (*yell-call, sad-unhappy, clever-helle* 'smart-bright'), co-hyponyms (*mug-cup, dog-cat, blau-orange* 'blue-orange'), hyponyms (*animal-dog, flower-rose*), associative score or frequency of co-occurrence (*fish-fowl, chicken-egg, hot-humid, König-Krone* 'king-crown') or are structurally similar to antonym pairs (*helpful-helpless, flammable-inflammable*) due to their morphological properties.

3.2 Corpus data: measuring frequency of co-occurrence

It is evident from the growing number of corpus studies that opposites fulfil important discourse functions and co-occur with much greater frequency than chance would predict. These co-occurrence patterns are generally considered very reliable indicators of antonymic strength (cf. Justeson & Katz, 1991; Fellbaum, 1995; Jones, 2002; Jones et al., 2012) and have also been used to detect antonyms and investigate novel opposite pairs (e.g. Jones, 2007; Davies, 2012). The degree of frequency of co-occurrence (FoC) is used as a measure of associative strength in this study, and the two corpora used for German and English and the analysis procedures are introduced below.

3.2.1 Corpora

Individual frequencies for all English lexemes in the questionnaire were extracted from the British National Corpus (BNC World) using the BNC concordancer Sara98. The BNC contains over 100 million words of written (90%) and spoken (10%) English from a wide variety of sources. The co-occurrence data for the German pairs was extracted from the corpus of the Institut für Deutsche Sprache (IDS Mannheim) using their web-based user interface COSMAS II.[1] This corpus is the biggest freely available German-language corpus and the part used in the present research[2] consists of over two billion word-forms.

3.2.2 Analysis procedure

Co-occurrence data was collected for both *lexeme1-lexeme2* and *lexeme2-lexeme1* combinations to allow for a later analysis of sequencing preferences. The aim was not to use particular syntactic frames as other studies have done but simply to establish co-occurrence rates in any syntactic structure, as any frequent co-occurrence of two items will lead to an entrenchment of the connection between them which may not necessarily be antonymic in nature. The total number of co-occurrences within a span of five words within the same sentence was used to calculate *t*-values which indicate whether the co-occurrence rates are greater than chance would predict. *T*-tests were used to compare the co-occurrence patterns both within and across languages (especially considering the size difference of the corpora). Despite the fact that *t*-values are sometimes considered less reliable in data sets with less statistical power, this method works satisfactorily in conjunction with mutual information scores and the observed/expected ratio which were also calculated but only *t*-values are reported throughout. As the crucial comparison, that of co-occurrence rate and judgement rating, is intralinguistic, the different size of the corpora should not affect the validity of the results. The complete co-occurrence data can be found in Appendices 2 (English) and 3 (German).

3.3 Assessing antonymic strength: a judgement task

Judgement tasks are a widely-used method in cognitive linguistics, especially when assessing the representativeness of a particular conceptual category (e.g. Rosch, 1973, 1975, 1978) in a goodness-of-exemplar (GOE) rating questionnaire. An adapted version of this method has been shown to be effective in collecting speaker judgements of antonymic strength (e.g. Charles et al., 1994; Paradis et al., 2009). In each language, the 210 antonym pairs were divided between two questionnaires for ease of completion, and two versions of each questionnaire were generated to allow for the presentation of each pair in both *item1-item2* and *item2-item1* order. Questionnaire I-1 contained 104 pairs, half in their prototypical order (insofar as a prototypical order can be determined; e.g. *up:down*) and the other half in the reverse order. Questionnaire I-2 contained the same pairs but in the opposite sequence (the same applies to Questionnaires II-1 and II-2, containing 106 word pairs each). The 210 pairs were divided into four groups of approximately 50 items depending on canonical antonymic strength as judged by a small pilot study using the English pairs. This resulted in a distribution of approximately 25% across four GOE-rating bands: Group I contained antonyms judged to be excellent examples, while Group IV contained control pairs which are not antonymous at all but are related and may display greater than chance frequency of co-occurrence.

3.3.1 Task and procedure

The questionnaires were created and distributed with the web-based questionnaire tool SurveyMonkey,[3] which enabled automatic randomisation of the order of presentation for each participant to avoid sequencing effects. Data was collected online and participants were recruited digitally in both the UK and Germany.

Participants were asked to rank each word pair on a Likert scale from 1–7 with '1' being *excellent* and '7' *very poor* depending on how good an antonym pair they judged them to be. The instructions furthermore asked participants to fill the questionnaire in swiftly and not to change their responses once they had made a decision to prevent over-rationalisation.

3.3.2 Participants

A total of 320 respondents participated in the questionnaire study (160 in each language; mean age 26.3 (18–60)). Out of these, 40 completed each of the separate sub-questionnaires. Incorrectly completed questionnaires (e.g. with the scale inverted or all pairs given the same rating) were immediately discarded during data collection.

Participants were all native speakers of English or German. Dialectal variation was not taken into consideration and English-speaking respondents were mainly speakers of British, Canadian and American English, while German-speaking participants were largely from southern Germany (137/160). All speakers reported education to A-level standard, and the majority had a university degree, with many in postgraduate education.

3.4 From best to worst: a judgement task analysis

This section presents the results of the GOE-rating questionnaires in combination with the corpus data in order to establish the part played by frequency of co-occurrence in antonym canonicity. After an initial overview of the best and worst scoring pairs (see Table 3.1), the data will be discussed using the criteria for good antonymy summarised in Table 2.2 to determine the effect of individual factors on antonymic strength. A detailed discussion of certain pairs is provided in the three case studies in Chapter 5 where data from the judgement task is combined with that from the behavioural experiments presented in Chapter 4.

For the analysis of the judgement task, the rating scale was divided into four bands as follows: Group I – excellent opposites (1–1.79; E: 64, G: 61), Group II – good opposites (1.8–2.99; E: 41, G: 48), Group III – medium opposites (3–4.99; E: 57, G: 58) and Group IV – poor opposites (5–7; E: 48, G: 45). The number of pairs in each group corresponds roughly to the predicted bands used to construct the questionnaire, which was designed to result in four groups of similar size. The distribution is relatively even and remarkably similar in the two languages. This suggests that, regardless of the ratings given for individual pairs, antonymic judgements are broadly similar in German and English regardless of lexical encoding (see Appendices 3 and 4 for complete results).

Table 3.2 displays the ten highest and lowest rated pairs in both languages. Despite the fact only 20 pairs are included, approximately half of the pairs in the top and bottom ten are the same in both languages (shaded grey in the table). Those pairs where the translation equivalent is not present are also all close in terms of scores. This shows the overwhelming overall correlation in antonym judgements between the two languages and provides the first evidence in support of the importance of conceptual evaluation in the judgement of opposition.

Before the following discussion of factors of good opposition, the suitability of frequency of co-occurrence as a predictor for antonymic strength is assessed. Subsequently, the corpus data is considered in relation to the ranking scores wherever relevant when assessing the impact of each of the following criteria: morphological relatedness (Section 3.4.2), symmetry and conceptual distance (Section 3.4.3), semantic range (Section 3.4.4), antonym order (Section 3.4.5), antonym type (Section 3.4.6), conceptual category structure and salience of the antonymic dimension (Section 3.4.7).

3.4.1 Associative strength as a predictor for antonymic strength

One of the central questions in antonym research has been the nature of the relationship of the two members of an antonym pair: conceptual or lexical. While recent research has firmly moved towards a cognitive

Table 3.2 Ten highest and lowest scoring pairs in the judgement task in English and German (pairs in bold print are present in both languages)[4]

ENGLISH				GERMAN			
Word 1	*Word 2*	*GOE*	*FoC*	*Word 1*	*Word 2*	*GOE*	*FoC*
false	**true**	**1.02**	**13.52**	**oben**	**unten**	**1.03**	**122.69**
up	down	1.04	50.31	hell	dunkel	1.04	33.69
soft	hard	1.07	8.64	**alt**	**neu**	**1.06**	**52.60**
right	**wrong**	**1.09**	**23.54**	groß	klein	1.08	123.71
fast	**slow**	**1.12**	**8.99**	**heiß**	**kalt**	**1.08**	**30.70**
top	**bottom**	**1.12**	**21.39**	jung	alt	1.08	197.12
cold	**hot**	**1.13**	**20.32**	lang	kurz	1.11	76.09
new	**old**	**1.13**	**21.78**	**falsch**	**richtig**	**1.12**	**52.11**
awake	asleep	1.14	5.17	**langsam**	**schnell**	**1.12**	**30.39**
last	first	1.14	13.00	schwer	leicht	1.13	24.30
good	**mediocre**	**4.82**	**2.59**	mangelhaft	angemessen	4.74	0
bland	hot	4.86	0	freundlich	kalt	4.78	6.18
dry	**sweet**	**4.87**	**3.06**	brilliant	mittelmäßig	4.87	0
occupier	**owner**	**4.93**	**4.56**	akzeptabel	furchtbar	4.90	0
next to	opposite	5.19	1.65	krabbeln	gehen	5.12	5.17
hungry	thirsty	4.24	5.42	**Besitzer**	**Bewohner**	**5.24**	**6.96**
buy	**spend**	**5.6**	**1.74**	**süß**	**trocken**	**5.51**	**7.20**
rent	let	5.62	3.27	**mittelmäßig**	**gut**	**5.62**	**9.03**
coffee	tea	5.9	21.43	jagen	ausbrechen	5.63	0.84
lukewarm	tepid	6.22	0.99	**ausgeben**	**kaufen**	**5.99**	**5.09**

basis for antonymy, the role played by the evidently strong associative relationship of many common opposite pairs should nevertheless be considered. If antonymy is indeed a relation which is largely (or in part) determined by a strong associative bond on the lexical level (as proposed by the WordNet group; Gross et al., 1989), co-occurrence rates should correlate well with speaker judgements on antonymic strength (especially out of context). This section presents two sets of antonym pairs which were deliberately included to represent stronger and weaker opposition as a starting point for the investigation of the relationship between associative strength as indicated by corpus data and judgement ratings.

The first set of results, displayed in Figure 3.1, contains gradable adjectival opposites on the TEMPERATURE scale and, even at first glance, the discrepancies between FoC and judgement rating are evident. The figures were plotted using the GOE-rating as the ranking measure and show no clear division between canonical and non-canonical opposites but a gradual decline of scores (except for *lukewarm:tepid*). This decline is not matched by the corresponding decrease in FoC which would be expected were it a 'perfect' predictor of antonymic strength. There does seem to be an overall correlation, however, especially at the extremes of the scale. The following analyses will show that the correlation of FoC and judgement scores is seen most clearly in gradable adjectival antonyms such as these.

The set of verbal converses (Figure 3.2) follows a similar pattern in terms of their judgement score distribution, which falls along a continuum from excellent opposition to poor (or non-) opposition. The associative strength measures, however, are less consistent here and do not seem to lend themselves to making accurate predictions about a verbal converse's place on the antonym continuum. It seems, therefore, that the lexical relationship of the two members of a pair plays a different role in certain antonym types and either contributes to the entrenchment of the antonymic relation to different degrees or only correlates well in cases of canonical opposition. This relationship and its interaction with the conceptual criteria for good opposition will be explored further below.

3.4.2 *Morphological relatedness*

As the only strictly lexical criterion, morphological relatedness will be discussed first. The effect of morphological relatedness on antonymic strength has not yet been explicitly investigated. Furthermore, as mentioned above, this factor is particularly relevant in psycholinguistic

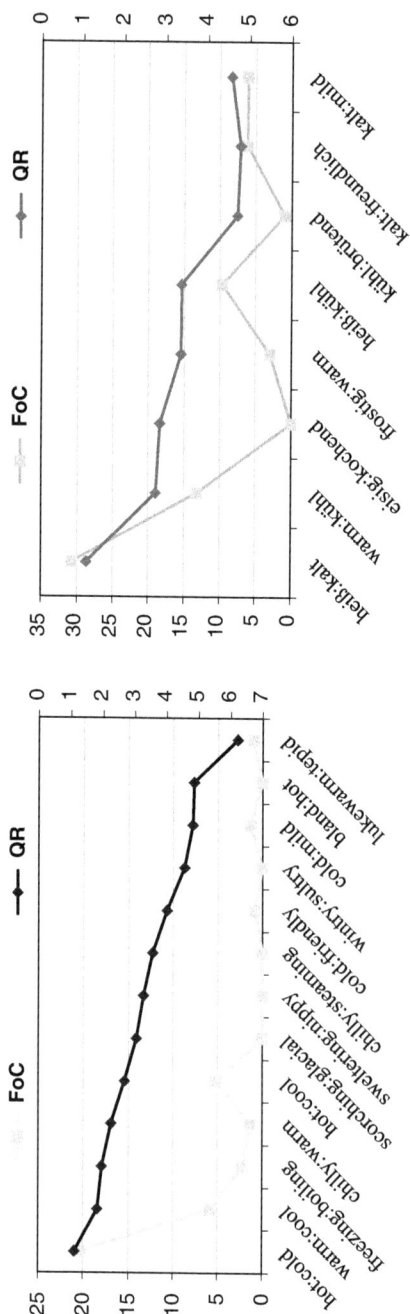

Figure 3.1 Antonym judgements (QR) and co-occurrence data (FoC) for English (left) and German (right) TEMPERATURE pairs.

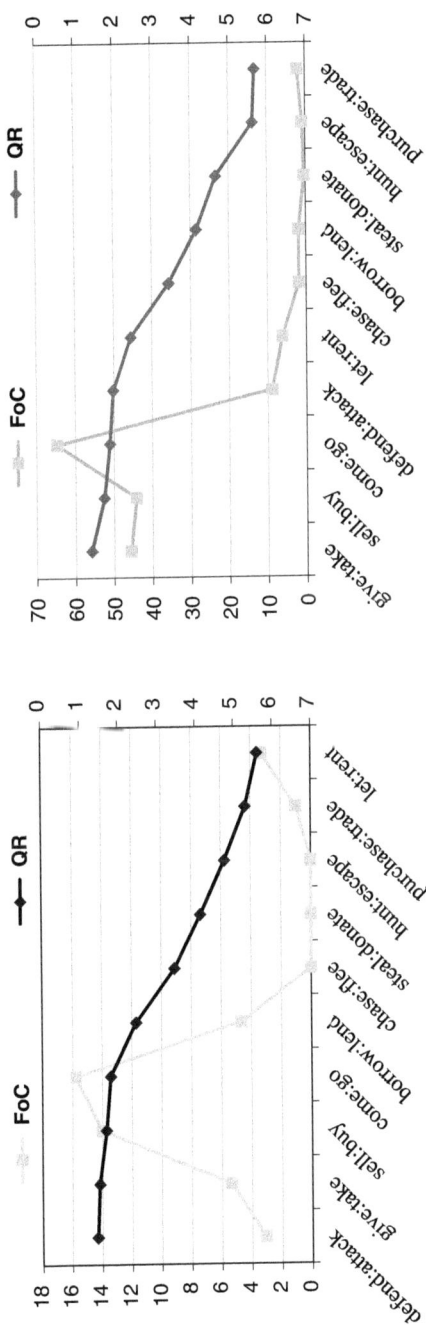

Figure 3.2 Antonym judgements (QR) and co-occurrence data (FoC) for English (left) and German (right) for verbal converses (German pairs provided in English translation).

approaches as there is much debate in the field regarding the storage and processing of morphologically complex items and whether items such as *unhappy* have their own lexical representation or whether their meaning is accessed via the root *happy* (see Section 6.3). While the highest scoring pairs are morphologically unrelated (e.g. *new:old/ neu:alt, big:small/groß:klein*) in both languages, almost all morphologically related pairs fall into Groups I and II.

To probe the effect of relatedness, the stimuli included pairs which were morphologically related in one language and unrelated in the other, as well as triplet sets which consist of one morphologically related pair and one conceptually similar but unrelated one (*happy:unhappy* and *happy:sad*). Table 3.2 shows GOE-ratings and FoC measures for pairs which differ in morphological relatedness in English and German but are conceptually equivalent.

There is no discernible systematic difference between the related and unrelated pairs which could indicate a pattern. In general, the top group of pairs in both languages consists of morphologically unrelated items, whereas no adjectival morphologically related pair (apart from pseudo-antonyms such as *easy:uneasy* or *hilflos:hilfreich*) scores worse than 2.08 (*interested:disinterested*).

Despite the inconclusive results, whether members of an antonym pair share morphological material remains an important factor in antonym judgements because the relationship is visibly encoded. However, affixes indicate different types of relationships, with negative prefixes providing the most overt antonymic clues while others, for instance *tutor:tutee* (3.39) in English and *König:Königin* 'king:queen' (3.66), the lowest-scoring nominal pairs, possibly highlight more strongly similarities. The lowest adjectival pairs are *married:unmarried* (1.97) and *interested:disinterested* (2.08) which shows that, overall, morphologically related pairs receive very high ratings, not simply because of the shared morphological material but equally because of strong conceptual opposition and, frequently, a large degree of shared semantic range as one item is derived from the other.

Pairs such as *landlord:tenant* and the German equivalent *Vermieter:Mieter* illustrate the role played by morphological relatedness, especially in pairs with otherwise medium-to-low antonymic strength such as these converses. The German pair, which is morphologically related, is judged to have significantly greater antonymic strength. The encoding of opposing concepts in morphologically related versus unrelated lexical items or even in the same lexical item will be the focus of Case Study I (Section 5.1), where the case of *borrow:lend* and German *leihen*, which encodes both 'borrow' and 'lend', is discussed.

3.4.3 Gradable opposites: the role of symmetry and conceptual distance

This section presents an evaluation of the effect of systematic violations of the criteria of symmetry and distribution on a uni-dimensional scale. The opposites used to illustrate the effect of these criteria are those on the TEMPERATURE scale. The pairs on the TEMPERATURE scale, centred on the highly canonical antonym pair *hot:cold,* comprise the biggest set overall and lend themselves well to cross-linguistic comparison as they are closely matched in English and German. Central pairs will be discussed first before more peripheral examples are considered which either do not meet some of the above criteria at all or fulfil them in a modified form. This will determine whether the criteria which proposed so far sufficiently account for the patterns observed in the data.

The central pair on the TEMPERATURE scale, *hot:cold/heiß:kalt,* is an example of antonymy proper in the Lyonsian sense, as it is a gradable, adjectival antonym pair. The co-occurrence and judgement task results for pairs along the TEMPERATURE scale are summarised in Tables 3.3 and 3.4.

There are more English pairs than German equivalents as one English pair, *lukewarm:tepid,* does not have a German equivalent since German encodes both senses in just one lexeme, *lauwarm.* Some of the more marginal English pairs, such as *wintry:sultry,* were also not included in German as there were not suitable translation equivalents. Overall, in terms of frequency of co-occurrence, Table 3.3 shows similarly distributed co-occurrence for English and German pairs. However, only three pairs are close in GOE-rating scores: the base pairs *hot:cold* and *heiß:kalt,* which are among the highest-scoring pairs overall, the asymmetric pairs *cold:mild* and *kalt:mild* which are unanimously seen as fairly poor examples of lexical opposition, and the pairs *cold:friendly* and *kalt:freundlich* which make use of the polysemous nature of *cold/kalt* and are thus not part of the TEMPERATURE domain. The five remaining pairs differ in their interlinguistic GOE-rating and German pairs are uniformly judged as worse opposites than their English equivalents.

The criterion of symmetry of distribution (equidistance from the midpoint) of a scale and of the resulting conceptual distance were proposed by Cruse (1986) and have been shown to have a strong effect

Table 3.3 Cross-linguistic differences in morphological relatedness

Word 1	Word 2	GOE	FoC	Word 1	Word 2	GOE	FoC
landlord	tenant	3.47	18.37	Vermieter	Mieter	2.52	48.74
employer	employee	2.85	10.39	Chef	Angestellter	3.08	8.21
king	queen	4.78	15.23	König	Königin	3.66	46.30
let	rent	5.62	3.26	mieten	vermieten	2.45	6.19
sell	buy	1.67	13.99	verkaufen	kaufen	1.74	44.15
borrow	lend	2.45	4.67	verleihen	ausleihen	4.15	1.83
interested	uninterested	1.42	0.94	interessiert	uninteressiert	1.57	0.92
interested	disinterested	2.08	1.36	interessiert	desinteressiert	1.52	1.62
sick	healthy	1.32	2.75	krank	gesund	1.22	25.39
unhealthy	healthy	1.33	1.98	ungesund	gesund	1.54	7.97
unhappy	happy	1.24	3.87	unglücklich	glücklich	1.28	13.51
sad	happy	1.22	5.42				

Table 3.4 Pairs on the TEMPERATURE scale ordered by English GOE-rating scores

Word 1	Word 2	GOE	FoC	Word 1	Word 2	GOE	FoC
hot	cold	1.13	20.32	heiß	kalt	1.08	30.70
warm	cool	1.84	5.78	warm	kühl	2.76	13.21
freezing	boiling	1.98	2.22	eisig	kochend	2.86	0
chilly	warm	2.27	1.34	frostig	warm	3.36	2.95
hot	cool	2.68	5.22	heiß	kühl	3.37	9.63
scorching	glacial	3.05	0				
sweltering	nippy	3.28	0				
chilly	steaming	3.57	0	kühl	brütend	4.71	0.98
cold	friendly	4.02	0.84	kalt	freundlich	4.78	6.18
wintry	sultry	4.57	0				
cold	mild	4.82	1.31	kalt	mild	4.57	6.14
lukewarm	tepid	6.22	0.99				

on judgements of the antonym canonicity of gradable opposite pairs in previous studies (e.g. Jones et al., 2012). This section will explore the effects of differing distributions on a scale and conceptual closeness or distance starting with an overview of the data for symmetrically distributed pairs.

In the TEMPERATURE set, there are three symmetrical pairs, where both members are the same distance from the midpoint of the scale, which differ only in degree: *hot:cold, warm:cool* and *boiling:freezing*. As expected, *hot:cold* and its German equivalent *heiß:kalt* are two of the highest-scoring pairs overall in both associative and antonymic strength and display all the properties expected from canonical antonyms. Despite much lower rates of co-occurrence, with *boiling:freezing* barely displaying a significant co-occurrence pattern (2.22) and the German pair *eisig:kochend* not co-occurring at all in the data, the GOE-scores of the two remaining symmetrical pairs in each language are remarkably similar. *Freezing:boiling* (1.97) is judged to have only slightly lower antonymic strength than *warm:cool* (1.84) and the German pairs *eisig:kochend* (2.86) and *warm:kühl* (2.76), while scoring significantly lower than their English equivalents, are rated almost identically. Both sets of pairs score significantly lower than their respective canonical pair. However, they are still judged substantially more antonymous than any of the asymmetrical pairs.

Most of the asymmetric pairs contain one member of the base pair which has been matched with a synonym of the other member of the base pair. These pairs have been designed to create asymmetrical distributions of varying conceptual distance on the relevant scale:

hot:cool, cold:mild and *warm:chilly* and their German equivalents. *Hot:cool* has the highest co-occurrence score of this group (5.22), which is roughly equivalent to that of *warm:cool*, and this is matched by the German pair *heiß:kühl*. However, their GOE-ratings (2.68 and 3.37 respectively) are considerably lower than those for *warm:cool* (1.84) and *warm:kühl* (2.76) and are also lower than those for English *warm:chilly* (2.26) despite the fact that *warm* and *chilly* only co-occur at chance level. The greater co-occurrence rate has not led to a higher GOE-rating score for *hot:cool* and *heiß:kühl* and this is in keeping with the hypothesis that, if one of the key criteria for good antonymy is violated, in this case symmetrical distribution, the result is a proportionately lower GOE-score. This holds despite the fact that the co-occurrence rate for *warm:chilly* is negatively influenced by the lower individual frequency of *chilly* and by their difference in semantic range.

Cold:mild, with a similar co-occurrence rate to *warm:chilly* (1.31), scores much lower on the GOE-rating (4.81). This is presumably due to the fact that *mild* is not strictly speaking a synonym of *warm* or *hot* and therefore is neither directly nor indirectly opposed to *cold*. They are, however, frequently used antonymically when talking about the weather, for example in this example from the BNC *Is it cold out? No mild.* (BNC KBH 918). Contextual support may however be necessary for a strong antonymic construal as the pair also differs in semantic range with both members of the pair also being polysemous, and thus the core component of any good antonym pair, minimal difference, is stretched too far in this case.

However, symmetry is not the only factor which emerged as relevant from the data in relation to the distribution of the members of antonym pairs along a scale. The **overall distance** between the concepts is also of importance. An analysis of pairs on the MERIT scale shows that concepts which are at a greater distance from each other, e.g. *excellent:bad* (2.64) or *mediocre:brilliant* (3.61), are rated as better antonyms than those which cover parts of the scale which are closer, such as *bad:satisfactory* (4.42) or *good:mediocre* (4.82), as this closeness decreases the salience of conceptual opposition.

The above analysis illustrates the importance of both symmetry of distribution and overall conceptual distance in the assessment of antonymic strength of gradable opposite pairs. The data shows that pairs located equidistant from the midpoint of the scale which structures the antonymic domain consistently score higher than pairs which are asymmetrically placed. This is also linked to minimal difference, because if the distance to the midpoint is identical, this also significantly reduces differences in semantic range and distribution. Thus, the effect of symmetry is not independent of the effect of semantic range and the resulting distribution of the lexical items in texts, which is discussed in the following section.

3.4.4 Semantic range and semantic generality

The degree to which the range of semantic applicability of the two lexical items in an antonym pair matches has been shown to be an influential factor in their antonymic relationship (Muehleisen, 1997; Murphy, 2003; Jones et al., 2012). Those pairs where members share the largest possible number of contexts they can be used in are generally considered the best opposites. The previous discussion of symmetry has already hinted at differences in semantic range as an explanation for some of the patterns observed, reinforcing the point that many of the factors affecting antonymic strength are interrelated. Semantic range can affect the degree of opposition either because the range differs between the two members of a pair or because both members of a pair are relatively restricted in their applicability (e.g. specialist terms). The restriction of (shared) semantic range also leads to lower co-occurrence and limits the chances of the two lexemes being used together.

For instance, while *warm:cool* and *boiling:freezing* are symmetrical, they are intuitively considered less canonical as their range is more restricted than that of the base pair *hot:cold*. However, as the semantic ranges of the members of both pairs still overlap substantially, especially in the case of *boiling:freezing* in English, it is still expected that they will co-occur more frequently than chance predicts. However, despite their closely matching opposed sub-senses, the distribution patterns of the two lexemes differ considerably. Out of the three subsenses for *freezing* in (3.1) below, *freezing* mainly appears in sense 2 ('(very) cold'), whereas sense 1a of *boiling* ('bringing/coming to the boil') in (3.2) is by far the most common one.[5] However, the LDCE and the OALD list *boiling* (adj.) as a separate sense which is overtly marked as the opposite of *freezing* in both dictionaries.

3.1 FREEZING

1a. to reduce temperature to achieve a change of state (liquid to solid)
*The **freezing** and canning process reduces the number of nutrients in food.* (BNC EX5 2006)
1b. (metaphorically) to halt something

*Between 1980/81 and 1982/83 the **freezing** of university places* [...]
(BNC FP4 479)
2. (very) cold but usually not literally at freezing point
[...] *draughty halls and **freezing** aircraft hangars.* (BNC ACE 2923)

3.2 BOILING

1a. bringing something (mainly liquid) to the boil (transitive/
intransitive)
*Return to heat and stir until **boiling**.* (BNC BN5 883)
1b. (metaphorically) uncontrollable emotions (anger/excitement)
[...] *she struggled to keep a check on her **boiling** emotions.* (BNC
HA6 472)
2. (very) hot
[...] *having tea in the shade on **boiling** afternoons.* (BNC AB4 1606)

This mismatch in the frequency of subsenses reduces the number of
occurrences in which the two lexemes can be found in close proximity
and this results in lower co-occurrence rates. The lexemes are also
individually less frequent compared to *warm:cool*, which has also been
shown to affect antonym canonicity (Jones et al., 2012).

Warm and *cool* are much less restricted in their application and
both lexemes have several subsenses which do not contrast directly
with each other, for example *warm* 'friendly' and *cool* 'stylish'.
However, this pair's rate of co-occurrence is still relatively high which
is not altogether surprising as all four lexemes share a significant
amount of semantic range and both *cold/cool* and *hot/warm* can be
used interchangeably in many contexts. Thus, overlapping semantic
range results in greater antonymic strength than the differences which
can be seen in the following pairs which were only included in the
English questionnaire.

In the above pairs both members were adjectives with the core
meaning on the TEMPERATURE scale, but the following pairs include
one of the base lexemes in a secondary meaning, thus forming a different type of indirect antonymy. *Cold:friendly*, German *kalt:freundlich*,
and *hot:bland* encode degrees of FRIENDLINESS and SPICINESS. As the base
lexeme included in each pair is always polysemous and covers a much
larger semantic range than the second lexeme, this results in a mismatch
of non-propositional meaning and a lesser amount of shared semantic
range which in turn results in fewer opportunities for co-occurrence. All
pairs score below four on the GOE-rating and none of them co-occur at
greater than chance rates apart from German *kalt:freundlich*. These
pairs are clearly not considered very good examples of opposition when

used uncontextualised. However, as in so many cases, both can easily be used contrastively in certain contexts which enhance the salience of the dimension along which they are opposed.

This effect of semantic range can also be seen particularly clearly in the cross-linguistic comparison of the data, where pairs which are matched for other criteria (e.g. distance from midpoint of the scale) show different ratings depending on the semantic range of each of the members of the pair and the degree to which this overlaps. For instance, the German equivalent of *good:disobedient, brav:ungehorsam,* shows significantly greater antonymic strength than its English counterpart. *Brav* 'well-behaved' and *ungehorsam* 'disobedient' are a much better match in terms of semantic range, whereas *good* has a much wider range than *disobedient,* which is as restricted in its usage to the same range of 'good behaviour' as both members of the German pair. In both languages, *disobedient* also has a morphologically related opposite: *obedient* and German *gehorsam* 'obedient', but as this is the case for both languages, it cannot explain the discrepancy in antonymic strength ratings.

The data clearly shows that semantic range plays an important part in antonym judgements, and that this criterion is another factor related to frequency of co-occurrence because a larger amount of shared semantic range will provide lexemes with more opportunities to co-occur and therefore strengthen their associative relationship. However, shared semantic range is first and foremost a result of a large amount of overlap in meaning as well as factors such as register. The greater the overlap between members of a pair, the more these criteria satisfy the need for minimal difference.

3.4.5 Antonym order

Sequencing of opposite pairs has been investigated by several scholars and criteria have been proposed which explain the preference of certain pairs to appear in a particular order (cf. Cruse & Togia, 1995; Jones, 2002; Croft & Cruse, 2004; Kostić, 2015a; Wu, 2017). Often, the unmarked property is preferred as the first member of the pair (e.g. *long:short, hot:cold*). In the judgement task, all pairs were presented in both sequences, but only a small number of pairs showed a difference greater than 0.5 in the resulting rating scores. This is to be expected as the offline, untimed judgement of antonymic strength is less reliant on sequencing than, for instance, timed behavioural experiments where greater differences may be expected.

While no principled statistical analysis was carried out for the sequencing differences in the judgement task, Table 3.5 lists 16 English

Table 3.5 Pairs with discrepancies greater than 0.5 in the English and German judgement task

Word 1	Word 2	FoC (1–2)	FoC (2-1)	GOE (1–2)	GOE (2-1)
English					
ask	answer	30	25	2.9	2.55
buy	spend	5	5	5.15	6.05
buy	sell*	157	48	1.93	1.43
child	parent	66	188	4.05	3.1
chilly	steaming	0	0	3.08	4.05
correct	mistaken	0	0	2.73	1.95
current	former	21	17	3.43	2.95
damage	repair	11	89	2.75	1.98
figuratively	literally	2	3	2.23	1.7
finish	continue	0	3	4.23	4.75
good	disobedient	0	0	3.05	3.7
lend	borrow	7	15	2.9	1.98
present	future	179	27	3.48	4.2
present	past*	107	494	2.43	3.13
sour	sweet	2	40	2.33	3.03
town	country	429	82	3.18	4.25
German					
akzeptabel 'acceptable'	furchtbar 'terrible'	0	0	4.58	5.21
Bulle 'bull'	Kuh 'cow'	17	17	2.98	3.58
dick 'plump, fat;	schmal 'slender, narrow'	5	2	3.43	4.21
falsch 'wrong'	passend 'fitting'	3	1	3.2	3.85
ganz 'whole'	halb 'half'	145	276	3.7	3.09
gegenüber 'opposite'	neben 'next to'	643	278	4.33	5.03
geschieden 'divorced'	verheiratet* 'married'	55	195	3.15	3.7
gigantisch 'gigantic'	mini 'miniscule'	0	0	2.2	3.27
heute 'today'	morgen* 'tomorrow'	43904	2059	4.65	3.55
höflich 'polite'	kurz 'short'	20	18	6.2	6.82
hungrig 'hungry'	satt 'satiated'	20	24	1.23	1.73
jagen 'chase'	ausbrechen 'escape'	0	1	5.88	5.38
kommen 'come'	gehen 'go'	5392	1189	1.53	2.24
Königin 'queen'	König 'king'	505	1664	4.08	3.23
kühl 'cool'	warm 'warm'	80	98	2.48	3.03
Lehrer 'teacher'	Schüler 'student'	10516	17928	3.23	2.58
lernen 'learn'	verlernen 'forget'	19	4	3.45	4.3

(*Continued*)

Table 3.5 (Continued)

Word 1	Word 2	FoC (1–2)	FoC (2-1)	GOE (1–2)	GOE (2-1)
lernen 'learn'	lehren 'teach'	337	488	3.13	2.45
miteinbeziehen 'include'	ausschließen 'exclude'	1	0	1.8	2.39
modisch 'fashionable'	traditionell 'traditional'	4	2	3.48	4.33
Mutter 'mother'	Vater 'father'	17797	14112	3.43	2.93
richtig 'right'	inkorrekt 'incorrect'	3	1	2.38	3.03
scharf 'hot'	fad 'bland'	3	0	3.53	4.18
Soll 'debit'	Haben* 'credit'	416	17	2.48	1.63
stehlen 'steal'	spenden 'donate'	2	1	3.98	5.35
Student 'student'	Dozent 'lecturer'	16	17	3.98	3.08
Tante 'aunt'	Onkel 'uncle'	478	572	4.1	3.33
Tochter 'daughter'	Vater 'father'	1878	7020	5.7	5.15
ungehorsam 'disobedient'	brav 'good'	1	2	1.78	2.38
irreal 'unreal'	real 'real'	1	2	2.5	1.94
Vergangenheit 'past'	Gegenwart* 'present'	4668	1207	3.35	2.3
verkaufen 'sell'	kaufen* 'buy'	292	1702	3.75	4.55
zufriedenstellend 'satisfactory'	schlecht 'bad'	11	6	4.2	4.7

pairs and 32 German pairs (out of 210) which display a clear preference for one sequence over the other. None of these are classical canonical pairs and the best ranked pairs displaying a strong preference are the English converse *sell:buy* and the pair *literally:figuratively* and German *hungrig:satt* ('hungry:satiated') and the converse *kommen:gehen* ('come:go'). Where there is a large difference in the frequency of co-occurrence between the two sequences, the judgement scores mirror this preference for the most part (cases where this does not apply are marked with *).

Nevertheless, most of the criteria for sequencing proposed in previous literature can be seen to have an influence here. The criterion of salience, for instance, is evident in the pairs *present:past* and its German equivalent *Gegenwart:Vergangenheit*. In both languages, *present* is the preferred first item, as it is the starting point for our thinking and thus the more salient concept. However, *former:current* does not correspond to this format because here chronology may provide the more salient motivation for the order, as it does for *sell:buy*, *former:current*, *present:future* and *hungrig:satt* 'hungry:satiated.' Most of the pairs are judged better when the derived members of a pair follows its base (e.g. *König:Königin* 'king:queen') and this also applies to pairs where the two items are unrelated but one is morphologically complex (e.g. good:disobedient); however, this could also be an example for positivity as a driving factor, which is also exemplified by the German pair *zufriedenstellend:schlecht* 'satisfactory:bad', or for frequency, as *good* is much more frequent than *disobedient*. Gender is also seen to have an effect in certain pairs such as German *Bulle:Kuh* 'bull:cow' or *Onkel:Tante* 'uncle:aunt', while there are no pairs in this list which are ordered by their phonology, but the English pair *town:country* is an example of idiomatic ordering.

3.4.6 Antonym type

Chapter 2 raised the question whether the differences in the logical relationship and types of construal which has led to classifications of opposition influence speaker judgements. The judgement task data does not show an overall correlation between antonym type and the judgement results. It is not the case, for instance, that gradable opposites are judged better than non-gradable pairs and, in fact, many of the top pairs are so-called complementaries (e.g. *true:false*, *right:wrong* or *awake:asleep*) or spatial opposites (e.g. *top:bottom*, *up:down*). Converses, however, behave slightly differently and are rated lower on average than the other types of opposition. As a sub-category of directional opposition in the structuralist classifications introduced in Section 2.2.1, it may well have been expected that they, like their spatial counterparts, would score rather better. One aspect to bear in mind here, however, is that most converses are not adjectival and the relation between the two members of a pair is conceptually more complex than a simple scalar dimension or bounded construal such as that in most of the pairs discussed so far. Converses nevertheless also show variable degrees of antonymic strength in judgement ratings and certain pairs are intuitively much more closely related than others (e.g. *above:below* vs. *charge:cost*; Cruse, 1986, p. 239). Due to the difference in the type of relationship between converses and the much greater variety of lexical categories, the factors affecting a converse pair's antonymic strength differ from those discussed so far and the patterns observed in the judgement task results also show clear differences in both German and English. As the data also differs between verbal and nominal converses, the converse data will be analysed in two parts.

Nominal converses form a cluster which spans roughly one point of the rating scale, whereas the judgements of antonymic strength for verbal converses are much more disparate. Cross-linguistically, the converse pairs are very similar in the speaker judgements of antonymic strength with very few pairs exceeding a difference of 0.5 on the rating scale. The two pairs which display the most striking differences between English and German, *borrow:lend* and *let:rent*, are analysed in detail in Case Study I.

Another striking observation in the GOE-rating of all converses is the overall greater standard deviation in the results for each pair[6] as well as larger differences between preferred and dispreferred sequences. The latter difference does not, as far as this can be established, stem from a greater preference for a certain sequence but simply from a greater amount of indecision on the part of the participants as to whether, for each informant, converses are part of antonymy. Converses do seem to have a particular standing within a speaker's awareness and therefore result in judgments different from those of 'regular' opposites.

3.4.6.1 Verbal converses

The four highest scoring verbal converse pairs in both languages are *defend:attack*, *give:take*, *buy:sell* and *come:go* and they form a cluster with high antonymic strength judgements (see Table 3.6). However, despite high co-occurrence rates (especially *come:go* and *buy:sell* in both languages and German *geben:nehmen* 'give:take'), they do not score as highly as many of the canonical adjectival pairs. Interestingly, the converse pair which scored best overall (*defend:attack*) does not have a very high co-occurrence rate in either language. Sequencing seems to play a stronger part in certain cases (*come:go, borrow:lend, sell:buy*) than in others where there is virtually no difference between the two orders of presentation (*give:take, steal:donate, hunt:escape*).

While the converse relation may prioritise different criteria to gradable adjectival pairs, for instance, effects of semantic range and overall item frequency can also be seen in some of the pairs constructed to violate these particular criteria. *Purchase:trade*, a pair constructed using synonyms of *buy:sell*, is not well-matched for register or semantic range and neither is the German equivalent of *hunt:escape, jagen:ausbrechen*, which scores significantly lower in German as the meaning of *ausbrechen* is more literal (escaping from a confined space) than that of *escape*.

Table 3.6 Verbal converses (ordered by English overall GOE-rating)

Word 1	Word 2	GOE	GOE1/2	GOE2/1	FoC	Word 1	Word 2	GOE	GOE 1/2	GOE2/1	FoC
defend	attack	1.44	1.50	1.38	3.07	verteidigen	angreifen	1.98	2.13	1.83	8.89
give	take	1.49	1.45	1.53	5.36	geben	nehmen	1.405	1.58	1.23	45.60
sell	buy	1.67	1.43	1.92	13.99	verkaufen	kaufen	1.74	1.93	1.55	44.15
come	go	1.79	1.65	1.92	15.74	kommen	gehen	1.885	1.53	2.24	64.73
borrow	lend	2.45	1.98	2.92	4.67	verleihen	ausleihen	4.15	4	4.3	1.83
chase	flee	3.46	3.33	3.59	0	jagen	fliehen	3.44	3.33	3.55	1.81
steal	donate	4.14	4.10	4.18	0	stehlen	spenden	4.665	3.98	5.35	0.37
hunt	escape	4.77	4.80	4.73	0	jagen	ausbrechen	5.63	5.88	5.38	0.84
purchase	trade	5.31	5.48	5.13	0.99	erwerben	handeln	5.69	5.6	5.78	2.01
let	rent	5.62	5.93	5.30	3.26	mieten	vermieten	2.45	2.3	2.6	6.19

Table 3.7 Comparison of verbal converses and canonical antonyms by FoC

Word 1	Word 2	GOE	FoC	Word 1	Word 2	GOE	FoC
buy	sell	1.67	13.99	true	false	1.01	13.52
defend	attack	1.44	3.07	dry	sweet	4.75	3.06
give	take	1.49	5.356	little	big	1.24	7.35
come	go	1.785	15.74	old	young	1.28	17.52
lend	borrow	2.45	4.67	badly	well	2.28	4.62

To determine how converses compare to other types of opposites with similar co-occurrence rates, Table 3.7 provides a list of the five highest-scoring converses in English and selected opposite pairs matched for associative strength only. The low co-occurrence rate of *defend:attack* does not seem to be detrimental to its antonymic strength while the matched pair, *dry:sweet*, scores significantly lower. *Dry:sweet* requires a very specific context to be successful as an antonym pair and the two lexemes, when used to describe wine or sherry, are without a doubt excellent opposites. However, in a context-free task the other meanings of these words distract from this very specific domain of opposition.

The opposite case is also shown in the table above: *buy:sell* and *true:false* have almost identical co-occurrence scores but *true:false* is the highest-scoring pair in the English data, whereas *buy:sell* is barely within the category of excellent antonymy. This comparison emphasises a point which has already been made in previous sections: frequency of co-occurrence, while without a doubt a factor contributing to associative strength, is not the strongest determining factor if conceptual criteria are violated.

As the converses discussed here are not adjectival, one factor which comes into play here is that of the complexity of the conceptual category (Paradis, 2005), or, in Cruse's (1986) terms *purity of opposition*. Compared to adjectives, which are conceptually simple, domains denoted by verbs or nouns usually contain a larger amount of conceptual information which may reduce the salience of the opposition. The patterns observed in the data for nominal converses provides even stronger support for this particular criterion.

3.4.6.2 Nominal converses

While the pattern of judgement rating scores for verbal converses is similar to that of other adjectival and verbal opposites in showing a gradual reduction in antonymic strength, the nominal converses in this study do not seem to fit the same pattern. As Table 3.8 shows, all

Table 3.8 Nominal converses (ordered by English overall GOE-rating)

Word 1	Word 2	GOE	GOE1/2	GOE2/1	FoC	Word 1	Word 2	GOE	GOE1/2	GOE2/1	FoC
employer	employee	2.85	2.95	2.75	10.39	Chef	Angestellter	3.08	3.12	3.03	8.206
pupil	teacher	3.15	2.90	3.40	11.40	Schüler	Lehrer	2.91	2.58	3.23	167.19
husband	wife	3.18	3.10	3.25	28.01	Mann	Frau	1.5	1.48	1.52	185.82
parent	child	3.59	3.10	4.08	15.66	Eltern	Kinder	3.65	3.5	3.79	250.24
victim	murderer	3.23	3.15	3.30	3.11	Opfer	Mörder	2.83	2.93	2.73	24.64
master	apprentice	3.23	3.20	3.25	2.17	Meister	Lehrling	3.05	3.18	2.91	16.06
doctor	patient	3.38	3.25	3.50	9.76	Doktor	Patient	2.96	2.98	2.94	6.824
landlord	tenant	3.47	3.68	3.25	18.37	Vermieter	Mieter	2.52	2.68	2.35	48.74
student	teacher	3.56	3.73	3.38	9.46	Student	Dozent	3.53	3.98	3.08	5.661

nominal converses have a judgement score between 2.85 (*employer:employee*) and 3.64 (German *Eltern:Kinder* 'parents:children'), which is an extremely narrow range in the middle of the rating scale. *Eltern:Kinder* and *husband:wife* have the highest co-occurrence scores in the two languages but their judgement scores do not even put them in the category of good opposites.

The two graphs in Figure 3.3 highlight two important aspects. Firstly, the difference between this set of converses and all others in this study. In all other sets a gradual increase in judgement scores was evident, whereas the judgement ratings of nominal converses only cover a very narrow range. Secondly, the co-occurrence data, on the other hand, shows some of the greatest variability in the whole study, with some pairs displaying extremely high associative strength. However, even for such pairs, the strong associative bond of the two lexemes does not seem to increase their antonymic strength. This is, once again, observable in both languages, which contributes to the need to search for an explanation beyond the lexical domain.

The data presented here has shown certain similarities between the data patterns for converses and other types of opposition. Certain criteria for good opposition, such as semantic range, hold for both types of converses and, as in the other examples presented earlier, judgement ratings pattern along a continuum. Most of the evidence thus indicates that converseness should be considered part antonymy. While nominal converses stray furthest from the prototypicality pattern seen in the results for verbal and adjectival opposites, the cause may not lie in the converseness of their relation but the conceptual category structure of the domains these items encode. The complexity of the domains involved in the construal of opposition and the effect on the salience of the opposite dimension will be the focus of the following section.

3.4.7 Extending purity of opposition: the effect of conceptual category structure

As is evident from previous research, adjectives are the perfect candidates for canonical opposition. This difference between opposite pairs of different lexical categories has been remarked upon by a number of scholars (e.g. Lyons, 1977; Cruse, 1986 and many others) and has been linked to the degree of complexity of the conceptual domains which are encoded by different word classes (Langacker, 2008; Paradis, 2005). While categories encoded by adjectives (and prepositions) are often very sparse in terms of their structure, with the

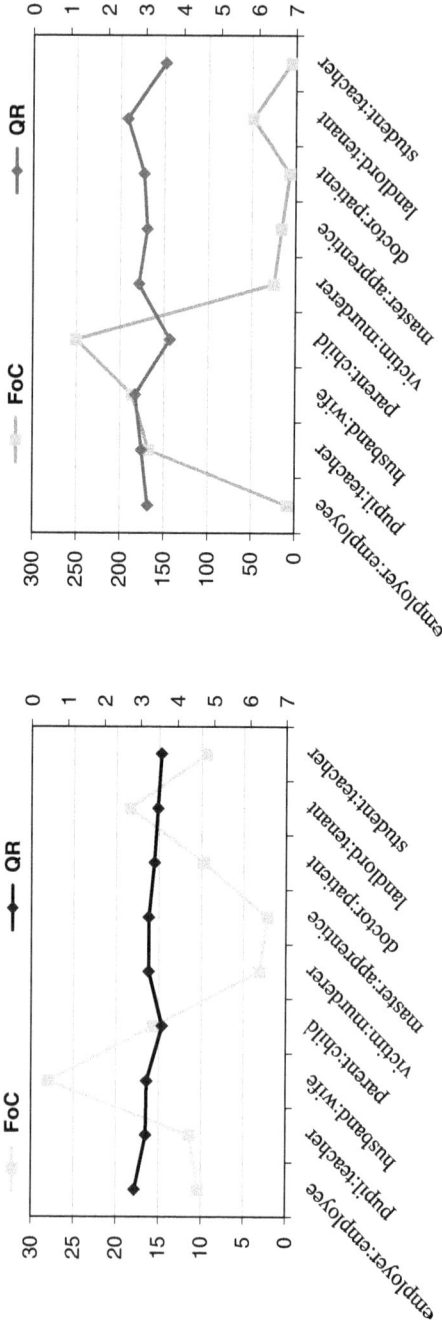

Figure 3.3 Antonym judgements (QR) and co-occurrence data (FoC) for English (left) and German (right) for nominal converses (German pairs provided in English translation).

opposing dimension often being the sole attribute (e.g. *hot:cold, fast:slow, big:little*), domains encoded by verbs and (concrete) nouns are often more complex, thus reducing the overt salience of the opposing dimension as well as possibly violating the criterion of minimal difference.

This difference in antonymic strength between lexical categories can be seen clearly in the judgement data presented so far. The vast majority of pairs judged excellent are adjectival in both languages. In the German data, only four (of 49) nominal (*Zwerg:Riese, Tod:Leben, Mann:Frau* and *Berg:Tal*) and five (of 24) verbal pairs (*nehmen:geben, ausziehen:anziehen, erlauben:verbieten, kaufen:verkaufen* and *fragen:-antworten*) were rated as excellent antonyms and in the English results two nominal (*giant:dwarf* and *life:death*) and eight verbal pairs (e.g. *exclude:include, succeed:fail, defend:attack, dress:undress, buy:sell*) fell into Group I. In the other groups, verbal and nominal pairs were roughly equally distributed in German, while in English, the nominal converses scored predominantly in the medium group (nouns: E: 5/21/16, G: 13/18/14; verbs: E: 3/4/8, G:7/6/6).

Cognitive proposals (e.g. Paradis, 2005; Jones et al., 2012) have recently provided more detailed theoretical explanations for the surface effect of word class on antonym canonicity (see Section 2.4.2) based on the structure of the underlying conceptual category. Nominal concepts, for instance, especially those which are concrete, are underpinned by experientially based rich cognitive models (Lakoff, 1987; Ungerer & Schmid, 2006). These models are not usually scientifically or factually accurate but reflect the interpretation and experience of an individual and are strongly influenced by culture. Thus, they also include encyclopaedic knowledge which influences not only decisions of category membership but also the associations, such as antonymy, formed by the concept and, by extension, the lexeme which encodes it.[7] These richer structures rely on a number of different attributes for their definition and the opposing dimension relevant for antonym construal may be less salient (and more contextually dependent). The sparse structure of adjectives makes them ideal for a relation which is, on the one hand, determined by minimal difference and on the other requires this difference to be the most salient semantic/conceptual feature.

To determine the internal category structure of certain nominal pairs, an attribute listing task (cf. Rosch & Mervis, 1975) was conducted. Each participant (E: n = 12; G: n = 15) was presented with only one member of a pair to avoid synchronisation of responses, and informants were asked to list as many attributes and characteristics of the given concepts as possible in one minute and not to change their responses once that time was over. The attributes listed were then weighted, with attributes listed first weighted at eight, those listed second at seven, down to attributes listed eighth and lower which were weighted at one.

One example of nominal pairs with relatively high antonymic strength is that of *giant:dwarf* (Table 3.9) and German *Riese:Zwerg* (Table 3.10). Neither of the two concepts in each pair elicited a large number of features and those listed are well matched across the two concepts. In English, if 'tall' and 'big' are combined to form one feature, and 'short' and 'small' likewise, neither concept has more than five features which were listed by two or more participants. Furthermore, the English concepts have two sets of antonymic features (*big:small* and *short:tall*) listed in the first three attributes. In both languages, the most prominent attribute is a size adjective.

This pair highlights three important aspects of nominal categories in terms of antonymic strength: the relatively simple overall structure

Table 3.9 Attribute listing results for giant and dwarf[8]

Giant		Dwarf	
huge/big/large	(12; 83)	**short/not tall**	(11; 87)
myth/fairytale	(7; 44)	**small/stunted**	(9; 70)
tall	(4; 26)	Snow White	(7; 43)
has two legs	(2; 13)	wears (funny) hat	(4; 24)
man/male	(2; 12)	beard	(3; 19)
		exaggerated features	(2; 14)

Table 3.10 Attribute listing results for RIESE and ZWERG

Riese		Zwerg	
groß 'big'	(12; 91)	**klein 'small'**	(15; 116)
Mythologie/Märchen 'mythology/fairy tale'	(9; 59)	(Zipfel)mütze '(pointy) hat'	(9; 51)
böse/gefährlich 'evil/dangerous'	(6; 33)	Märchen 'fairy tale'	(5; 34)
Gegenteil von Zwerg 'opposite of dwarf'	(3; 22)	Garten 'garden'*	(5; 28)
David & Goliath	(3; 20)	Bart 'beard'	(3; 19)
stark 'strong'	(2; 13)	frech 'cheeky'	(2; 13)

Notes
* *Gartenzwerg* is German for *garden gnome*.

with a limited number of key features, the salient position of the opposing dimension (here that of SIZE) and an overlap of certain other
features contributing to fulfil the criterion of minimal difference.

Other nominal pairs, in particular those differing along the dimension of SEX/GENDER, score much lower in the judgement task (e.g.
mother:father; E: 4.55; G: 3.18) despite very high co-occurrence scores
(E: 29.99; G: 177.12). *Mother:father* scores lower than, for instance,
the related pair *man:woman/Mann:Frau*. Compared to *mother:father*,
the underlying category structure of *man:woman* may well be much
sparser and the additional attributes of *mother:father* may obscure the
dimension of biological sex, as this is also presumably not the most
salient feature. It is worth noting here that the base pair, *male:female*,
scored surprisingly low in the judgement task despite having long been
considered an excellent pair when referring to biological sex. However,
English and German both conflate sex and gender in the lexemes
male:female and *männlich:weiblich*. As there are no separate words
to refer solely to biological sex, this is mixed together with 'social'
gender and therefore carries a number of connotations and additional
encyclopaedic knowledge, which is not usually the case with other
adjective pairs. The gender pairs, including attribute listing results
for *man:woman* and *mother:father*, are discussed in detail in Case
Study III.

Thus, in terms of category structure and conceptual evaluation of
the antonymic relationship, the overall density or richness of the internal category structure (i.e. the number of attributes), the amount of
overlap between attributes of the two concepts and the ranking of the
salient opposing attributes are of importance in relation to antonymic
strength. The richer the category structure, the more difficult it is to
identify the salient axis, especially when the salient distinction is not
the most prominent attribute in the conceptual structure. Whether
these factors are equally relevant in explaining the patterns observed in
the behavioural data is discussed following a short summary of the
most influential factors which account for the patterns observed in the
judgement data.

3.5 Conclusions

The main aim of the analysis above was to establish whether the
factors proposed for good opposition could be shown to explain the
patterns observed in speaker judgements on antonymic strength.
Overall, conceptual factors seem to have greater explanatory power
than lexical effects such as morphological relatedness or frequency of

co-occurrence. The criteria drawn from the literature were evaluated and the data presented here largely supports previous findings with the effects of the following factors evident in the judgement data:

1. symmetry in the distribution on a scale
2. distance between concepts on the continuum
3. semantic range or generality
4. complexity of category structure
5. salience of the opposing dimension

On the lexical level, the main question was whether associative strength, as indicated by co-occurrence data from corpora, is a reliable indicator of antonymic strength. If, as some claim, canonical opposition depends on a strong associative relationship entrenched by high frequency of co-occurrence (e.g. Gross et al., 1989; Charles & Miller, 1990; Justeson & Katz, 1991), judgement data on antonymic strength should show a clear correlation with co-occurrence data. However, as the analyses here have shown very clearly, this is not the case. There are, of course, instances where the associative strength and antonymic strength of a particular pair correlate, but it remains unclear what role highly frequent co-occurrence plays in antonym judgements and whether it may simply be a consequence of particularly high antonymic strength (e.g. Jones et al., 2012). Matching antonymic and associative strength occurs mainly with highly canonical antonym pairs (e.g. *hot:cold, large:small, good:bad*) and the role of this lexical effect is further explored with the dataset of behavioural data in the following chapter. This third measure will allow for insights into the representation of antonymic items in the lexicon, for instance whether the members of an opposite pair are linked in the mental lexicon on the lexical level or whether their antonymic relationship has to be evaluated based on conceptual similarity or difference.

Notes

1 www.ids-mannheim.de and https://cosmas2.ids-mannheim.de/cosmas2-web/
2 Public part of the Archiv der Geschriebenen Sprache (W – öffentlich) http://www.ids-mannheim.de/cosmas2/projekt/referenz/archive.html (last accessed 10.03.2021)
3 www.surveymonkey.com (data collected between May 2008 and April 2010)
4 The GOE-rating score presented is the mean of the scores of both directions of presentation (i.e. *up:down* and *down:up*) unless otherwise indicated.
5 Data taken from the BNC World (accessed November 2008 – www.natcorp.ox.ac.uk)

6 In the questionnaire data overall, the standard deviation is relatively low and decisions seem largely homogeneous. However, with items which are rated in the middle of the continuum there is a larger amount of indecision and thus difference in the scores. This tendency seems to be particularly strong in the case of converses.

7 For a detailed introduction to cognitive models see Lakoff 1987, and for an overview Ungerer and Schmid (2006).

8 Figures only include attributes mentioned by more than one participant and the numbers in brackets refer to the number of participants who listed the attribute in question and the overall weighting of this attribute. Thus, the attributes at the top were those listed first by the largest number of participants.

4 Processing opposite pairs: an antonym decision task

The behavioural experiments discussed in this chapter were designed to further investigate the strength of the relationship between the members of different opposite pairs and the extent to which this is influenced by the conceptual and lexical factors proposed by the previous literature. The diverging patterns of co-occurrence data and antonymic strength found in the offline measures are taken as the starting point for the experimental investigation to determine whether 'online' data from a timed behavioural task matches 'offline' speaker judgements. In contrast to the offline methods used to establish antonymic strength, the online measure of reaction time (RT) provides information regarding the degree of entrenchment of these relations in speakers' lexicons, through repeated conceptual construal or habitual co-occurrence, which may result in their automatic co-activation.

Together with the antonymic strength data from the previous chapter, the experimental data will be used to investigate the processing and representation of antonym pairs in the lexicon and assess the contribution of individual factors of antonymic strength to the degree of entrenchment and resulting faster access of opposite pairs. The key questions here are first whether antonyms are stored as such or whether they are at least to some degree computed 'online' through, for example, a process of feature matching on the conceptual level (e.g. Hutchison, 2003). A second aim is to determine whether the data allows for a differentiation of the contribution of conceptual and lexical factors and if it supports a clear distinction between direct and indirect antonyms (cf. Gross et al., 1989) or provides evidence for a continuum approach to antonymy. Before the data is presented, the methodology and analysis procedure is outlined.

DOI: 10.4324/9781003026969-4

4.1 Rationale and design

This study employs a task similar to a lexical decision task but involves antonym/non-antonym judgements instead of word/nonword judgements. In a lexical decision task, participants are asked to decide whether an item presented to them (either visually or auditorily) is a real word in a given language or not. Lexical decision tasks are often used in combination with priming, where a prime word is presented at a certain interval before a target word to establish whether this prime leads to a change in the speed of activation of the target. In semantic priming, for instance, presenting the prime *warm* before the target *HOT*[1] would lead to faster reaction times to *hot* because these two items are semantically related, and activation is assumed to spread automatically between related items along semantic and form-based links (e.g. rhyming words) which operate on different levels of the lexical representation (e.g. Levelt, 1989; Bock & Levelt, 1994).

This mechanism of spreading activation is considered to underlie priming effects (e.g. Harley, 2013) and is a subconscious and automatic process which facilitates access to related words in the lexicon (which may, for instance, be needed in a conversation about a particular topic). This is based on decades of experimental research[2] using lexical decision tasks and word association and elicitation experiments which have also been used successfully in previous studies on opposition (among many others Deese, 1964, 1965; Paradis et al., 2009; Willners & Paradis, 2010; van de Weijer et al., 2012).

To be able to assess the contribution of the experimental data, the question of the mechanisms generating semantic priming has to be addressed. Antonymy falls into the category of semantic priming, which is based on co-activation of related meanings and has been explained in the literature as being either purely due to associative strength (Harley, 2013) or due to a matching of features of the two concepts during processing (e.g. Jeon et al., 2009; Hutchison, 2003). Hutchison (2003), in a very thorough investigation of a large number of priming experiments and their results, concludes that both associative strength and feature overlap have an influence on semantic priming. His category of 'functional associates' (Hutchison, 2003, p. 785) – synonyms and antonyms – supports a theory based on feature overlap, whereas mediated priming paradigms seem to indicate that there is at least some level of automatic associative priming. It is assumed that automatic associative facilitation as result of the entrenchment of close associates with great associative strength will play a role at the top end of the antonymic strength continuum.

Opposite pairs which do not possess this added 'boost' of associative strength, however, will be computed by a process of evaluation on the conceptual level of representation.

Thus, the question in terms of the relationship between antonyms is whether retrieving one member of an antonym pair automatically activates the other member by virtue of their strong associative relationship (i.e. simply 'looking up' a stored/entrenched relationship) or whether the conceptual similarity of the two items is assessed during processing ('working out'; Aitchison, 2012). As introduced in Section 2.5, antonym processing has been investigated in a number of studies (e.g. Charles et al., 1994; Paradis et al., 2009; Willners & Paradis, 2010) and recent evidence (e.g. Paradis et al., 2009; van de Weijer et al., 2014) supports differences between certain highly frequent canonical pairs which may be stored as opposite pairs based on strong associative relations, whereas other pairs are conceptually related and constructed when necessary by feature comparisons. This highlights the same categorical division between canonical and non-canonical antonyms prominent in the previous literature (among others Lyons, 1977; Cruse, 1986; Gross et al., 1989; Charles et al., 1994; Murphy, 2003) and more recently by Mohammad et al., 2008; Paradis et al., 2009; Jeon et al., 2009; van de Weijer et al., 2014). Previous research has thus proposed several different underlying mechanisms which may lead to facilitation in online psycholinguistic tasks using opposites depending on the precise relation between members of an antonym pair: associative strength (e.g. Paradis et al., 2009), distributional closeness (e.g. Mohammad et al., 2008)or activation of bundles of shared features (e.g. Jeon et al., 2009), while studies such as van de Weijer et al. (2012) did not find any independent effect of co-occurrence frequency in their priming experiments.

In this study, native speakers of English and German were asked to make a meta-judgement on the relationship between two lexical items rather than a simple decision on the lexical status of one item. Thus, if the decision is based on conceptual similarity or, for instance, a feature-matching process (e.g. Hutchison, 2003; Jeon et al., 2009), this would necessitate full activation of a lexical entry's semantic and conceptual material (e.g. Bock & Levelt ,1994) rather than simply being driven by, for instance, co-occurrence frequency which does not necessarily require full conceptual activation depending on the task[3]. The data presented here assesses the relative contributions of lexical and conceptual factors and informs a psycholinguistic model of the representation of opposition in the lexicon (see section 6.3).

4.1.1 Task design

The tasks consisted of 120 visually presented word pairs in English (Experiment 1) and German (Experiment 2): 60 opposite pairs and 60 control pairs. Both words were presented at the same time in the following format: WORD1-WORD2 (e.g. HOT-COLD) in capital letters (font size 36) in white on a dark grey background in the centre of a computer screen. Each pair was displayed for 1000 ms with 2050 ms between pairs. The order of pairs was pseudorandomised to avoid presentation of more than four clear yes-responses in a row. The task was divided into two lists per language, with each antonym pair appearing once in its preferred and once in its dispreferred order with the number of pairs in each order counterbalanced across the two lists.

The stimuli were presented to participants on individual monitors in the English experiment, while in the German experiment words were presented via a data projector. Reaction times were recorded on individual custom-made yes/no button boxes. The participants, who were tested in small groups of two to twelve, wore headphones to prevent distraction and were asked to use their thumbs to respond (dominant hand for yes-response). Participants received written and verbal instructions and, after providing written consent, completed a 10-item practice task before the main experiment.

4.1.2 Stimuli

The selection of the word pairs used in this task was primarily guided by the judgement task results discussed in the previous chapter. Those pairs which displayed potentially informative discrepancies between associative and antonymic strength measures, for example the *male:female* cluster, were included along with gradable pairs which displayed clear testable effects of certain criteria (e.g. symmetry). As an under-researched category of opposition, and with differing patterns in the judgement task data, converses also accounted for a sizeable proportion of the test pairs.

The control items were matched to test items in frequency, word class, number of phonemes, syllables and letters as well as image-ability.[4] The pairs resulting from combinations of these control words were 50% completely unrelated (e.g. *subject:town*), 25% related by association (e.g. *heavy:full*) and 25% synonymous (e.g. *pale:light*) to allow for different degrees of non-antonymic relatedness between the control words. A full list of test stimuli and their matched control items for both languages can be found in Appendix 4.

4.1.3 Participants

In Experiment 1, 38 native English speakers (aged 18–37), all students at the University of Oxford, participated in the experiments. For Experiment 2, 32 native speakers of German (aged 18–21) were recruited in a secondary school in Munich, Germany. All participants had corrected-to-normal vision and did not report any reading or hearing deficits. They participated in the study voluntarily and were compensated accordingly for their participation.

4.1.4 Data cleaning and analysis procedure

Participants were excluded based on error rates greater than 10% (E: n= 6; G; n = 4), which resulted in 32 participants in the English experiment and 28 for the German experiment. Reaction times (RT) outside ± 2 standard deviations from the individual participant's mean were excluded as outliers. The design of this experiment, especially the selection of stimuli, complicates the setting of an appropriate cut-off point for error rates since some of the word pairs used as targets (e.g. *debit:credit, tea:coffee, chase:flee*) are not considered opposite pairs by all speakers. Thus, items which generated extremely high error rates and long reaction times due to non-canonicity (e.g. *bull:cow*) were excluded from the main analyses.

For the individual factor analyses, FoC measures were converted into categorical variables (very high (t-score > 30.0), high (*t*-score 10.0–30.0), medium (*t*-score of 2.0–10.0) and low (*t*-score < 2.0) and judgement ratings were divided into the four groups introduced in Section 3.4 (excellent (1.0-1.79), good (1.8-2.5), medium (2.5-4.0) and bad (4.0–7.0)).

4.2 Overview of results

Before the results of individual factors are discussed, antonym type, co-occurrence rates and judgements scores are examined with regard to their correlation with reaction times. Here co-occurrence (medium to very high) and judgement data (good and excellent) were considered continuous variables and analysed using a mixed linear regression model in order to determine the effect of judgement scores and co-occurrence on RT. The interaction between the two factors is significant ($p < .001$), as are individual factor analyses (co-occurrence: $p < .001$; judgement ratings ($p < .001$). This shows that, overall, both the degree of co-occurrence and antonymic strength affect participants' reaction times. The data also shows an overall correlation between the two independent factors.

In terms of antonym type, the interaction with the judgement task data provided results supporting the classical distribution of antonym types. The analysis showed that gradable pairs with excellent judgement ratings were recognised fastest overall, while complementaries and converses are clustered together with more similar reaction times. FoC also had an added effect on the antonymic strength of the pairs with very high co-occurrence rates. As expected, the fastest times are achieved by gradable adjectival pairs with very high co-occurrence rates and excellent antonymic strength. However, the distribution below this initial top level is not influenced by any one of these factors alone but by combinations of different factors to varying degrees. It therefore seems that associative strength, a measurement of the lexical link, and antonymic strength, a measure of the conceptual link, do not interact in a straightforward manner. The following discussion of the effects of the individual factors on reaction times provides a more fine-grained analysis of the behavioural results which show effects of most of the proposed criteria in at least some groups of opposite pairs.

A series of individual analyses[5] was conducted using the statistical software JMP. Table 4.1 presents an overview of the effect of each factor on participants' reaction times before the analysis for each criterion is presented in greater detail.

4.2.1 Antonymic strength (judgement task scores)

As explained above, the continuous judgement results were divided into the four groups proposed in Section 3. 4, *excellent* (1.0–1.79), *good* (1.8–2.99), *medium* (3.0–4.99) and *poor* (5.0–7.0), to provide categorical variables for the RT analysis. These groups are solely based on the results of the judgement tasks and have not been changed for the statistical analysis in this chapter. Thus, there are some idiosyncrasies stemming from the judgement data which result in some unusual distributions of reaction times. Pairs in the poor category were excluded from all analyses as there was insufficient data for statistical analysis.

Figure 4.1 shows the comparison of the mean RT in the different groups. The analysis of the English data showed that the distribution below is significant, and a further comparison shows that the differences between all three conditions are significant (*excellent*: 752ms; *good*: 818ms; *medium*: 850ms). In the German data, the effect of judgement rating is also significant overall and, as in English, all three categories differ from each other (*excellent*: 859ms; *good*: 910ms; *medium*: 988ms).

Table 4.1 Summary of behavioural results for individual factors

Factor	Language	Overall*	
Judgement task	English	$F (2, 1385) = 14.2788; p < .001$	excellent < good < medium
	German	$F (2, 774) = 35.9552; p < .001$	excellent < good < medium
Frequency of co-occurrence	English	$F (2, 1385) = 33.5398; p < .001$	very high < high < medium
	German	$F (3, 774) = 52.6106; p < .001$	very high < high = medium
Sequence	English	$F (1, 1347) = 3.866; p = .049$	no significant difference
	German	$F (1, 1205) = 1.9228; p = .166$	no significant difference
Symmetry	English	$F (1, 632) = 29.0858; p < .001$	faster for symmetrical pairs
	German	$F (1, 774) = 23.4779; p < .001$	faster for symmetrical pairs
Morphological relatedness	English	$F (1, 1301) = 61.8392; p < .001$	faster for related
	German	$F (1, 702) = 13.7086; p = .0002$	faster for unrelated
Word class	English	$F (2, 1500) = 32.3821; p < .001$	adjectives < nouns < verbs
	German	$F (2, 775) = 46.1962; p < .001$	adjectives < nouns < verbs
Antonym type	English	$F (2, 1529) = 29.7352; p < .001$	antonym = complementary < converse
	German	$F (2, 775) = 32.4671; p < .001$	antonym < complementary < converse

Note
* In all tables < indicates a significantly faster RT for the item on the left while = indicates no difference.

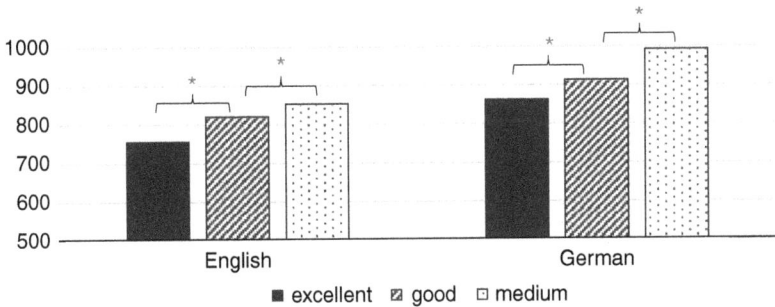

Figure 4.1 RT (in ms) by judgement rating for English and German.

The distribution of RT in the analysis by antonym type is quite similar to that in English with the conditions excellent and good resulting in faster reaction times than medium and poor in the analysis of both antonyms and complementaries. The case of converses, however, differs from the English distribution as the differences in reaction times between the conditions in the category of converses is not significant (p = .7418). This reflects the distribution of nominal converses seen in the judgement task in both English and German but is not reflected in the English behavioural data. The fact that those pairs which obtained relatively fast reaction times in the converse group in English (e.g. *husband:wife*) despite having low GOE-ratings were rated much higher in the German GOE-data will also have played a part in these more even results.

This is an expected distribution and supports the judgement task ratings as a reliable indicator of antonymic strength. In a more detailed analysis, certain pairs showed surprising differences between their judgement scores and RT, for instance nominal pairs in the *male:female* cluster such as *king:queen*. These pairs will be examined in greater detail in Case Study III in Chapter 5.

Table 4.2 RT by judgement ratings and antonym type (*denotes statistical significance)

	Excellent		Good		Medium	Overall
English						
Antonym	752 ms	<	818 ms	<	850 ms	p < .001*
Complementary	767 ms	<	803 ms	=	817 ms	p = .004*
Converse	822 ms	<	927 ms	=	872 ms	p < .001*
German						
Antonym	816 ms	<	847 ms	=	869 ms	p = .188*
Complementary	860 ms	=	864 ms	<	973 ms	p < .001*
Converse	971 ms	=	947 ms	=	987 ms	p = .803

Table 4.2 shows mean RT by judgement rating split according to three antonym types: *antonymy* (in the Structuralist sense), complementarity and converseness. The data shows that, as predicted, the congruence of GOE-rating and RT is greater in the *antonymy* and *complementary* categories than in the converse category.

All gradable opposite pairs in both languages show significant differences between the three rating categories ($p < .001$), with those rated excellent recognised fastest and those in the medium category slowest. In the case of the complementaries, the pattern is not as clear-cut. The English analysis still displays a strong degree of overall significance ($p = .004$) but planned comparisons show that the difference between good and medium pairs is not significant while in the German data, medium pairs are significantly slower than both excellent and good pairs, which do not differ. The reasons for this distribution and their implications will be discussed below in Section 4.2.7.

The RT distribution for converses shows a pattern which diverges from that seen in the judgement tasks in both languages. The English analysis for converse pairs shows strong statistical significance between the excellent and good and the excellent and medium GOE-rating categories, while the good and medium categories do not differ significantly. The faster reaction times in the medium category may be explained by the results for the pairs around the base pair *male:female,* which displayed a strikingly different pattern from the judgement data and will be discussed in more detail in Section 4.2.6. In the German data, there was no significant difference between the three groups (p = 0.742). This reflects the very narrow range of judgement scores for the nominal converses in both English and German, but this effect does not surface in the English RT data. This may be partly due to certain English converse pairs (e.g. *husband:wife*), which elicited comparatively fast reaction times despite low judgement scores as their German equivalents were rated much higher in the judgement task (see Section 4.2.7).

4.2.2 *Associative strength: frequency of co-occurrence*

It is indisputable that both individual frequency and frequent co-occurrence and subsequent entrenchment of certain lexical items or relations influence the strength of these relationships and the reliability of their connection in the mental lexicon (e.g. Traxler, 2012; Aitchison, 2012). However, the question is whether associative strength is the key factor in the speed and ease of antonym judgements or whether the degree of opposition between the two concepts involved is more crucial to the evaluation of the relationship. Given that in this task, participants are

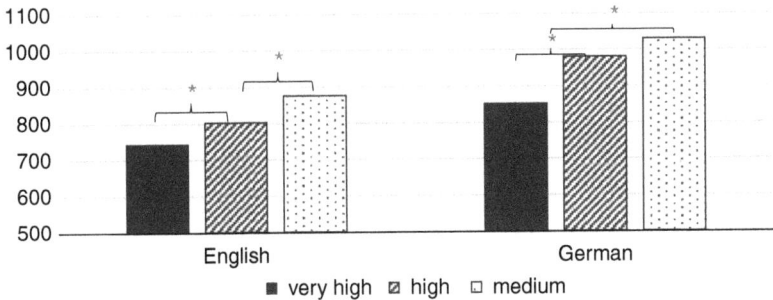

Figure 4.2 RT (in ms) by frequency of co-occurrence.

required to make decisions as quickly as possible, we may see an effect which prioritises pairs with strong associative connections which may not generally be judged as strongly antonymic in judgement tasks as they may be automatically co-activated regardless of their specific relation.

The statistical analysis of the effect of frequency of co-occurrence was carried out in three stages: first for the overall data set, second divided by antonym type and last by judgement rating score. All three analyses are first presented and subsequently discussed.

Figure 4.2 illustrates the results of the analysis for the whole data set in both languages which show a similar pattern. The overall analysis is significant in both ($p < .001$) and shows greater co-occurrence rates resulting in faster RT. The English data shows significant differences between the categories *very high* (742 ms) and *high* (802 ms), as well as *high* and *medium* (876 ms). In the German data, however, only the category *very high* (852 ms) is significantly faster than all other categories while *high* (981) and *medium* (1030 ms) are not significantly different. They are, however, still numerically different, and in a data set with higher statistical power the pattern might have been more similar to that seen in English.

The division of the data set by antonym type (Table 4.3) results in markedly different patterns. In the English data, gradable opposites – which include the largest proportion of canonical adjectival pairs – show a 'classic' distribution with significant differences between all three conditions. The German data shows the same pattern but there is no statistically significant difference between the high and medium categories.

The English complementary analysis also shows overall statistical significance, but this is driven by the slower reaction time in the *high* category (863 ms) compared to *very high* (734 ms) and *medium* (765 ms)

Table 4.3 RT for antonym types by frequency of co-occurrence for English and German

	Very high		High		Medium	Overall
English						
Antonym	690 ms	<	757 ms	<	908 ms	p < .001*
Complementary	734 ms	<	863 ms	>	765 ms	p < .001*
Converse	834 ms	=	836 ms	<	1032 ms	p < .001*
German						
Antonym	794 ms	<	891 ms	=	975 ms	p < .001*
Complementary	843 ms	<	968 ms	=	1024 ms	p < .001*
Converse	902 ms	<	1038 ms	=	1057 ms	p = .0003*

which do not differ. Thus, complementaries with high co-occurrence scores elicit a significantly slower RT than those with medium co-occurrence rates, while very high co-occurrence rates resulted in similar reaction times to the medium pairs. Here, the question to what extent the absolute, rather than relative, frequency of co-occurrence is crucial in antonym (or other relational) judgements arises. This will be revisited in the discussion below as well as in Chapter 6. As for antonyms above, the German data showed a difference only for *very high* pairs, with *high* and *medium* pairs showing no significant difference.

The overall analysis for English converses is significant but there are no differences between the *very high* (834 ms) and *high* (836 ms) conditions. Pairs in both of these conditions are recognised significantly faster than those in the *medium* category (1032 ms). In the German dataset, only the converse pairs with very high co-occurrence show a significant facilitation effect compared to those with high or medium co-occurrence. This data suggests that the degree of strength of the association does not have as direct an influence on these less conventionalised pairs. However, very high co-occurrence rates do seem to have a significant facilitatory effect.

The last set of analyses divides the data by judgement rating category to assess the effect of frequency of co-occurrence in pairs which are judged to have similar antonymic strength (see Table 4.4). The English excellent set showed a classic distribution with significant differences between all three conditions. In the German data set, this pattern is repeated. This is, again, an expected distribution because opposite pairs rated excellent do occur more frequently in context.

For those opposite pairs with a good rating, the English data shows an overall significant difference but only the *medium* category differs significantly. In the German dataset, those opposites with very high co-

Table 4.4 RT for pairs by antonymic strength and frequency of co-occurrence for English and German

	Very high		High		Medium	Overall
English						
Excellent	703 ms	<	776 ms	<	847 ms	*p* < .001*
Good	813 ms	=	801 ms	<	853 ms	*p* = .004*
Medium	787 ms	<	890 ms	<	1083 ms	*p* < .001*
German						
Excellent	816 ms	<	940 ms	<	1039 ms	*p* < .001*
Good	824 ms	<	968 ms	=	948 ms	*p* < .001*
Medium	911 ms	<	1033 ms	=	1054 ms	*p* = .002*

occurrence are responded to significantly faster than those in the *high* and *medium* conditions, which do not significantly differ from each other.

In the category of pairs rated as having *medium* antonymic strength, there are still a significant number of pairs with high or very high co-occurrence rates, which in itself raises the question of the reliability of the correlation between frequency of co-occurrence and antonymic strength. These pairs show the same pattern as those rated *excellent* with all three conditions differing significantly. The German data, once again, shows a significantly faster RT for the *very high* condition only.

The fact that co-occurrence influences reaction times to a significant degree in the overall analysis of the data is not surprising as it has been demonstrated by numerous corpus studies that antonyms do indeed occur more frequently in the same context than chance would predict (see Jones et al., 2012 for an overview). It seems that extremely high frequency of co-occurrence does have a considerable influence on the speed with which a word pair is judged as an opposite pair but also that this very strong associative relation aids recognition in general. This makes it more difficult to determine the cause of the faster reaction times as the results are heavily influenced by associative strength. Overall, it is clear that while co-occurrence rates do have an influence on RT, antonymic strength also plays an important role since the different categories of antonymic strength display progressively slower reaction times and the reaction times for the excellent pairs, for instance, are broadly similar, despite variable co-occurrence rates.

4.2.3 Antonym sequence

While sequencing preferences of certain opposite pairs are evident in corpus studies (e.g. Jones, 2002; Kostić, 2015a; Wu, 2017), previous

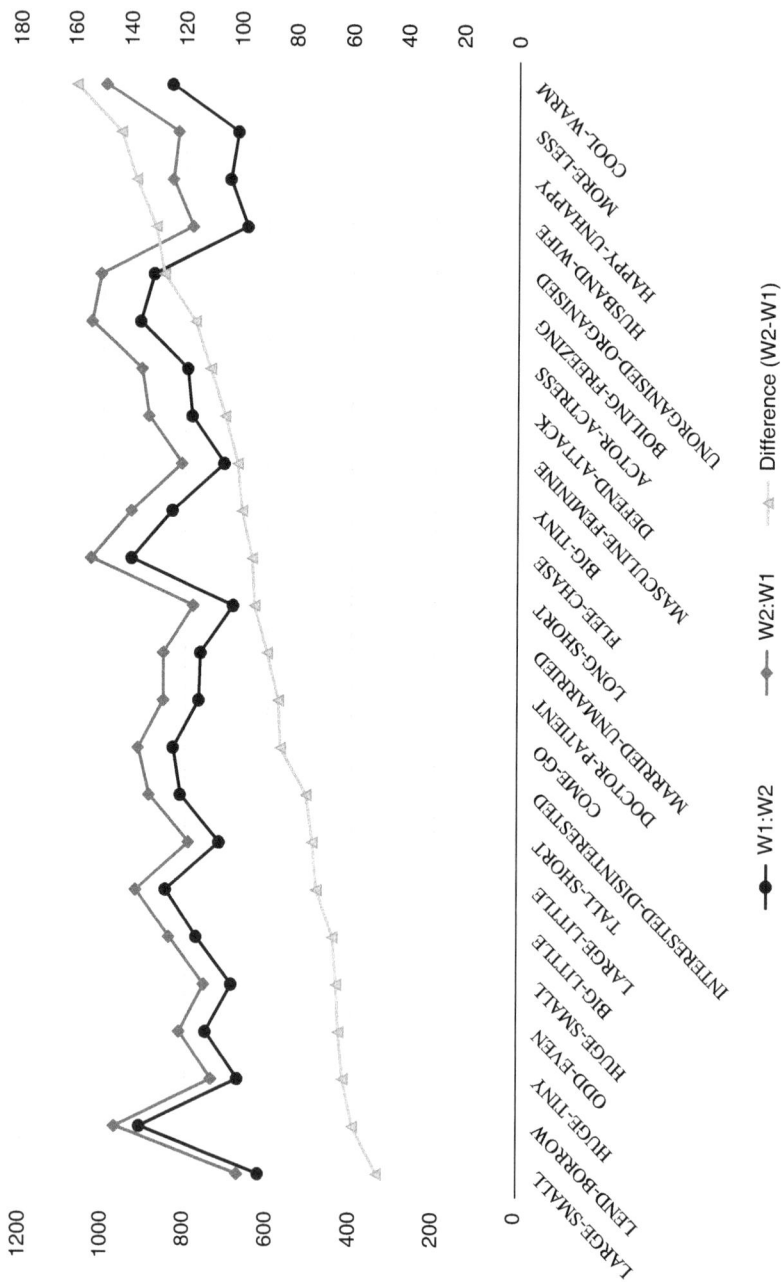

Figure 4.3 **RT** (in ms) for English pairs with a difference > 50ms between sequences.

psycholinguistic research has not found any difference in, for instance, judgement tasks (e.g. Paradis et al., 2007) between antonym pairs displayed in their preferred and dispreferred sequence. Here, all pairs which showed a considerable discrepancy in co-occurrence in the two sequences[6] were coded as preferred/dispreferred in the experiment to detect potential differences in the behavioural results. As discussed earlier, the judgement task data only showed discrepancies of antonymic strength for a small number of pairs, and none of those were highly canonical (Section 3.4.5).

The overall analysis of the English data barely reaches statistical significance ($p = .049$), while the difference in the German pairs is not significant ($p = .166$). However, the differences between sequences for some pairs differ substantially and are statistically significant while others display no difference at all. RT differences range from 0.4 ms for *old:young* to 144 ms for *more:less* and 159 ms for *cool:warm*. This pattern is repeated in the German data, and both data sets show faster reaction times for those pairs which do have an ordering preference compared to those that do not. However, many of those pairs which show a preference in this task are the more canonical pairs (e.g. *big:little, odd:even, long:short*) while this was not the case in the judgement task.

Figure 4.3 illustrates these differences for English pairs with a difference of more than 50 ms between the two sequences. The grey line plots the difference (in ms) on the right-hand axis in ascending order. It is clear that there are pairs in which the order of presentation does affect the response speed of participants as one direction leads to greater facilitation than the other.

Overall, the results of the behavioural experiments corroborate both previous results which have not shown overall differences based on sequencing in antonym judgements (e.g. Paradis et al., 2009) and support the criteria put forward for ordering preferences as those pairs which do display a preference do conform to these criteria. Furthermore, all pairs in the experimental study, if they show any difference at all, are slower in the dispreferred order as indicated by corpus data. Whether these ordering differences for some of the canonical pairs are relevant in terms of the lexical representation and access of opposite pairs will be discussed in Section 6.3.

4.2.4 Symmetry of distribution

As symmetry only applies to gradable opposites, the analysis of the effect of symmetry was carried out on this subset of the data. The overall results show that symmetrical pairs are responded to significantly more quickly in both the English ($p < .001$; 757 ms vs. 856 ms) and German ($p < .001$; 819 ms vs. 838 ms) data. This finding ties in with the analysis of the results of the judgement task in Section 3.4.3, which showed very clearly that gradable pairs which are equidistant from the midpoint of their scale are judged to be better examples of antonymy than those which are asymmetrically distributed.

4.2.5 Morphological relatedness

As previously discussed, there is general agreement that the 'best' antonyms are morphologically unrelated (e.g. Cruse, 1986; Paradis et al., 2009). However, as the judgement task scores showed, while unrelated opposites are spread across the whole canonicity continuum, morphologically related pairs are only found in the top third. The behavioural data should therefore reflect the fact that both the most and the least strongly related opposite pairs are morphologically unrelated, while the related pairs are usually considered good opposites with much greater consistency.

The analysis of the complete English data set showed a significant result for morphological relatedness ($p < .001$), with unrelated items approximately 60 ms slower than related ones (related: 837 ms vs. unrelated: 771 ms). The German data shows significantly faster RT for unrelated items ($p = .0002$; unrelated: 883 ms vs. related 933 ms). To minimise the effect of item length (as morphologically related pairs are often longer than unrelated ones), a second analysis was carried out in both languages with all items longer than 18 characters removed. In this second analysis, the English data no longer shows any significant difference between related and unrelated items ($p = .141$) while the German data remains stable.

These results (Figure 4.4) are initially counterintuitive from a psycholinguistic perspective, as morphologically related items should result in reliable priming due to both their semantic and form overlap as long as the semantic relatedness is transparent (e.g. Marslen-Wilson et al., 1994). There are several reasons for the differences observed in the German data: for instance, the German set of morphologically related pairs includes a larger proportion of nouns and verbs (while the English items are largely adjectival), which displayed slower reaction times overall. It seems that, in this kind of task, a significant amount of form overlap does not result in faster reactions, which may be due to the simultaneous presentation of the items or the nature of the task, which requires full lexical access to conceptual information. In both

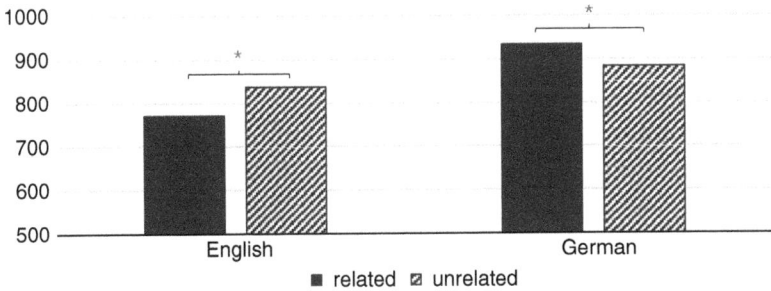

Figure 4.4 RT (in ms) by morphological relatedness for English and German.

languages, the overall distribution of related and unrelated items is broadly similar in both the GOE-rating and the behavioural data.

One result which is in keeping with the results of previous studies is that, in both English and German, the pairs with the fastest reaction times are morphologically unrelated (cf. also Gross et al., 1989; Charles et al., 1994; Paradis et al., 2007, 2009). The overall distribution of related and unrelated items is broadly similar in both languages for judgment scores and the behavioural data. The effect of morphological relatedness and the lack of a clear pattern of facilitation will be revisited in Chapter 6 in the context of the proposed model of antonym processing.

4.2.6 Word class

As the complexity of the internal category structure of the two members of an opposite pair is difficult to determine accurately, word class has been used here to determine the effect of complexity as word class and conceptual complexity have been shown to correlate strongly. While adjectival pairs provide the largest proportion of opposite pairs, in both languages a significant number of verbal and nominal pairs were included for purposes of comparison. Many of these pairs, both nominal and verbal, are converses, and two separate analyses were conducted (one with and one without converses) in order to establish whether differences were due to word class or antonym type. As the two analyses resulted in the same pattern, only the results for the complete dataset are illustrated in Figure 4.5.

The analyses in both languages showed word class to be a highly significant predictor of RT (English: $p < .001$; German: $p < .001$). In both languages, all three conditions differ significantly, with adjectives

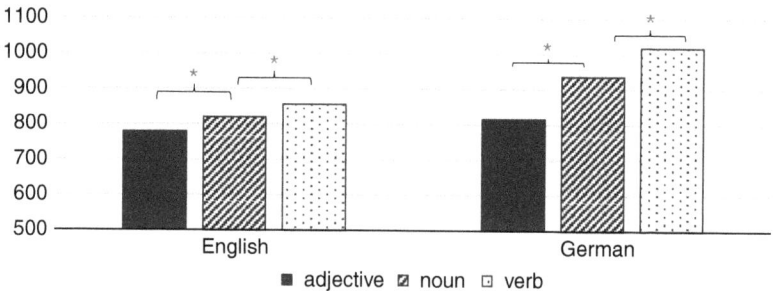

Figure 4.5 RT (in ms) by word class for English and German.

fastest and verbs slowest. These results do not match the judgement scores because, in that data set, verbal converses showed much greater variability and overall higher antonymic strength than their nominal counterparts. The pattern observed in the behavioural data, however, may reflect the fact that certain nominal pairs, most notably those in the *male:female* cluster, elicited much faster RTs than their judgement rating would predict. Therefore, a second analysis was carried out excluding pairs with very high co-occurrence scores and disproportionately lower judgement scores. This resulted in the removal of the following four pairs and their German counterparts: *mum:dad, mother:father, man:woman* and *king:queen.*

While the overall analyses in both languages still show word class to be a significant predictor for RT, there is no longer a significant difference between nominal and verbal pairs in either language with adjectival pairs still recognised significantly faster. Despite the fact that this is based on a small dataset, this seems to be a very robust result, which is partly due to the large number of good and excellent adjectival pairs in the judgement tasks and highlights the privileged status of adjectives in antonym formation.

4.2.7 Antonym type

The analysis of antonym type shows a distribution of results which is unsurprising in light of the foregoing discussion. The overall analysis for antonym type is significant in both languages (English: $p < .001$; German: $p < .001$) and participants were significantly slower to recognise converse pairs (E: 849 ms; G: 981 ms) than either antonyms (E: 783 ms; G: 857 ms) or complementaries (E: 784 ms; G: 909 ms). In German, the difference between antonyms and complementaries is also

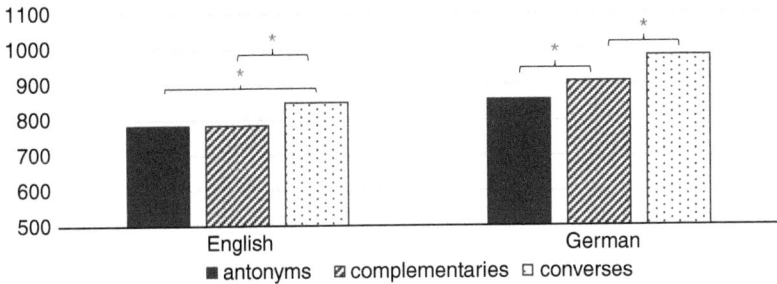

Figure 4.6 RT (in ms) by antonym type for English and German.

significant (52 ms), with complementaries being recognised more slowly (Figure 4.6).

This division between the more canonical categories on the one hand and converses on the other is one also seen in the judgement rating. There are several possible reasons for this including the increased complexity of the conceptual structure and relationship between the two members of a converse pair and the absence of certain criteria of good antonymy. While the difference in the size of the conditions in the experiment (with converses making up a much smaller proportion of stimuli) may make emerging patterns more difficult to detect, when the data is considered from a qualitative perspective it becomes clear that there is more at play than simply a task-based effect.

The analysis of the distribution of judgement ratings for converses resulted in different patterns within and between nominal and verbal converses, and the behavioural data shows slower reaction times for both types when compared to other opposite pairs. The judgement data shows a clear difference in patterns between nominal and verbal converses, which was initially attributed to the more complex conceptual structure of nominal pairs and thus the greater difficulty of accessing the binary dimension necessary for antonym construal. The behavioural data shows no such distinction between verbal and nominal pairs. It seems that, despite the fact that many verbal pairs received better ratings in the judgement task, those pairs obtain slower reaction times.

However, when reaction times are directly compared to both co-occurrence rates and judgement scores a possible pattern emerges. Figure 4.7 illustrates this for English converse pairs and it is noticeable that verbal converse pairs show a greater correlation between RT and judgement scores than nominal pairs. In part, this can once again be attributed to the much faster reaction times of certain

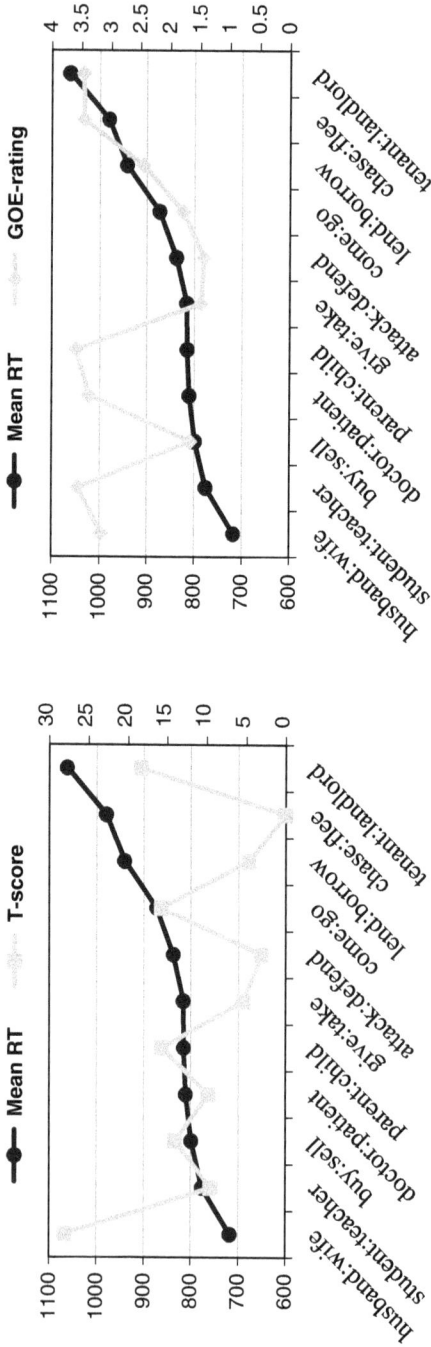

Figure 4.7 Comparison of RT (in ms) and co-occurrence (left) and judgement scores (right) for English converse pairs.

nominal pairs with very high co-occurrence scores which do not match speaker assessments of their antonymic strength. This indicates that the weighting of the criteria for good opposition is somewhat different in a judgement task from a behavioural experiment task where decisions about antonymicity are made under time constraints.

4.3 Conclusions

The data from the behavioural experiments contributes both methodological insights and evidence which supports previous accounts of antonymy as a prototype category, with pairs that pattern along a canonicity canonicity continuum. Each pair's place on this continuum is determined by certain factors which influence its antonymic strength.

Given the previous literature, the data shows some clear and expected patterns in terms of the overall correlations of judgement ratings and co-occurrence patterns which both significantly affect reaction times. In general, pairs with the highest judgement ratings and co-occurrence rates also elicit the fastest the reaction times and many of these pairs are similar across the two languages (e.g. *new:old/neu:alt* and *big:small/ groß:klein*), and the pairs where the three measures align best are those which are called canonical in the literature.

However, as the individual analyses show, the data also highlights the complexity and interdependence of the factors which influence antonymic strength and illustrates that antonymy is not a relation determined by a single factor. Most of the individual factors show an overall effect on reaction times (see Table 4.1 for a summary of significant effects) but the patterns in planned comparisons are not always straightforward.

Pair ordering, for instance, was only very marginally significant in the English data and did not affect reaction times significantly in German which supports the previous findings (e.g. Paradis et al., 2009; Willners & Paradis, 2010). However, there are a number of pairs in the data which show a significant difference in reaction times depending on the order of presentation (as illustrated in Figure 4.4 for English). The effect of morphological relatedness also does not significantly influence the lexical decision task results in English but in the German data, related items elicited significantly longer RTs which initially seems counterintuitive but may be explained by the variable distribution of pairs from different lexical categories in the two languages.

The effect of word class in the experimental data is clear and antonym type is closely related to lexical category in this data set, especially with regard to converses because most converse pairs in the experiment are verbal or nominal while a large proportion of antonyms and complementaries consists of adjectival pairs. Both these factors showed significant effects on reaction times, with the canonical combination of adjective and antonym/complementary resulting in the fastest reactions.

The picture which emerges with regard to co-occurrence initially seems very clear but the results obtained in the more detailed analyses do not always match the scores obtained for antonymic strength. It was already noted in the analyses of word class and antonym type that several pairs which obtained the some of the fastest reaction times in both languages were not considered highly antonymic in the judgement task. These pairs were mainly nominal (e.g. *king-queen*; *husband-wife*) and all pairs co-occurred extremely frequently. This shows that the influence of frequency of co-occurrence and subsequent entrenchment of the connection of the two members a pair is of greater weight in a behavioural experiment than in 'offline' judgements such as the judgement task, where the conceptual relation plays a more prominent role. This can be explained by the nature of the processing taking part in the two different tasks.

If we assume that the lexicon is structured in such a way that lexical and conceptual information are stored separately at least to some degree (e.g. Levelt, 1989; Bock & Levelt, 1994; Levelt et al., 1999), and we suppose that fast, automatic processing mechanisms initially tap into the lexical relationship rather than the rich conceptual representation during language comprehension (e.g. Norris et al., 2006), the greater effect of associative strength in a timed online task such as the experiment presented here is unsurprising. However, if the faster reactions are due to the entrenchment of a relationship between the two lexical items in an antonym pair rather than their conceptual antonymic relationship, this cannot be considered indicative of their antonymic strength. This may explain cases where high associative strength makes a considerable difference in reaction times in pairs which are not judged to be very strongly related in the judgement task.

To what extent the exact value of the *t*-score (or the absolute rather than relative frequency of co-occurrence) influences antonym (or other relational) judgements is difficult to determine. A higher than chance co-occurrence ($t > 2.0$) seems to have an overall effect, whereas the extreme facilitation seen in some of the examples mentioned above only occurs with an extremely high *t*-score ($t > 25$; see also van de Weijer et al., 2014). This further supports the hypothesis that there are certain pairs which are very strongly associatively connected and, in a task which crucially depends on speed, this effect aids both the recognition and possibly the subsequent conceptual assessment of pairs with great associative strength. This difference in the type of connection and entrenchment forms part of the model of antonym representation proposed in Section 6.3.

While the above could suggest a categorical difference between certain types of opposites, the empirical evidence in this study, like much recent work (e.g. Jones et al., 2012) supports a continuum approach to antonym canonicity rather than a binary division into central and peripheral antonymy. However, the question whether certain factors allow us to predict where on this continuum an antonym pair will fall is not a straightforward one. The comparison of offline and online measures has provided useful insights into the structure and nature of antonymy. For instance, cases of mismatch, both between languages and between the three data sets, show the role played by individual factors (e.g. semantic range) as well as differences in weighting of factors depending on the task as certain factors have a more significant impact in the online tasks (e.g. associative strength). This raises the question whether the relationship between the two members of a pair is judged on the basis of lexical or conceptual criteria (or both) and which of these play the bigger part. Thus, it remains to be determined whether the increased importance of associative strength is simply a by-product of the online task or whether it is a genuine factor in antonym judgements.

Returning briefly to methodological considerations, the benefits of a cross-linguistic approach have been highlighted throughout. In addition to providing a richer data set, the comparison of antonym behaviour in two language systems allows for more reliable generalisations and, crucially, offers an opportunity to distinguish between lexical and conceptual effects. It has emerged very clearly from the data that most factors influence antonym judgements in a similar way in both languages while effects differ according to task demands. The cross-linguistic comparison of lexical opposition presented here has resulted in remarkable similarities in all datasets, which cannot be coincidental. This adds to the empirical basis on which models such as the cognitive proposal of antonymy put forward by Jones et al. (2012) are built, and stands in contrast to the position of the 'lexical categorical model' (e.g. Gross & Miller, 1990) supported by many earlier approaches to antonymy.

The recent conceptual approaches and the evidence in this book suggest that antonym judgements are made on the basis of conceptual similarity and opposition but that the recognition and processing of highly conventionalised pairs at the top of the scale may well be aided by the entrenchment provided by frequent lexical association.

In Part III, the combined data, in addition to the results of previous antonym studies, will be used to model the representation and processing of both canonical and non-canonical opposites in the mind and brain on the basis of both psycholinguistic and cognitive theories regarding lexical storage, processing and entrenchment. This model will be used to explain the prototype effects seen in the judgement of non-canonical opposition as well as the special status of canonical opposites. Before this, in Chapter 5, three case studies are presented to allow for a more qualitative analysis of certain phenomena which highlight particular aspects crucial to antonym construal and processing.

Notes

1 To distinguish primes and targets in visual tasks, targets are usually presented in capital letters in languages which distinguish lower case and upper case letters.
2 Harley (2013) and Traxler (2012) are both accessible introductions to psycholinguistic with comprehensive chapters on experimental methods and language processing.
3 A more detailed description of the structure of a lexical entry and possible activation patterns is provided in Section 6.3.
4 Matched control items as well as imageability data were taken from the MRC Psycholinguistic Database (Wilson ,1988).
5 In the analyses, participants were included as a random factor and targets nested under the fixed effect.
6 For this purpose, preferred and dispreferred orders were determined by the BNC (English) and COSMAS (German) co-occurrence data.

5 Case studies

The following three case studies cover three different sets of opposites: two pairs of verbal converses, gradable opposition (SIZE) and a set of complementaries (*male:female*). The data here is presented in greater detail with a more fine-grained analysis of individual pairs and a greater focus on cross-linguistic differences than in the overview provided in Chapters 3 and 4. Furthermore, each case study will highlight particular criteria which play a role in antonym judgement. Case study I focuses on the lexical encoding of opposition in one or two lexical items while Case Studies II and III deal with larger sets of pairs and revisit criteria such as semantic range, conceptual category structure and the differing effects of co-occurrence on judgement and behavioural data.

5.1 Case study I: *borrow:lend* and *rent:let* – a cross-linguistic comparison

The two verbal converse pairs *borrow:lend* and *let:rent* display the biggest cross-linguistic difference in antonymic strength in the converse set. They are, in fact, opposite manifestations of the same phenomenon. In the case of *borrow:lend* and *verleihen:ausleihen*, English encodes each direction of this converse opposition in a separate lexeme, whereas the distinction made by prefixation in German is somewhat artificial as the German lexeme *leihen* (and its prefixed form *ausleihen*) can mean both 'borrow' and 'lend.' Meanwhile, in the case of *let:rent* and *mieten:vermieten*, German uses two lexemes, whereas in English speakers have two lexemes at their disposal but they can be used interchangeably (much like *leihen* in German). Lexeme such as these which have two opposing sub-senses (e.g. also *dust* 'to cover in dust' or 'to remove dust' are called referred to as antagonyms and are not usually considered within the antonym canon (see Lutzeier, 1997, 2001).

DOI: 10.4324/9781003026969-5

The pair *lend:borrow* is generally considered an opposite pair by speakers of English but not one of the canonical pairs due to its converse nature. There are some dialect areas in the UK and other English-speaking areas (e.g. the USA) which use either lexeme for both concepts (cf. Example 5.1) but in most varieties, including Standard British English, the separation is fairly rigid and 'mistakes' are very noticeable.[1]

5.1   North West Wales

> ***Borrow** me a quid*   *vs.*   *I **lent** it off him.*

This causes difficulties for native speakers of German who are learning English because German uses a single lexeme for both directions of the process. In fact, German does have two lexemes to cover this word field, but both can be used to denote *lend* **and** *borrow*, namely ModG *borgen*, which derives from the same root as *borrow* (OHG *borgên*), and *leihen* which can be traced back to OHG *līhan* (MHG *līhen*). *Lend* is not a direct cognate of *leihen* but comes from OE *lænan*, which comes from the OE noun *læn*. German has a derivate from the same nominal root, namely *lehnen* 'to enfeoff.'[2] *Lehnen*, in this meaning, is extremely rare and is not considered a lexical choice for the concepts under discussion.

5.2   *lend/borrow* vs. *leihen/borgen*

    *Kannst   du   mir   das   Buch   **borgen/leihen?***
    can2SgP youNOM meDAT DefArtN bookACC lendINF
    'Can you lend me the book?'

    *Kann   ich   mir   das   Buch   **borgen/leihen?***
    can1SgP INOM meDAT DefArtN bookACC borrowINF
    'Can I borrow the book?'

From the examples in 5.2, it can be seen that both *leihen* and *borgen* can be used for either process. The distinction between the two is dependent on register and region; *borgen* is more colloquial and used mainly in northern Germany, whereas *leihen* is the more standard form which is used throughout the German-speaking area. As can be seen from the examples above, there is little room for ambiguity as the syntax of the sentence makes clear which meaning is intended. However, this is also the case in English, which nevertheless uses two lexemes. Interestingly, both German lexemes can be modified morphologically by adding the prefix *aus-*, but this does not disambiguate between the two senses since *ausleihen* can still be used for both *lend* and *borrow* (cf. 5.3).

5.3   *Kann*   *ich*   *mir*   *das*   ***ausleihen?***
       can1Sg INOM meDAT   thisACC borrowINF
       'Can I borrow this?'
       Ich   *habe*   *dir*   *das*   *Buch*   ***ausgeliehen.***
       INOM   have1Sg youSG.DAT DefA bookACC   lend (PP)
       'I have lent you the book.'

The only alteration which makes it completely clear which direction of the exchange the speaker is focusing on is the addition of *ver-*. This is only an option with *leihen,* but the form *verleihen* is not used very frequently. The corresponding noun, *Verleih,* however, for a rental agency (providing cars, skis etc.) is extremely common.

    The pair *rent:let* operates in the same way but is the reverse case. *Rent* could conceivably form an antonym pair with *let,* which covers a similar semantic area, but because neither is completely restricted to either direction of the 'letting/renting exchange' this antonymic pairing is rather weak, a hypothesis which has been substantiated by the low antonymic strength this pair displayed in the GOE-rating questionnaire. *Let* seems more restricted in usage but, as was shown in the case of *ausleihen:verleihen* above, only one of the two lexemes needs to be bi-directional for the opposition to be weakened. In the case of *rent,* the directionality is occasionally made clear by forming a prepositional construction with *out* – *to rent out*. However, as the examples in (5.4) show, it is perfectly possible for *rent* to operate on its own for both perspectives which could have been encoded by a converse antonym pair.

5.4 *rent*
     *He **rented** the cottage to them.* vs. *They **rented** the cottage from him.*

        Sense 1: *trans.* To let (property) for rent or payment; to hire *out* [sic] to someone. Freq. with the person as indirect object. (c1447/1546)
        Sense 2: *trans.* To pay rent for (land, buildings, etc.); to take possession of, hold, occupy, or use, by payment of rent. (1530)

In German, the situation is different; *mieten:vermieten* form a morphologically related antonym pair and the directionality is signalled by the prefix *ver-*, which is often, but not exclusively, a marker of converseness (e.g. *kaufen:verkaufen* 'buy:sell'). There is no flexibility in the usage of either *mieten* or *vermieten*; each covers its own part of the relevant semantic field, and using one for the other would have much the same effect as it would to use *buy* and *sell* the wrong way around (see 5.5).

5.5   *mieten* vs. *vermieten*

    Er   **vermietete**   *seine*   *Wohnung.*
    heNOM   rent3SgPRET   PossP3SgMACC   flatACC
    'He rented out his flat.'
    Sie   **mietete**   *ein*   *Ferienhaus.*
    sheNOM rent3SgPRET   IndefAACC   holiday homeACC
    'She rented a holiday home.'

This pair is readily recognised as an antonym pair by speakers of German (as much as any converse pair in the language) and does not encode weaker opposition than any other pairs of its kind. Thus, it seems plausible that speakers perceive concepts as standing in weaker opposition when they are antagonymically encoded than when the same concepts are encoded antonymically. This also has consequences for storage and processing as, in one case, both meanings are linked to one lexeme which is accessed repeatedly in the experimental task, while in another the encoding is distinct and the two items are closely linked (see Chapter 6).

5.2 Case study II: *a matter of size*

The domain of size is structured around highly canonical gradable antonym pairs in both English and German. However, English has two base pairs, *big:little* and *small:large*, while German has one, *groß:klein*, which not only covers almost the complete semantic area of *small*, *little*, *big* and *large* (except the 'overweight' sense of *big/large*) but also parts of the lexical field covered by *tall* and *short* in English (most notably HEIGHT). Therefore, of the eleven English pairs in the original questionnaire, only seven have German equivalents. Overall, English and German pairs are considered relatively similar in judgements of antonymic strength despite certain differences in associative strength.

Before a detailed discussion of the data, the relationship between the two central English pairs will be examined more closely. The pairs are of nearly equal standing and can be used interchangeably in many contexts. Despite the two lexemes denoting the upper end of the scale (*large, big*) generally being considered good synonyms and those at

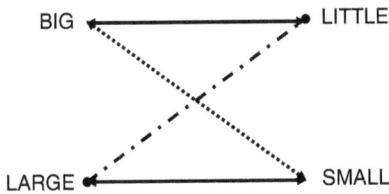

Figure 5.1 Antonymic relationships between big, large, small *and* little.

the opposite end (*small, little*) likewise, native speakers show a strong preference for two specific pairs (cf. Figure 5.1).

There are two pairs (*big:little* and *large:small*) which are more conventional (connected with solid lines in Figure 5.1) while of the less conventional pairs, *big:small* is judged better than *large:little* (dashed line).[3] These native speaker intuitions are also supported by empirical evidence. Miller (1998, p. 52), for example, states that '[...] the pair *large* and *little* are simply not accepted as antonyms. Overwhelmingly, association data and co-occurrence data indicate that *big* and *little* are considered a pair and *large* and *small* are considered a pair.' Gross et al. (1988) and Miller (1998) claim that this distribution gives support to the theory that antonymy is an associative relation on the lexical level, as the conceptual contrast in the other pairings is of similar strength.

An analysis of the semantic range of each of the four adjectives, however, illustrates their distributional differences.[4] Muehleisen (1997, pp. 104ff.) shows that *little* does not share a large amount of semantic range with *large*, whereas *small* and *large* seem to occur in similar contexts and collocational combinations much more frequently. She explains the better match between *big* and *little* by a greater shared semantic range compared to *large:little* and the fact that the connection of *large:small* is such a strong one, which leaves *big* as the only available option for *little*. However, Muehleisen's corpus data also shows that, statistically speaking, *big* and *small* have more semantic range in common than *big* and *little* (1997: 112) and that therefore, *big:small* should be the better antonym pair. As an explanation for the stronger perceived connection between *big* and *little*, she proposes reciprocity, as *small* is found primarily in the same environments as *large* and shares less semantic range with *big* but still more than *little* shares with *big*. In the following analysis we will see whether these patterns, based on semantic range and associative strength, are evident in the results.

Of the eleven English pairs on the SIZE continuum (Table 5.1) ten involve adjectives and one, *giant:dwarf*, is a nominal pair. As in the TEMPERATURE

Table 5.1 Data for pairs on the size continuum (ordered by English judgement score)

Word 1	Word 2	GOE	FoC	RT (ms)	Word 1	Word 2	GOE	FoC	RT (ms)
big	small	1.23	10.79	625	groß	klein	1.08	123.71	701
small	large	1.24	25.67	648					
big	little	1.24	8.13	806					
giant	dwarf	1.45	1.72	777	Riese	Zwerg	1.29	11.82	829
tiny	huge	1.49	3.90	705	winzig	riesig	1.34	5.37	
colossal	miniscule	1.51	0	1084	kolossal	unscheinbar	4.2	0	1197
big	tiny	2.04	1.82	882	groß	winzig	2.73	4.56	967
large	little	2.05	−3.72	885					
small	huge	2.25	1.53	721	klein	riesig	2.8	5.87	795

examples in Section 3.4.3, pairs were selected to violate certain criteria for good opposition and, in this case, all possible combinations of the central four lexemes were included to investigate their complex relationship. The German stimuli contained the same nominal pair, *Riese:Zwerg*, as well as all available translation equivalents of the English pairs.

The antonym judgements for the central pairs are similar in both languages. German *groß:klein*, scores highest, and is one of the pairs with the highest antonymic strength overall, which, given its extensive shared semantic range and high co-occurrence frequency, is unsurprising. The fact that there are several possibilities in English may contribute to the slightly weaker antonymic strength displayed by the English because as they are, individually, more restricted in their range than the German pair (Muehleisen, 1997).

While *small:large* (25.67) has the highest FoC (compared to 8.13 and 10.79 for *big:little* and *big:small* respectively), the judgement ratings for the first three pairs are virtually identical. While this is expected for the conventionalized parings, there is also no difference in perceived antonymic strength between *big:little* and *big:small*. Thus, according to speaker judgements, there are not two but three central pairs on the English SIZE continuum. *Little:large,* with a judgement score of 2.05 and chance level co-occurrence scores, does not follow the same pattern as it simply does not seem to have enough shared range to allow the lexemes to co-occur at a sufficient rate and therefore does not benefit from the added entrenchment of the lexical relationship despite showing a conceptual opposition. While the conventional pairings are readily identified by native speakers, highly proficient non-native speakers often show a preference for *big:small*[5] which may be based on the individual items' higher frequency.

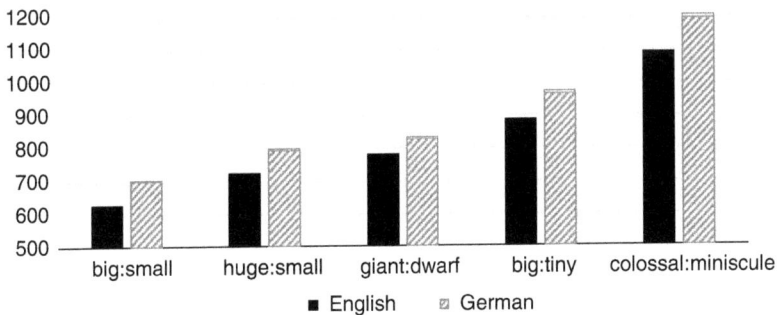

Figure 5.2 Comparison of RT (in ms) for pairs on the SIZE continuum in English and German.

This preference is reflected in the behavioural data (see Figure 5.2) where despite the almost identical results for *big:little* and *big:small* presented above, their reaction times differ with *big:small* resulting in considerably faster RTs than *big:little* (625ms vs. 806ms). It seems that seeing big generated an expectation for *small* rather than *little*, which resulted in an inhibitory effect for *big:little* and led to a slower RT. *Small:large*, on the other hand, is relatively similar in RT to *small:big* (648 ms) while *large:little* is significantly slower (885 ms). These results do not completely reflect either the judgement scores or co-occurrence rates and support the hypothesis that the weighting of criteria in antonym judgement may be affected by task type.

An overall comparison of co-occurrence rates and judgement ratings (see Figure 5.3) shows substantial variability for FoC while judgement scores are generally fairly high. While the top scoring pairs also display the highest co-occurrence rates, it seems that beyond a certain co-occurrence rate, the impact of an increase in frequency of co-occurrence does not directly translate into an increase in antonymic strength. This suggests that judgement ratings are only susceptible to changes in co-occurrence rates within a certain range and, at a certain point, an increase in FoC is no longer reflected in speaker judgements. It may also be that pairs with mid-range conceptual antonymic strength may benefit most from frequent co-occurrence.

The behavioural experiments show a relatively linear distribution of reaction times in both languages, with no clear break between canonical and non-canonical pairs (see Figure 5.2). Given the demonstrated effect of symmetry on antonym judgements, it is surprising to see the comparatively fast RT for *huge:small* in the behavioural task, which is faster than that of certain symmetrical pairs, most notably *big:little*. The corresponding German pair also elicits the second fastest reaction times in the German SIZE set. This cannot be attributed to high FoC or extremely high judgement scores as *giant:dwarf*, for instance, scores higher in both measures in English and German. Thus, RT alone does not reliably reflect either antonymic strength or associative strength, as illustrated in Figure 5.4.

The other symmetrical pairs included in the judgement task in both languages were *tiny:huge* and *colossal:miniscule* and the nominal pair *giant:dwarf*. Both *tiny:huge* and its German equivalent, *winzig:riesig*, as well as the nominal pairs *giant:dwarf* and *Riese:Zwerg*, are almost identical in terms of their judgement scores. These non-central symmetrical pairs are judged to be more antonymic than similar pairs on the TEMPERATURE and MERIT scales (e.g. *freezing:boiling:* 1.97, *warm:cool:* 1.84, *excellent:atrocious:* 2.14). *Tiny:huge* and *winzig:riesig* both co-

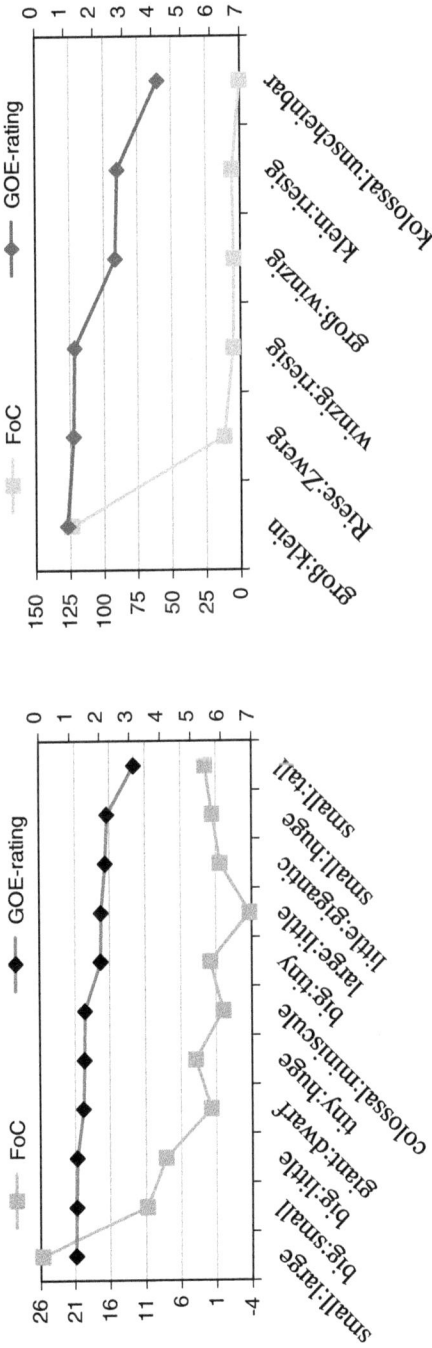

Figure 5.3 Judgements scores and co-occurrence rates for pairs on the SIZE continuum in English (left) and German (right).

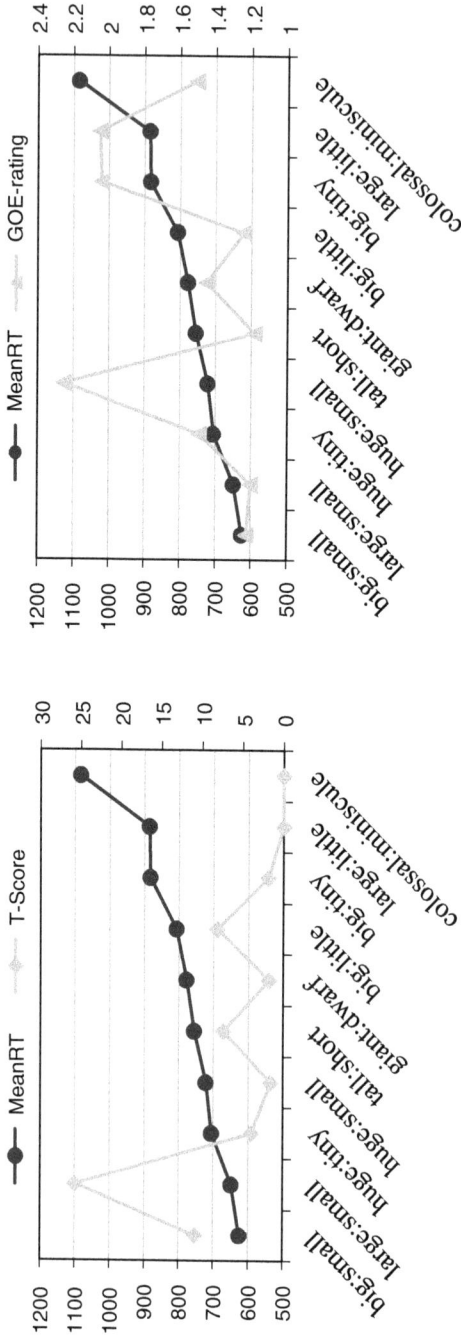

Figure 5.4 Comparison of RT (in ms) and co-occurrence (left) and judgement ratings (right) for English SIZE adjectives.

occur at greater-than-chance levels but their associative strength is not very high. The difference between the judgement rating of *colossal:miniscule* (1.51) and that of *kolossal:unscheinbar* (4.2) is largely due to the fact that opposition between *kolossal* and *unscheinbar* 'inconspicuous' in German is very weak and this is not an ideal translation equivalent.

The English questionnaire included three asymmetric pairs – *big:tiny*, *small:huge* and *little:gigantic* – two of which, *small:huge* and *little:gigantic*, were translated with the German pair *klein:riesig* because there is only one equivalent for *little* and *small*. *Riesig* is the only common equivalent for *huge* and also for *gigantic* and is also derived from *Riese* 'giant.' The third English pair, *big:tiny*, corresponds to the German *groß:winzig*. Despite FoC differences between the languages which should favour the German pairs, all English pairs score more than 0.5 higher than their German counterparts in the judgement task even with co-occurrence rates at, or below, chance level. Many pairs with similarly low t-scores, morphologically related pairs aside, score much lower in the judgement task despite strong conceptual opposition (e.g. *chilly:warm*, *cold:mild*). The one 'structural' difference between these pairs is that members of the asymmetrical pairs on the SIZE continuum are a greater distance from each other than those on the TEMPERATURE scale as the latter consist of a base member and one that is closer to the centre of the scale. Overall distance between the concepts may be the critical factor here as this increases the salience of the conceptual contrast.

Giant:dwarf, the only nominal pair, scores surprisingly high in the judgement task in both languages (E: 1.45; G:1.29) despite being a nominal pair with the resulting increased complexity in category structure. The pair contains other features apart from the salient SIZE distinction, a fact which should lead to a weakening of the salient axis. One reason for this could be that those additional features for *giant:dwarf* include dimensions of opposition apart from *big:small*, for example *strong:weak* and, certainly in German, *stupid:clever/sly*, which may further strengthen the opposition between the two concepts. They also occur in relatively restricted contexts, for instance in fairy tales, and are often portrayed as diametrically opposed. This hypothesis will be investigated further in the following case study where pairs based on the domain of SEX/GENDER are discussed.

The examples above show clearly that there are considerable similarities in both the judgement scores and behavioural data of the SIZE adjectives in German and English. These similarities strengthen the argument for antonymy as a fundamentally conceptual relation. However, the data also shows that both the associative relationship, reflected by FoC here, and the antonymic strength of a pair have an effect on reaction times. Unlike in an 'offline' task, in the behavioural experiments several processes are at work in antonym recognition, as the decision whether a pair is antonymic or not has to be made under time constraints. A close associative connection on the lexical level can thus have a stronger effect in a task which relies more heavily on automatic processing.

Overall, this case study of gradable adjectival opposite pairs highlights the same key criteria which affect the judgement of lexical opposition as those which emerged as crucial in the analyses of associative and antonymic strength. Some of the factors, for example differences in antonymic strength for different word classes, have been supported by the data discussed in this section. Others, for example FoC, have proven to be a more significant factor in the behavioural experiment than in the judgement task. However, this does not answer the question whether frequency of co-occurrence determines or enhances antonymic strength or whether it is a result of the strong antonymic relation of the two lexemes involved. The relative contribution of associative strength and conceptual opposition and the difference between task types will be discussed further in the following case study.

5.3 Case study III: *complementaries: pairs clustered around* male:female

Male:female is frequently cited as one of the best examples of complementary opposition (e.g. Lyons, 1977; Cruse, 1986; Lehrer, 2002)[6] and it is therefore assumed to be part of the category of canonical antonymy. Generally, complementaries score very highly (e.g. English *true:false* (1.02), *right:wrong* (1.09); German *falsch:richtig* (1.12) or *awake:asleep* (1.14)). The English judgement results, in particular, are thus quite surprising as *male:female*, with an overall rating of 2.06, does not fall within the group of excellent antonyms. Other pairs, such as *man:woman* and *mother:father,* were also expected to score higher, especially if FoC is considered an adequate predictor of antonymic strength. Some of these pairs, however, elicited very fast reaction times in the behavioural experiment. As Table 5.2 shows, the pairs in this group ranked among the highest in terms of frequency of co-occurrence in both languages. The discrepancy between the judgement scores and the measures of associative strength provides a useful starting point for the search for additional factors underlying these differences.

The overall distribution of pairs is similar in English and German in both the judgement task and the behavioural experiments. In the

Table 5.2 Opposite pairs based on male:female (ordered by English GOE-rating)

Word 1	Word 2	GOE	FoC	RT (ms)	Word 1	Word 2	GOE	FoC	RT (ms)
male	female	2.06	32.54	677	männlich	weiblich	1.23	51.60	782
masculine	feminine	1.81	8.94	758	maskulin	feminin	1.30	6.24	935
man	woman	2.11	28.67	781	Mann	Frau	1.5	185.82	820
husband	wife	3.18	28.01	718					
brother	sister	3.42	17.43		Bruder	Schwester	2.92	54.76	818
mum	dad	3.5	26.47	660	Mama	Papa	2.88	70.16	806
cow	bull	3.76	2.18		Kuh	Bulle	3.28	5.80	
nephew	niece	3.96	3.60		Neffe	Nichte	3.78	10.90	
actor	actress	4.4	2.96	851	Schauspieler	Schauspielerin	4.47	6.04	1165
aunt	uncle	4.53	10.15		Tante	Onkel	3.72	32.37	
mother	father	4.55	29.99	677	Mutter	Vater	3.18	177.12	727
king	queen	4.78	15.23	688	König	Königin	3.66	46.30	952

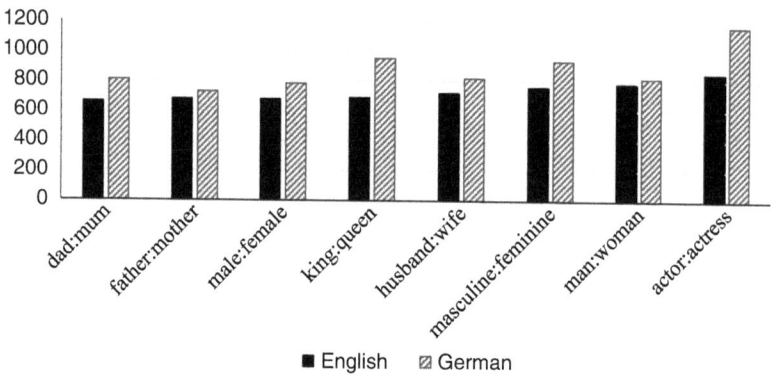

Figure 5.5 RT (in ms) for GENDER pairs in English and German.

judgement task, all nominal pairs are roughly the same distance from the base pair(s) for this cluster. However, when comparing the judgement scores cross-linguistically, it is noticeable that all German pairs but one, *Schauspieler:Schauspielerin*, are judged as having greater antonymic strength than the corresponding English pairs. Thus, the question why some of these pairs, and especially the base pair *männlich:weiblich*, are considered considerably better antonyms in German warrants closer investigation.[7]

Figure 5.5 shows the mean reaction times of all gender pairs included in the experiment for both languages. It is evident, even at first glance, that these results are markedly different from the antonymic strength results (Table 5.2). This applies especially to English where not even the two adjectival pairs scored in the *excellent* category in the judgement task (*male:female* 2.06 and *masculine:feminine* 1.81). The two English pairs which result in the fastest reaction times, *mum:dad* and *mother:-father*, were both rated in the *medium* category of the GOE-rating while in German *Vater:Mutter* and *männlich:weiblich* 'male:female' are the pairs with the fastest RT, closely followed by *Mama:Papa* 'mum:dad.'

The two pairs which show a difference in morphological relatedness between the two languages, *king:queen* and *actor:actress* (*König:Königin* and *Schauspieler:Schauspielerin*), behave quite differently. While *Schauspieler:Schauspielerin*, at 4.47, is almost identical to *actor:actress* (4.4), *König:Königin* is judged to have more antonymic strength in German than in English, perhaps in part due to its shared morphological material. In terms of reaction times, the German pairs are the slowest overall, while in English, *king:queen* elicits substantially faster

RTs than expected. However, these examples show that morphological relatedness also does not have a uniform effect on all opposite pairs and interacts with other factors.

In the following, more qualitative discussion of the data, the focus will first be on the comparison of judgement task data and co-occurrence followed by the behavioural results. As is evident from the distributions shown in Figure 5.6, while there is some correlation between antonymic and associative strength, especially at either end of the canonicity scale, there are also some significant discrepancies. These are analysed below and possible causes are suggested for the lower judgement ratings obtained for some, seemingly canonical, pairs starting with the adjectival base pairs in both languages.

Although *male:female* is commonly considered the base pair, in the English data *masculine:feminine* is the pair with the best GOE-rating result despite a much lower *t*-score. In the German questionnaire, the adjectival pairs are both ranked among the best antonyms in the entire judgement task at 1.23 (*männlich:weiblich*) and 1.295 (*maskulin:feminin*). As the two pairs are similar to their English equivalents in terms of semantic range, the cause of this discrepancy is not immediately obvious. Possible hypothesis might invoke cultural difference in emphasis on gender roles between the two societies or the fact that German has retained grammatical gender[8]. However, another possible cause is a difference in semantic range: *weiblich* and *männlich* also cover a certain amount of the range covered by *feminine* and *masculine* in English, for example in cases such as (5.6) below.

5.6 *Er   zeigt   gerne   seine   **weibliche** Seite.*
he<small>NOM</small> show3<small>PSG</small> gladly his<small>ACC</small> feminine side<small>ACC</small>
'He likes showing his **feminine** side.'

If one were to suggest that the relatively low antonymic strength of *male:female* is due to the fact that it does not solely encode biological sex which is, at least in everyday thought considered an excellent complementary pair, but also gender, which is not binary, this should also hold true for *männlich:weiblich*. In fact, judging by the examples above, it might be expected to have an even stronger impact on the German pair because this seems to include more of the range of *masculine:feminine*, a pair which is used in both languages to denote a more gradable and variable property than biological sex. However, this is not what we find and instead there seems to be a general tendency in this cluster towards greater antonymic strength in German

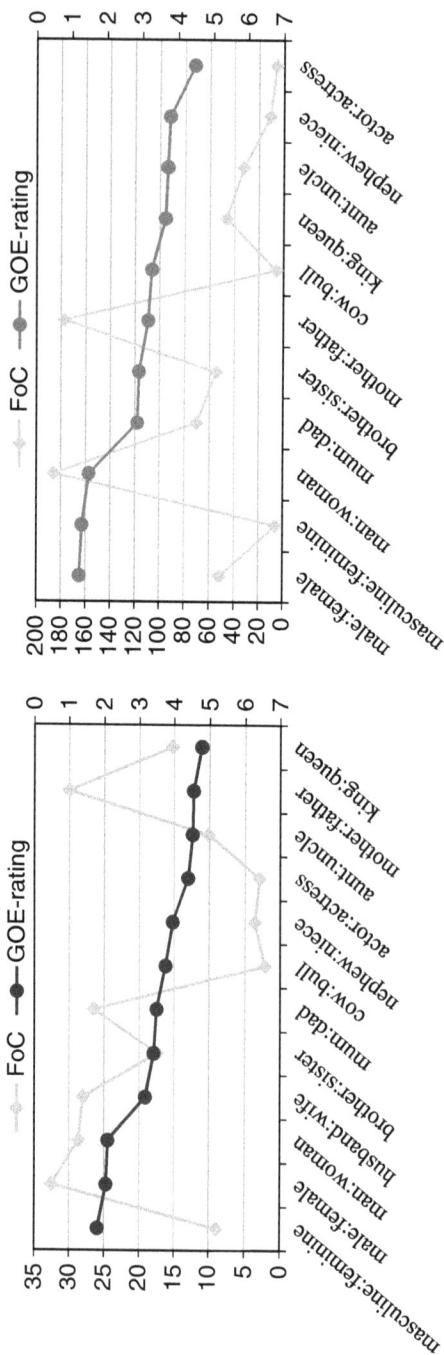

Figure 5.6 GOE-rating and FoC for pairs based on male:female in English (left) and German (right).

than in English. This is also borne out in the analysis of the remaining pairs in this group.

The remaining pairs are all nominal, and although these pairs tend to receive lower judgement scores, a fact previously attributed to more complex underlying category structure, the difference between adjectival and nominal pairs is not as substantial here because both adjectival pairs score comparatively low. In both languages, *man:- woman* receives a score close to one of the adjectival pairs, and German *Mann:Frau* is even judged to constitute an excellent opposite pair (1.5).

Two pairs which score relatively highly in English, *husband:wife* and *brother:sister*, display reciprocal logical relationships between the concepts enconded by the individual lexemes. Logically, in a male-female couple, if A is B's husband, B is A's wife. By the same token, *mother* should be paired with *child, son* or *daughter* (as a converse) and not with *father*, as there is no logical relationship which holds between these two concepts; this also applies to *aunt:uncle* and *nephew:niece*. However, *mother:daughter* and *father:daughter* (the logically 'correct' combinations) score even lower than *mother:father* in the judgement task (E: 5.08 and 5.42 respectively; G: 4.82 and 5.43) despite high co-occurrence rates (15.33 and 9.96; G: 110.17 and 92.63). It thus seems that a logical opposition does not necessarily result in a conceptually salient opposite distinction.

The pairs presented here provide an opportunity to illustrate the effect of category structure using the results of the attribute listing task introduced in 3.4.7 for the pairs *mother:father* and *man:woman* in both languages. Recall the example of *giant:dwarf* presented in Chapter 3 which, despite being a nominal pair, showed a relatively simple conceptual structure with the opposing dimension, that of SIZE, clearly the most salient. In the first pair discussed here, *mother:father*, the attributes listed are much more varied and the results differ considerably between FATHER/VATER and MOTHER/MUTTER (Table 5.3) although the difference is more striking in English. Overall, there were far fewer responses to FATHER/VATER and many were highly subjective (e.g. *mine is great*) which resulted in fewer attributes being listed by more than one participant. However, it is clear from the listing that 'male' and 'female' are not very prominent as attributes of either concept. Both are mentioned by the same number of informants (four in each case in English and three and five in the German data) with roughly equivalent weightings.

The category MOTHER is much richer in both languages and has a considerable number of attributes which are considered more

Table 5.3 Attribute listing results for father, Vater, mother, Mutter

Father		Vater	
has children	(6; 43)	**ist ein Mann/männlich**	(5; 35)
is a man/male	(5; 38)	ist ein Erzeuger	(4; 31)
provides	(2; 15)	ist fürsorglich/liebevoll	(4; 27)
is old	(2; 14)	beschützt	(5; 26)
		ist Oberhaupt der Familie	(2; 14)
		ist ein Vorbild	(2; 14)
		ist streng	(2; 13)
		sorgt für Familie	(2; 7)

Mother		Mutter	
has children/gave birth	(10; 71)	ist fürsorglich	(11; 74)
is caring	(7; 46)	ist warm/lieb	(7; 53)
is loving/loves	(6; 41)	hat geboren	(5; 34)
is warm/gentle	(7; 49)	erzieht	(3; 19)
nurtures/nourishes	(5; 33)	**ist weiblich**	(3; 18)
is a woman/female	(4; 27)	ist immer da	(4; 17)
comforts	(3; 23)	hilft/unterstützt	(3; 13)
works/hard-working	(3; 17)	schimpft	(2; 10)
cooks	(3; 12)	lacht	(2; 7)
listens	(2; 11)	kocht	(2; 5)
teaches	(2; 4)		

noteworthy than 'female', whereas FATHER only has four attributes in total which were mentioned twice or more and while VATER has more attributes, none of these are very highly weighted. Both the number of attributes listed and the discrepancy between the results for MOTHER and FATHER show a more complex picture than in the case of *giant:dwarf,* and these richer conceptual categories reduce the salience of the opposing dimension. Interestingly, while many of the features listed for MOTHER refer to the stereotypical and idealised role of a mother in the family unit, the role of the father as provider is less clear from the responses.

The German category of VATER is much more similar in structure to MUTTER than FATHER is to MOTHER. While the English list of attributes limits itself mainly to attributes which refer to biological properties ('has children,' 'is male,' 'is old') and only contains one feature which refers to other properties ('provides'), the German category is much richer in attributes, especially where nurturing features like 'caring' and 'protective' are concerned. These features match those listed for the category MOTHER and thus highlight the similarity of the two

Table 5.4 Attribute listing results for woman, Frau, man, Mann

Woman		*Frau*	
has children	(8; 42)	**weiblich**	(7; 51)
mother(hood)	(3; 22)	schön	(4; 28)
beauty/beautiful	(3; 19)	kann Kinder bekommen	(5; 24)
female	(2; 16)	hat Brüste	(3; 22)
feminine/femininity	(2; 15)	liebevoll	(3; 18)
breasts	(2; 15)	feminin	(2; 16)
nurturer/nurturing	(2; 12)	weich	(2; 13)
skin	(2; 8)	trägt Kleider/Röcke	(2; 13)
smells good/nice	(2; 6)	zierlich/kleiner als Mann	(2; 10)
		Mutter	(2; 10)
		macht Haushalt	(2; 5)
Man		*Mann*	
male	(7; 55)	stark	(8; 55)
strong/firm	(6; 41)	groß	(7; 53)
has a penis	(5; 31)	**Frau/Gegenteil von Frau**	(4; 30)
not woman/opposite of woman	(4; 29)	hat einen Bart	(3; 21)
human	(3; 20)	ist ein Mensch/menschlich	(2; 16)
testosterone	(4; 16)	verdient Geld	(3; 15)
taller than women	(2; 13)	praktisch	(2; 11)
mankind/humanity	(2; 12)	hat einen Penis	(2; 10)
has two legs	(2; 11)	trinkt Bier	(2; 7)
facial hair	(2; 10)	**männlich**	(1; 7)
has two arms	(2; 9)		

categories which, given that antonymy is a relation of minimal difference, may well be a contributing factor to the German pair's better judgement rating.

The second set of pairs which will be considered contrastively is *man:woman* and *Mann:Frau* (Table 5.4). Both sets of equivalents are fairly similar in their overall category structure and in the number of attributes listed by more than two participants for each of the categories. Alongside the biological characteristics, there are several important elements in both the male and the female set which are listed early on for both languages (e.g. 'beauty,' 'has children' for WOMAN/FRAU and 'human,' 'tall' and 'strong' for MAN/MANN). In the list for English *man*, we also find attributes referring to its other meaning of 'human' (e.g. 'mankind/humankind,' 'has two legs' and 'has two arms').

The antonymic pairs of features, *male:female* and *männlich:weiblich*, are distributed differently in terms of their weighting in the two languages. In the results of the English listing task, only two participants list 'female' as a feature of WOMAN, whereas 'male' is considered the most important characteristic of the category MAN. In German, this is reversed, with 'weiblich' coming top of the list while 'männlich' was only mentioned by one participant and thus should technically not even be included. While this discrepancy is interesting, it does not have any bearing on antonymic strength in the present case. Despite the fact that the English categories, and the differences and similarities between them, are closely matched by their German counterparts, the German antonym pair scores significantly higher on the judgement task, as has been discussed previously.

Both members of the pair are reasonably well matched for structural complexity in both languages and they are still relatively complex. The antonymic features are slightly more central to the category structure than for MOTHER and FATHER, which means *man:woman* would be expected to form a better antonym pair than *mother:father* where other, non-antonymic features are in focus in both members of the pair. However, the cross-language comparison does not reveal a convincing explanation for the greater antonymic strength displayed by the German pairs clustered around *male:female*.

These results of the attribute listing task highlight the importance of the salience of the antonymic features (in this case 'male' and 'female') as crucial to the conceptual construal of antonym pairs. As the features in question do not rank particularly highly in the attribute-listing results, and thus may be less central to the overall structure of the category, *mother:father* would not be predicted to be a particularly good opposite pair. Furthermore, the difference in complexity of the categories is problematic for antonym construal for two reasons: firstly, the concepts in question are clearly not sufficiently minimally different and, secondly, the structural complexity reduces the weight of every individual feature, thus further diluting the salience of the potentially antonymic features.

Overall, the judgement data does not lend support to the claim that a word pair which has antonymic 'potential' becomes entrenched as an antonym pair through frequent co-occurrence, since some of the above pairs have very high co-occurrence rates, as well as encoding a potentially salient opposition, but still are not judged to be very good opposite pairs. It seems more likely that the frequent co-occurrence of two members of an antonym pair is, as previously indicated, a consequence of greater overlap of their conceptual opposition and minimal difference and the resulting shared semantic range, which makes these lexemes more likely to appear in the same contexts.

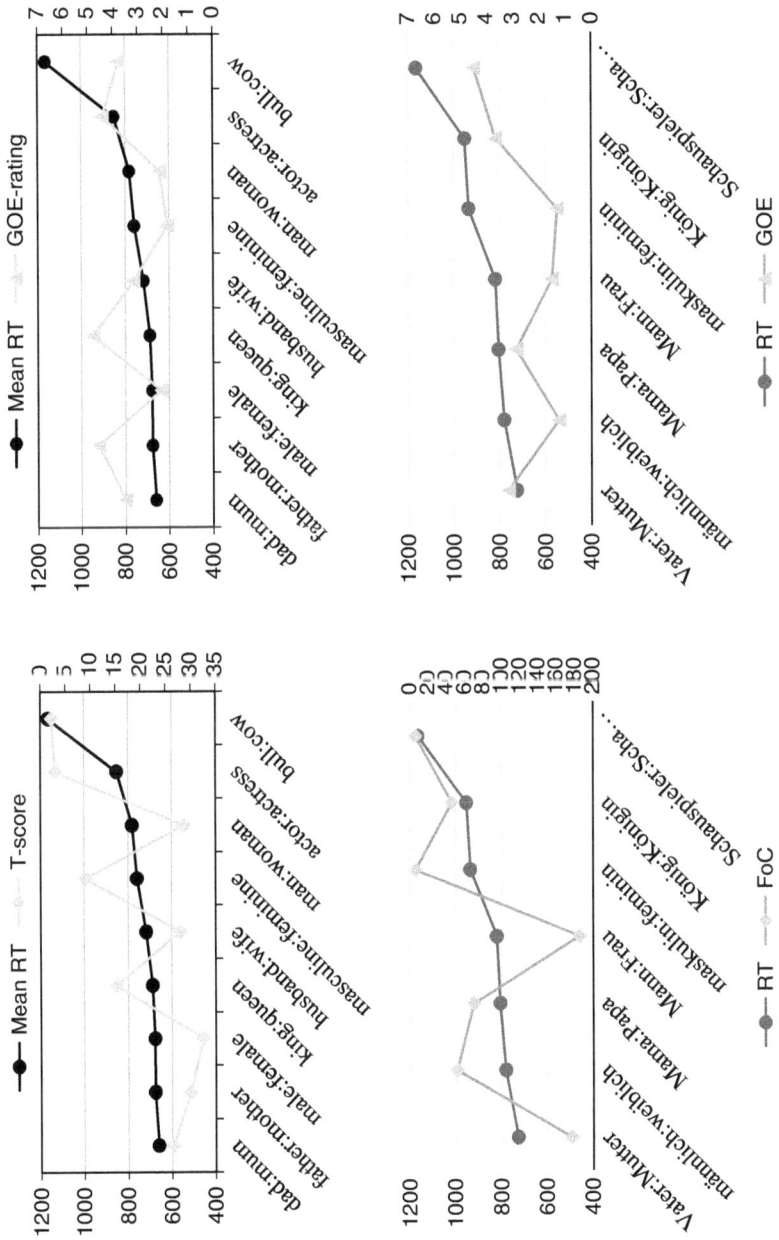

Figure 5.7 Comparison of **RT** (in ms), co-occurrence rates and judgement ratings of GENDER pairs for English (top) and German (bottom).

114 *Empirical Investigation*

The behavioural data shows a different pattern. Despite the fact that Figure 5.7 does not show a perfect correlation between RT and co-occurrence rates, these measures correspond much more closely than FoC and judgement scores. This supports the stronger effect of co-occurrence in timed behavioural experiments. The extremely high associative strength of certain pairs (e.g. *dad:mum*, *mother:father*, *man:woman*) facilitates processing and results in faster reaction times than would be expected based on the pairs' antonymic strength. It may even be the case that a feature matching process of antonym recognition is superseded by associative strength in cases with very strong lexical associations, as they may benefit from automatic co-activation even though the primary lexical relationship may not be based on antonymy. However, in processing the lexical link is readily available whether antonymic or not, and it leads to very fast co-activation of the two items which then facilitates a faster decision on their opposition. The proposal of a model of the representation and processing of opposites put forward in the following chapter is based on the empirical evidence presented here as well as on previous research and will also include the entrenchment of cognitive aspects of conceptual construal.

Notes

1 Both the OALD and the LDCE make a particular point of indicating the correct usage of *borrow* and *lend*.
2 'To invest with a fief; to put (a person) in possession of the fee-simple or fee-tail of lands, tenements, etc.' (www.oed.com – 22.12.2009)
3 This section is based on discussions with the participants of the questionnaire study as well as judgements by native speakers of English who were asked to pair up the four lexemes.
4 For a detailed analysis of the four central lexemes on the size continuum, see Muehleisen 1997 (Chapter 2 – http://www.f.waseda.jp/vicky/dissertation/pdf.html).
5 A small survey among highly proficient non-native speakers of English showed that most considered *big:small* an excellent opposite pair. These informants paired *small* with *big* as well as with *large*.
6 Much of this research was conducted some time ago and does not take into account changes in both language and society to become more inclusive of diverse gender identities.
7 The pair *Mann:Frau* means both 'man:woman' and 'husband:wife' in German and therefore may benefit from the greater shared semantic range and resulting frequency of co-occurrence.
8 The question whether the fact that German has grammatical gender whereas English does not influence these judgements will not be discussed here because there is no evidence in the current study to evaluate this theory.

Part III
Theoretical Implications

6 Antonyms in mind and brain: towards a psycholinguistic model of opposition

The rich data presented in the empirical investigation in Part II has provided substantial support for theoretical proposals arguing for a conceptual basis of antonymy and has further confirmed the influence of a number of factors on the degree of opposition displayed by individual pairs. In the analyses, these criteria were discussed in relation to their observed effect (or lack thereof) on the data and the overall theoretical implications of the observed patterns form the first part of this chapter (Section 6.1).

In the second section (Section 6.2), the nature of the antonymic relationship is considered to determine whether the standpoint of antonymy as a fundamentally conceptual notion is supported by the evidence presented in Part II and whether lexical and conceptual contributions can be teased apart.

On the basis of this discussion and the data presented here, the third part of this chapter (section 6.3) focuses on the proposal of a model of the lexical representation of opposites. This model aims to explain the patterns observed in the data presented here, as well as that in previous psycholinguistic studies (e.g. Paradis et al., 2009; Paradis & Willners, 2011; van de Weijer et al., 2012, 2014), based on both cognitive theories of conventionalisation and entrenchment and psycholinguistic theories of lexical representation, activation and competition.

6.1 Antonym canonicity: what makes an opposite pair canonical?

Throughout this book, canonicity has been understood as the degree to which a given pair of words is considered antonymous, and it was thus very closely linked to antonymic strength, the two terms often being used interchangeably here. The notion of a continuum of canonicity rather than a binary distinction between canonical and

DOI: 10.4324/9781003026969-6

non-canonical opposite pairs is not a new one, as early studies of antonymy also remarked on the gradability of antonymic strength (e.g. Herrmann et al., 1986; Mettinger, 1994). One definition which encapsulates two key components of 'good antonymy' – which in turn are dependent on a number of factors – is that by Murphy (2003. p. 31), who states that '[c]anonicity is the extent to which antonyms are both semantically related and conventionalized as pairs in language.' This view, that both conceptual factors and some degree of conventionalisation are important in antonym canonicity, is one that has gained traction as a result of the renewed interest in antonyms as an object of investigation (e.g. Jones et al., 2012). The degree to which conventionalisation on the lexical rather than the conceptual level plays a role in antonym judgements, especially with regard to lexical representation and processing, is still not entirely clear but there is still strong support for a small category of canonical opposites which elicit different patterns in a number of methodologically different studies.

The aim of the empirical methods used in this study was to determine which factors influence the canonicity of opposite pairs and to establish whether the contribution of a lexically entrenched link for certain opposite pairs could be isolated. In Section 2.6, a set of criteria for canonical antonymy was put forward, consisting of factors collected from several separate investigations of antonymy (Cruse, 1986; Muehleisen, 1997; Murphy, 2003; Jones, 2002, 2007; Paradis et al., 2009), and these criteria provided the framework for the data analysis presented in Part II. In the analyses, each factor was found to have a different degree of explanatory power for the patterns observed in the data, with certain factors – most notably frequency of co-occurrence, showing different effects in offline and online tasks. A number of key factors are discussed here and their contribution is evaluated in light of previous theoretical accounts.

6.1.1 *Minimal and sufficient difference*

The fact that the relation of opposition is dependent on minimal difference has been considered one of the most important factors in determining which antonyms are judged to be good examples (e.g. Cruse, 1986; Murphy, 2003). The empirical evidence convincingly shows that the more easily definable and containable the conceptual and semantic differences between the two members of an antonym pair are, the greater its antonymic strength. However, the criterion of minimal difference only seems to apply to the conceptual similarities and not to the lexical items which encode them. Recall that Lyons (1977) claims that the most common opposites are morphologically unrelated because this difference highlights the distinctness of the two members of a pair. While there are certain related pairs which are judged to have a very high degree of canonicity (e.g. *accurate:inaccurate* or *include:exclude*), on the whole the data lends support to this idea of minimal conceptual difference paired with maximal lexical difference. One particularly clear example is that of the cross-linguistic converses discussed in Case Study I. The analysis of *borrow:lend* and *rent:let* and their German counterparts (*ausleihen:verleihen/leihen* and *mieten:vermieten*) shows that the question whether two opposing concepts are encoded antonymically or antagonymically is not dependent on the type of opposition, nor is it the case that the conceptual opposition itself is intrinsically 'weaker' in antagonyms than in antonyms because the same concepts may be encoded antonymically in one language and antagonymically in another. However, in the case of an antagonym, the conceptual opposition is encoded as distinct sub-senses of the same lexical item. While antonymy is generally considered a relation between sub-senses of two lexemes rather than between the lexemes themselves (see for example Miller, 1998: 49), it seems that the fact that two opposing concepts are encoded in the same lexical form weakens the overt opposition of these two concepts. Speakers do not 'automatically' perceive antagonyms as opposites because the lexical aspect – the encoding of two opposing concepts in two lexical forms which are frequently used together, especially in contrastive constructions (e.g. Jones, 2007; Jones et al., 2012) – is missing and the lack of overt difference between the lexical forms makes the difference too minimal.

The case of antagonyms which are perceived as only weakly antonymous, if at all, supports the claim that antonymy has a strong lexical component. This does not mean, however, that antonymy is dependent on differences on the lexical level but may simply mean that this lack of distinction in lexical encoding obscures the salience of the conceptual opposition. As opposite construal is fundamentally binary, it requires **two** opposing items rather than **one** with meanings which are opposed on a more specific level. Minimal difference is a crucial criterion for good opposition, especially in conceptually (section 6.1.3), but the lexical encoding of the conceptual difference also plays a role.

6.1.2 Morphological relatedness

Following on from the previous point regarding the importance of the binary encoding of opposing concepts on the lexical level, in morphologically related antonym pairs the opposition is overtly encoded in two items which are lexically minimally different. There are a large number of morphologically related opposites in both English and German (and, of course, many other languages) and several productive derivational processes to create these, such as prefixation with a negative prefix (e.g. *in-, un-, dis-, non-*) or suffixation with a feminine suffix (*actor:actress*) or *-full-less* (*useful:useless*).

The stimulus set in this study contained pairs from the following categories:

a. prefixation with a negative prefix (e.g *happy-**unhappy***)
b. suffixation with a gendered/relational suffix (e.g. *actor:actress* or *employer:employee*)
c. affixation with contrasting or opposite affixes (e.g. *include:exclude* or *helpful:helpless*)
d. pseudo-antonyms (*flammable:inflammable* and *easy:uneasy*)

In the judgement task, morphologically related pairs form a more homogeneous group than their unrelated counterparts, which are distributed much more widely. This may be in part due to their derivational nature, as the semantic range within these pairs is generally very similar (e.g. Muehleisen, 1997) and while the derived item is sometimes narrower in use, it often covers a similar range to that of its base. This would mean that not only the similarity in form but also the greater overlap in meaning and usage contribute significantly to the greater antonymic strength and more consistent nature of the results observed for these pairs.

The influence of morphological relatedness on judgements can be seen in the results of the two pseudo-antonymic pairs: *easy:uneasy* (3.68) and *flammable:inflammable* (3.46). While these results are by no means 'good', they are significantly better than expected because the former is usually considered barely antonymous (other than in a very specific context) and the members of the latter pair are technically synonyms. These pairs display a larger standard deviation (participants chose either the very top or bottom of the scale, with few responses at 3 or 4), indicating that some participants were misled by the overtly antonymic morphological relationship, which once again points towards a lexical contribution to antonym construal.

The behavioural data, however, does not reveal any clear patterns in a comparison of the morphologically related pairs and their unrelated counterparts. The related pairs display marginally longer RTs which could be accounted for by the increased item length but also by the fact that one (or both) members of the pair are morphologically complex. The effect of morphological complexity in language processing in relation to antonym processing will be introduced in greater detail in 6.3, where the processing effects of complex items are integrated into the proposed model.

6.1.3 Purity and salience of opposition

Moving from lexical to purely conceptual factors, the effect of the salience of the dimension along which opposites differ has long been recognised as an important factor. In early research, this was referred to as purity of opposition, which is closely linked but not identical to the ease of construal of a unilateral scale (e.g. Cruse, 1986; Herrmann et al., 1986, pp. 134f.) and evidently very influential. With the rise of cognitive linguistics, these early criteria have been extended and more precisely formulated on the basis of cognitive theories of construal (e.g. Paradis, 2005; Jones et al. 2012; Paradis et al., 2015).

In the present dataset, the bulk of the evidence for the effect of category structure comes from the analysis of the GENDER pairs. Pairs where the antonymic dimension or scale is the primary attribute of the conceptual categories involved in construal are very readily identified as good opposites (e.g. *big:little* or, theoretically at least, *male:female*). Those pairs which rely on richer conceptual categories with a greater number of attributes which increase the difficulty of the construal of a binary scale result in more varied antonymic strength judgements (e.g. *work:play*, *credit:debit*, *landline:mobile*). Most of the 'impure' pairs in the present study are nominal, although verbal pairs are also possible (e.g. *walk:run* or *meander:sprint*) and there may even be adjectival pairs which are more complex than the base pair they are derived from (e.g. *feminine:masculine*?). The lesser degree of antonymic strength can clearly be seen in categories with a richer conceptual representation, and this is closely related to lexical category as certain word classes, most notably concrete nouns, are underpinned by more complex conceptual structures (Langacker, 2008).

The construal of a clear, often binary, scale along which the two antonymous concepts differ is a key factor which allows speakers to assess the oppositeness of the features in question. Theoretical accounts of opposition (e.g. Cruse, 1986; Lyons, 1977) proposed inherent binarity as a prerequisite of good. And this is, indeed, one factor which makes gradable adjectival pairs such good examples of opposition. In cases such as *hot:cold*, for example, there is no need for the construal of a scale as this comes 'ready-made' as an integral part of the concepts. Furthermore, the criterion of inherent binarity provides an explanation for the lack of antonymic strength between co-hyponyms such as *cat:dog* or *red:green*, which are weakly opposed and can be construed as binary with the appropriate contextual support but are not usually considered antonyms 'proper' (i.e. canonical antonyms) due to their lack of inherent binarity (Cruse, 1986). Inherent binarity may thus be considered a prerequisite for canonical antonyms.

However, in the category of non-canonical opposition, inherent binarity is less crucial as a uni-dimensional scale can be construed between two concepts with a greater or lesser degree of ease. The degree of difficulty in identifying and construing the dimension which represents the salient opposition between two concepts is consistently reflected in the judgements of antonymic strength. Context (both linguistic and situational) can strongly affect the ease of construal of this binary scale, as certain features can be foregrounded which lead to facilitation or inhibition of the construal of a specific scale (e.g. *coffee:tea* in the context of a dinner party).

6.1.4 Symmetry

Another criterion which is closely related to the construal of a scalar opposition is that of symmetry. In the subgroup of gradable opposites which evoke a scalar dimension, the importance of the symmetrical distribution of the members of an antonym pair along the relevant scale can clearly be seen in all datasets. Symmetrical pairs co-occur more frequently, are rated more highly in the judgement task and are recognised faster than their asymmetrical counterparts. Three fields, each centred on a particular base pair, were constructed to investigate this feature (as illustrated in Table 3.1) and the data for the TEMPERATURE and SIZE clusters was discussed in detail in Part II.

In the judgement data overall, symmetrical pairs score better than asymmetrical ones. However, symmetrical distribution in relation to the midpoint of a scale is not the only criterion affecting the antonymic strength as far as scalar opposites are concerned. The overall distance from the midpoint also plays a role: there seems to be an ideal distance from the midpoint which coincides with the 'basic level' of the scale (e.g. *hot:cold* on the TEMPERATURE continuum) where the distinction is most salient. These are generally the pairs encoded by the most common lexemes, which have the greatest overall semantic range. Those pairs, which are here called 'basic level' pairs, are also those which are first acquired by children, a factor which is considered an integral part of the basic level distinction (cf. Rosch, 1978;

Ungerer & Schmid, 2006). The neutral case of a scale – or midpoint – is often not fixed since different contexts presuppose different 'neutral' settings, for example for temperature or, to take a classic example, size. The neutral size of an elephant is very different from the neutral size of a mug, for example. Furthermore, the judgement task results confirm previous claims that the members of the pair are required to be on opposite sides of the midpoint rather than on the same side (Osgood et al., 1957; Herrmann & Chaffin, 1986) and ideally equidistant from the mid-point of the dimension (Herrmann et al., 1986, pp. 134f.). This partly explains the results for pairs such as *tepid:lukewarm* as most native speakers would place both concepts on the HEAT continuum rather than the COLD continuum, which locates them on the same side of the mid-point. Thus, in addition to the symmetrical distribution of the two concepts, overall distance from the midpoint also affects antonymic strength.

6.1.5 Semantic range and generality

The clearest support for the importance of semantic range, which includes Cruse's match of non-propositional meaning (1986) and Jones et al.'s (2012) semantic generality, in antonym judgement comes from the cross-linguistic data. For instance, the lack of a suitable translation equivalent for *boiling:freezing* necessitated certain concessions when translating this pair into German. The differences in semantic range between *boiling* and *kochend*, in addition to the lack of relatedness and symmetry between the two lexemes in the pair *kochend:eisig*, resulted in a substantially lower judgement score for the German pair.

Furthermore, all asymmetrical pairs, especially those containing one member of the base pair (e.g. *hot:cool* or *bad:excellent*), differ in semantic range as they cover a different part of the scale and the range of the base pairs is generally much broader than those of the lexemes on the more extreme parts of the scale. However, this is also strongly determined by context. In certain contexts, pairs which would be considered decidedly mismatched in terms of semantic range display extremely high antonymic strength. This can be illustrated with pairs such as *open:laprascopic* (cf. Paradis et al., 2007) where the first member is an extremely frequent lexeme with broad semantic range while the second member is a very restricted technical term. This pair obtained extremely high co-occurrence scores in the corpus study carried out by Paradis et al. (2007) since it is an excellent opposite pair in a surgical context and appears frequently in contrastive constructions. It is, however, unlikely that *open* would elicit *laprascopic* in a general elicitation task while the reverse is much more likely. Thus, pairs with a mismatch in semantic range may also frequently display asymmetric elicitation or priming patterns.

Fundamentally, however, semantic range is determined by the conceptual structure of the individual members of a pair. The more closely the conceptual structures and features of these concepts match, the better the antonymic relation will be – provided, of course, that these features contain a binary opposition. Pairs such as *hot:cold* are therefore also further strengthened by the opposition of their metaphorical extensions where one member of the pair has an additional, metaphorical meaning (e.g. *hot* 'stolen') and the meaning of the other member of the pair is extended to cover the matching opposing concept (e.g. *The trail has gone cold.*). In addition, sharing a larger amount of semantic range, covering the same contexts and belonging to the same register creates more opportunities for co-occurrence and thus also increases the associative strength between the two lexemes.

6.1.6 *Associative strength: a result of frequent co-occurrence*

As laid out in Chapter 2, the effect of the degree of associative strength of an opposite pair on the lexical level on its antonymic strength and the causality of this relationship has been the subject of much debate. The question whether the root of the antonymic relationship lies in the degree of associative strength of the lexemes involved in the relation or in the degree of conceptual opposition – or, indeed, in a combination of the two – is further explored after this discussion of associative strength.

The results of the judgement task data presented in Part II clearly show that, while a rating which implies high antonymic strength most often goes hand in hand with a high associative score (here generated from co-occurrence frequencies in the BNC and Cosmas corpus), it is not a prerequisite for a good opposite pair to co-occur frequently. On the flipside, the data also showed that high co-occurrence alone, even in the syntactic frames suggested by previous antonym research (e.g. Jones, 2002; Jones, 2007; Davies, 2012), does not necessarily result in high antonymic strength. The discussion of verbal and nominal converses and the GENDER pairs (Case Study III) illustrate this particularly clearly. Here, nominal pairs which obtained extremely high co-occurrence scores (e.g. *husband:wife, mother:father, king:queen*) score very low in the judgement tasks, reflecting a much lesser degree of antonymic strength than their high co-occurrence rates would suggest. Thus, while high antonym judgement ratings often correlate with highly frequent co-occurrence, the reverse does not seem to be as reliable. This points towards frequent co-occurrence of opposites as a consequence of their antonymic strength rather than its cause. However, it is only possible to investigate the chain of causation with the more recently employed multi-method approaches as co-occurrence rates are also very strongly reflected in reaction time tasks and without a conceptual measure of antonymic strength (such as a judgement task) this may lead to distorted results.

As mentioned in Chapter 4, this greater correlation between co-occurrence and reaction times in the behavioural study may be at least partly an effect of the nature of the task. The fast presentation of the stimuli and the time constraints require a different type of reaction which relies more strongly on the automatic activation of certain pathways in the lexicon. If associative strength had as great an influence on antonymic strength as is sometimes attributed to it in the literature (Gross et al., 1989; Miller, 1990; Justeson & Katz, 1991), there should be a higher level of agreement between all three measures.

The data in this study showed a greater correlation between reaction time and co-occurrence measures than for the judgement task. Had this only applied to excellent antonyms it would most likely not have been noticeable because these would have obtained fast reaction times in any case, with the higher associative strength simply boosting reaction times further. However, some of the pairs included in the study were not judged to be excellent opposites but had extremely high co-occurrence rates nonetheless (e.g. *mother:father*). These pairs resulted in disproportionately fast reaction times, which suggests that a certain level of associative strength is required for the level of facilitation seen in those nominal pairs, for instance, and this will occur regardless of their antonymic strength. This means that pairs with very high co-occurrence rates but without a similar degree of antonymic strength may skew the results of a behavioural task. Thus, the degree of influence of associative strength on antonym judgements varies according to the task, pointing to the existence of different underlying mechanisms.

It is clear that associative strength plays an important role in the behavioural data as it contributes to faster activation and recognition of items which are very strongly associatively related. However, while pairs such as *mother:father* display the same degree of co-occurrence as many excellent opposites and elicit similarly fast reaction times, this in itself does not make their relation antonymic. Two independent factors are at work here and it is important that these effects be kept separate. There seems to be a component of automatic activation which is facilitated by the close associative relation and lays the groundwork for faster recognition and decision in timed behavioural tasks of this type. This automatic associative relationship will be explained in terms of language processing in 6.3.

6.2 Opposites in the mind: cognitive construal and entrenchment of opposition

The most recent theoretical proposals regarding the nature of antonymy propose a conceptual basis of opposition which is rooted in the binary construal of two concepts in an opposite relation (see Jones et al., 2012 and Paradis et al., 2015 for the most recent cognitive accounts). In these proposals, the category of antonymy no longer only includes canonical (gradable) adjectival pairs, but opposites form a prototype category in the cognitive sense with an internal structure closely matching that of other such categories, with category members distributed along a continuum of goodness-of-fit (cf. Lehrer, 1990; Grandy, 1992; Paradis et al., 2009, p. 414). A set of highly canonical opposites at the top end of the continuum may constitute an exception and form a separate set within this category (e.g. Paradis et al., 2009). Proposing such a structure for antonymy allows for the flexibility necessary to include less canonical examples and ad hoc pairings which are construed within a particular context. In the following, we will first examine the empirical evidence for a continuum approach before discussing the data in light of the cognitive construal account (Jones et al., 2012).

6.2.1 Antonymy as a prototype category

Despite the proposal of binary distinctions such as direct and indirect or canonical and peripheral opposites, much of the evidence does not unequivocally support such a categorical division. The notion of a canonicity continuum has recently been supported by mounting empirical evidence but is by no means new. Mettinger (1994, p. 162), for instance, pointed out that the involvement of encyclopaedic knowledge increases on a scale and proposed three categories – systemic, terminological and encyclopaedic opposites – with the first needing the least amount of encyclopaedic knowledge for construal and the last almost entirely dependent on it. This could be extended to four by adding contextual opposites as a category which requires even language-external support beyond encyclopaedic knowledge as situational and cultural context may also play a role. Such a four-part distinction is representative of the patterns in the data if these subtypes are not taken as categorical but as distributed on a continuum from no necessary encyclopaedic knowledge to a large amount of encyclopaedic, cultural and contextual knowledge. This scale would then be inversely proportional to antonymic strength. The special status of highly canonical pairs would then have to be considered separately with the strong conventionalised connection on the lexical level as an essential feature of the most canonical pairs. However, as the language system is dynamic, new pairs can be added here but established pairs can also become less entrenched if their frequent lexical association is not continuously reinforced by frequent co-occurrence or if meanings change (e.g. Schmid, 2010, 2020).

The data collected in the present study supports a continuum approach to antonymy. Neither the judgement task data nor reaction times in the behavioural experiment indicate a clear division between canonical and non-canonical opposite pairs. If plotted in a graph, there is no point where a clear cut-off point is indicated and this matches data from previous multi-method studies such as Paradis et al. (2009), although they chose a categorical rather than continuous presentation of their data which highlighted the difference between canonical and non-canonical opposites. The comparison of German and English data points to a highly homogeneous set of canonical antonym pairs which lends further support to the definition of antonymy as a prototype category with a highly prototypical centre point made up of canonical antonyms.

Canonical pairs aside, the datasets for the two languages also show more similarities than differences. Most of the cases where the ratings differ significantly between the two languages have already been discussed in Part II, for example *lend:borrow* and *ausleihen:verleihen* (cf. Case Study I). These are, on the whole, easily explained and usually directly attributable to the violation of one or more of the central criteria for good antonymy. Thus, the data presented here supports previous proposals of opposition as a gradable property with antonym pairs patterning along a continuum of antonymic strength. The factors which determine the place of any given opposite pair on this continuum were illustrated above and they are crucial to the cognitive construal of opposition and the possible subsequent entrenchment of this relation in the lexicon.

6.2.2 *The conceptual construal of opposites*

What has been evident in the summary of the data, as well as in the outline of previous literature, is that the factors which affect antonym canonicity are not easily separable and their individual contribution to an opposite pair's degree of antonymic strength is often difficult to assess and may be cumulative. In the following section, an integrated approach from a cognitive perspective is proposed based on the conceptual properties of the members of an opposite pair.

The basic assumption here, as in the work of Jones et al. (2012), is that antonymy is a fundamentally conceptual relation and that the specific structure of the conceptual categories involved in the construal of opposition is crucial to the degree of antonymic strength an opposite pair displays. Some of the proposed criteria for good opposition are directly related to category structure while others are contingent on this construal or are a result of it. Jones and colleagues, in their cognitive construal account, propose that each instance of antonymy necessarily involves a BOUNDED binary construal of a domain (2012, p. 143) regardless of the underlying BOUNDED or UNBOUNDED nature of the opposition (e.g. non-gradable or gradable opposites). Thus, certain content domains, those which are inherently binary and favour a bounded construal, lend themselves particularly well to opposite construal. The degree to which a particular domain lends itself to this type of construal is affected by the 'salience of the meaning dimension' and 'semantic generality' (Jones et al., 2012, p. 141) and this accounts for the prototypicality pattern of antonyms on a canonicity continuum. The salience of the meaning dimension is affected by the structure of the conceptual categories involved in the construal, which is therefore an important factor. The flexibility of category-internal structure is well-attested in psychological and now psycholinguistic research (cf. Lakoff, 1987, pp. 83ff.) and this flexibility is also crucial here.

Each member of an antonym pair represents a conceptual category delimited by certain attributes whose structure is influenced by underlying cognitive models which may be cultural, contextual or dependent on register. The match between the structure of the two concepts in an opposite pair determines its antonymic strength. Within this framework, there are several factors which influence the quality of this match and thus the degree to which concepts are perceived as antonymic.

6.2.2.1 Complexity of category structure

The data of the empirical study supports the proposal that lexemes encoding more complex categories are less likely to be judged to be good antonyms (e.g. Paradis, 2005; Jones et al., 2012). This ties in directly with purity of opposition and the construal of a uni-dimensional scale and often surfaces in a word-class effect. Lexemes of certain word classes, such as adjectives or abstract nouns, are less likely to encode meanings underpinned by a rich conceptual structure. In terms of antonymic strength, this is an advantage because there are fewer additional attributes which could reduce the salience of the binary antonymic dimension.

All accounts of opposition agree on one point: adjectives make the best antonym pairs and the vast majority of highly canonical pairs are adjectival. Adjectival categories are often structurally very simple and in most of the canonical adjectival pairs the opposite dimension is the only attribute and thus maximally salient by default. Certain directional opposites encoded by prepositions (e.g. *up:down*) are also very simple in structure but some which are spatially more difficult to construe (e.g. *next to:opposite*, have a less clearly antonymic dimension and are judged as less antonymic as a result.

Nouns and verbs generally encode more complex concepts and are linked to richer underlying cognitive models (e.g. Paradis, 2005). The larger number of overall attributes in the conceptual categories can detract from the antonymic dimension and thus reduce its salience. Generally, it can be said that the more complex the category and the greater the number of determining features, the weaker the antonymic strength of the pair in question. As previously stated, complexity is not necessarily tied to word class and some adjectival pairs, such as *male:female* for instance, are not as conceptually simple, because the cognitive model underlying them is relatively complex.

As mentioned above, the bounded construal is easiest in simple categories where the opposed features are easily accessible and conceptually salient. Naturally, there are pairs for which this dimension is more easily identifiable – for instance, all gradable opposites come with a 'ready-made' scale which is pre-construed and highly conventionalised, while others require more effort for this construal regardless of the complexity of the category structure. In conceptual categories where the scale is easier to identify and a salient property of the concept, antonymic strength will be greater than in those where the opposite dimension is not primary or is obscured by a large number of other features.

However, it is not simply the complexity of the internal structure which matters, but also the degree to which the structures of these categories match. Lexemes encoding conceptual categories which share a large number of attributes overall and are of a similar density in structure (criterion of minimal difference) usually make better antonym pairs. Similarity in the underlying models is also an important criterion (cf. semantic range and match of non-propositional meaning) as the underlying models determine the contexts the lexeme is likely to appear in; this, in turn, will influence the rate of co-occurrence of the two items encoding the concepts.

6.2.2.2 Salience and context effects

However, while the overall structure and number of features is certainly important, the determining factor is that of salience (e.g. Rosch, 1975; Rosch & Mervis, 1975; Schmid, 2020). The attributes or features of the concepts in the antonymic relation must differ along a salient dimension for the opposition to be recognised. As established above, the degree of salience of a certain dimension is partly dependent on the complexity of the category structure as it is easier to establish the salience of a certain scale in a less complex environment. If the categories in question are rich in attributes, the dimension along which the two pairs differ must be of greater salience than in a category with a simpler structure and thus the opposition may be more difficult to establish. This was observed in many of the nominal and verbal pairs (e.g. Case Study III) which overall show greater complexity in their category structure and whose semantic range is also constrained by the underlying models to a greater degree than that of their adjectival counterparts. The reason some nominal and verbal opposite pairs were judged to be excellent opposites is that the opposing dimension in these concepts involves the most salient attributes in the neutral setting they were presented in (e.g. *giant:dwarf* and *Tod:Leben/death:life*).

However, antonymic salience is not determined only by the (inherent) binarity of two features of a concept, which may be more or less readily evident depending on the complexity of the overall category structure. Contextual, cultural and register effects all have considerable influence on the salience of a given property. One advantage of a cognitive approach is that, with flexible conceptual categories underpinning antonym construal, it can account for the contextual phenomena found in antonym judgements. The context determines which cognitive models a concept relies on and thus which features are of particular importance. If the antonymic dimension is foregrounded by a particular context, the pair is likely to be considered to have more antonymic strength in this particular context than it might in a neutral setting. A poem by Wilbur (2000) illustrates this context-dependence by first introducing the opposite of *white* in a neutral context – *black* – but then modifying the context to that of EGGS in which case the opposite of *white* changes to *yolk*. Without the specific context provided and the encyclopaedic knowledge provided by the models which underpin these concepts, it would require much greater effort to construct a binary opposition between *white* and *yolk* and they may only be judged as very faintly antonymic in a context-free judgement or association task.

These context-dependent opposites are, of course, not highly canonical since they are conceptually opposed but do not fulfil certain other criteria, such as morphological relatedness or frequent co-occurrence, which link particularly strong opposites in addition to their conceptual opposition. However, both of these criteria are also linked to the cognitive relationship between the conceptual opposites and thus also determined by it. A morphologically related opposite pair will match very closely in category structure and differ only along a salient dimension because these pairs are lexically constructed to be opposites. This also works on an ad hoc basis, for example by the modification of a verb with a reversative prefix in a productive derivational process (e.g. the recent addition of *unfriend* to the English lexicon). A high degree of associative strength is dependent on an excellent match of the concepts and their semantic range as this allows for usage in the same contexts. Register is also accounted for in a similar manner since the cognitive models which underpin the concepts as well as the conceptual structure will change according to register, resulting in a change of the level of salience of some of the features involved.

6.2.2.3 Conceptual entrenchment

The mechanism underlying antonym judgement would have to be such that the relation is evaluated on a conceptual level, with its features examined for a possible opposite dimension which results in a binary contrast. It seems intuitively sensible that this might be an easier process and thus more swiftly accomplished if the attributes in question were foregrounded either because of the structure of the category, i.e. their centrality of position in the conceptual structure, or by the context in which the concept occurs. However, this approach so far assumes full conceptual evaluation as a default mechanism which does not necessarily represent all patterns observed in the data. One relevant feature, which has already been much debated on a lexical level, is repeated association. Frequent patterns in language, whatever their nature (e.g. collocations, idiomatic language) or underlying cause (e.g. phonologically or conceptually determined), become conventionalised and their use becomes habitual.

The term *entrenchment* has been used in many of the studies mentioned in this chapter but has not usually been defined as a specific process. In recent theoretical work which combines cognitive and psycholinguistic theories, Schmid (2020) proposes entrenchment as a key process in a dynamic linguistic system. He defines this as 'the continual reorganisation of linguistic knowledge caused by repeated usage activities in usage events', which consists of four cognitive processes: 'activation, association, routinization and schematization' (2020, p. 205).

In his dynamic system approach, Schmid (2020) integrates cognitive and psycholinguistic approaches to provide a comprehensive account of the language system and the role played by the cognitive processes of conventionalisation and entrenchment. Entrenchment is triggered by conventionalised usage which activates certain patterns of association and it is these patterns (rather than the conventionalised utterance itself) that become entrenched. Entrenchment then leads to automatisation in processing whereby a certain structure is no longer constructed but becomes a single unit (see also Langacker, 2008). Once a process becomes automatised, this results in a number of different effects including very fast and accurate processing and greater efficiency, resulting in reduced cognitive load (Hartsuiker & Moors, 2017 for an overview).

We are all aware of certain frequent connections between lexical items which have become entrenched and lead to automatic activation (e.g. in collocations such as *heavy traffic* or *torrential rain*), but this process also applies to conceptual constructions which have been conventionalised through repeated usage. They become entrenched and no longer need to be evaluated and construed as the pattern of activation of one concept automatically spreads to another.

The consequences of entrenchment and automatisation are faster spreading activation or simultaneous unconscious activation as the necessary level of activation can be attained quickly due to frequent co-activation (e.g. MacWhinney, 2017, p. 345). Thus, the speed at which a certain conceptual pattern can be retrieved depends on the level of entrenchment and competition during the activation process. Crucially, long-term representations are experientially based, meaning that they are not fixed and are context-sensitive (e.g. Kiefer & Pulvermüller, 2012); this can be seen in the context-sensitive behaviour of opposites and allows for changes in the degree of antonym canonicity of a particular pair resulting from changes in meaning of patterns of use. While the notion of entrenchment is well established in cognitive linguistics and is a fundamental aspect of cognitive models of language processing, it also plays an important role in psycholinguistic and neurolinguistic models of language (although it is often referred to in different terms). In the following section the mechanisms of conceptual entrenchment and automatisation sketched above are integrated into a psycholinguistic model of the representation and processing of antonymic relations in the mental lexicon.

6.3 Antonymy in the brain: a psycholinguistic model of representation and processing

Before outlining the proposal for the representation of antonyms in the lexicon, certain fundamental concepts regarding the representation and processing of words and their meanings are briefly introduced. This builds on the concept of spreading activation introduced in Chapter 4 and provides the foundation for the theoretical approach taken here. There are many different (sometimes competing) theories regarding the representation and access of information in the mental lexicon, and the overview presented here does not aim to distinguish between these competing approaches but to equip the reader with an understanding of the fundamental ideas regarding the storage of lexical, semantic and conceptual knowledge and how this is accessed during language comprehension.

6.3.1 Lexical entries and the mental lexicon

Our mental lexicon is where we store information about lexical items, such as their pronunciation, orthography, morphosyntactic properties and meaning. One way to conceive of this that this information is stored in a system of nodes which are organised on different levels and are connected by links which result in activation or inhibition during processing (e.g. Bierwisch & Schreuder, 1992; Traxler, 2012). There is, as yet, no consensus regarding the precise nature of these representations or the level of detail in which this information is stored. From a neurolinguistic perspective, representations are clusters of nerve cells which are strongly connected but can be distributed across different areas of the brain (e.g. Pulvermüller, 1999, 2013).

Most models of the mental lexicon assume a continuous flow of activation through the lexicon in reaction to a lexical or conceptual stimulus (e.g. when you hear or read a word or see an object; e.g. McClelland & Rumelhardt, 1981; McClelland & Elman, 1986). Lexical access is very fast (MacGregor et al., 2012), and it is assumed that from any entry point into the lexicon – a visual, auditory or other sensory stimulus – activation spreads along connections between nodes of a network and nodes which are directly and indirectly linked to the entry node are activated to greater and lesser degrees (e.g. Collins & Loftus, 1975; McNamara, 1992). Activation spreads over time and decreases with increasing distance from the entry node (cf. McNamara & Altarriba, 1988; McNamara, 1992) and this activation is not modality-specific in that related auditory primes also lead to facilitation of visual targets and vice versa. The original *Spreading Activation Model* (Collins & Loftus, 1975) argued for a purely meaning-based lexicon within which activation would spread via semantic links. However, evidence from speech error research and experiments shows that activation also spreads via phonological or structural similarity (e.g. McNamara, 1994; Aitchison, 2012).

How information is stored in the lexicon and, in particular, how many distinct levels of representation there are is a contentious topic. Most proposals agree on a differentiation of the word form, also sometimes referred to as the *lexeme* (e.g. Levelt, 1989; Bierwisch & Schreuder, 1992), which encodes lexical information such as orthography and phonology and the *lemma*, which includes morphosyntactic properties (e.g. word class, number, grammatical gender) as well as argument structure (the types of complements necessary for a particular verb) and a conceptual level which encodes meaning. The distinction between lexical information and meaning components has also been supported by neurolinguistic evidence which finds cell clusters in different brain areas representing these different types of information, with grammatical components sometimes proposed to be generated by the connections or activation patterns between the cell assemblies (e.g. Pulvermüller, 1999). Where opinions diverge, however, is on the question whether there is a distinction in representation between semantic and conceptual information, with the former part of the lemma (e.g. Bierwisch & Schreuder, 1992) and specific to a particular language (e.g. Pavlenko, 2000)[1] and the latter language-independent. Others propose an approach where word meanings are part of conceptual representations (e.g. Roelofs, 2000) and so-called 'lexical concepts', those concepts which are lexicalised in a particular language, form a subset of all conceptual representations.

While this is not an issue which can be addressed here, it is not trivial with regard to antonym processing as a separate semantic level, as proposed in certain accounts (e.g. Bierwisch & Schreuder, 1992) proposes that lexical relations manifest on the semantic level, which is separate from the conceptual structure. As it is not clear what exactly a separate semantic level would encode (e.g. de Groot, 2000) and data in the present study cannot explicitly contribute to the debate on the separation of lexical and conceptual knowledge, the model outlined here is informed by that of Levelt and colleagues (Bock & Levelt, 1994; Levelt et al., 1999) which assumes three distinct levels of nodes linking to each other (see Figure 6.1). For the current purpose, we will restrict ourselves to the necessary levels: the level of the *lexeme* includes lexical information such as orthography and pronunciation while the *lemma* stores morphosyntactic properties and the *conceptual* level is where meaning is represented with lexicalised meanings as a subset of all conceptual meaning).

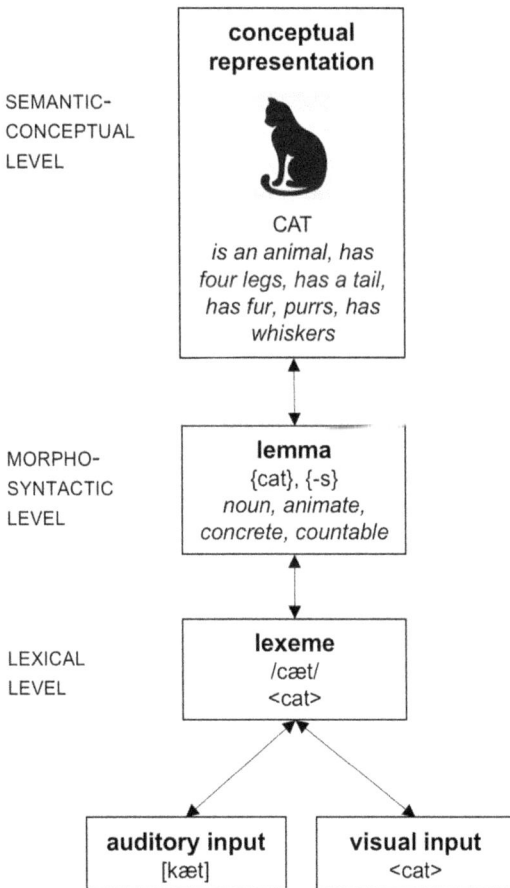

Figure 6.1 Levels of lexical representation in the mental lexicon (based on Bock & Levelt, 1994; Levelt et al., 1999).

This separation into form, syntactic and meaning components has been established experimentally (e.g. Levelt et al., 1999; Norris et al., 2006 among many others) with incoming input (speech or writing) activating the lexeme which, in turn, activates the corresponding lemma and thus the semantic/conceptual information. There is much debate regarding the discreteness of these levels and the interaction between them but most agree on a continuous flow of information between the levels. Work such as that by Norris et al. (2006) has shown that conceptual activation and semantic priming is dependent on the type of processing necessary to achieve understanding (or to complete a task). Phonological and orthographic representations and conceptual representations, while linked by a continuous flow of information in most models, can be activated independently and activation of one does not necessarily lead to (full) activation of the other (e.g. Cutler, 2012, p. 91). In addition, according to approaches which assume a flexible retrieval of conceptual information, not all information is activated in each instance as the activation of conceptual features depends on contextual constraints (e.g. Kiefer & Pulvermüller, 2012)[2]. Thus, access to conceptual information is dynamic and only necessary and relevant features are activated.

Another important point here is that, in language comprehension, phonological and orthographic representations are activated first (e.g. Huettig & McQueen, 2007) and activation then spreads quickly to related items (e.g. embedded words) and an item's corresponding conceptual information is activated continuously rather than only when an item has finally been recognised/chosen. Thus, while the representations for form and conceptual knowledge are separate, activation spreads very quickly between these to allow for effective communication (e.g. Cutler, 2012, p. 95).

In language comprehension and production, activation not only flows between the different nodes of representation of one lexical entry but also spreads along links between words at different levels. For instance, that is why it is easy to respond with a rhyming word (*sun -> fun*) when asked to do, as they share phonological material which is already activated, but we can also very speedily produce semantically (*moon*) or associatively related (*hot*) items which rely on activation travelling through links at a different level. These links vary in strength and are reinforced through repeated association, for example as a result of frequent co-occurrence in texts, which results in the entrenchment of these particular links and therefore faster facilitation. On a neurological level, the repeated co-activation of the cell assemblies which support the processing of a particular word-meaning mapping or a certain structure (e.g. an idiom or common phrase) results in the continuous reinforcement and resulting strengthening of the synaptic connections involved, which leads to fast and automatic co-activation of these entrenched patterns (e.g. Pulvermüller, 1999, 2013).

In order to make an antonym judgement regarding two words at the conceptual level, the speaker/listener has only to activate both individual entries fully but also to evaluate the type of relation between them. However, if the members of an opposite pair are strongly connected on the lexical level, full conceptual access may not be necessary or, alternatively, may be achieved faster. Depending on the task, the speed and ease of an antonym decision may be affected by differences in the types of links (e.g. lexical or semantic) between the two items and their respective strength.

6.3.2 *Looking up or working out?*

One of the questions investigated by psycholinguists is whether we do actually need to compute all information during language processing or whether some is simply stored for wholesale retrieval. This was also raised in early antonym research, where Gross and Miller (1990, p. 274) propose indirect opposites to be relations which are computed rather than stored while direct opposites are linked in the lexicon. Cognitive construal of opposite pairs requires access to the semantic/conceptual information in a lexical entry to determine whether the members of a pair are opposites or not.

One area of research which serves to illustrate the division between storage and computation is that of the processing of morphologically complex words (e.g. *un-happy*). The question whether speakers take morphologically complex words apart in processing (decomposition) or whether they are stored as separate entries (full storage) has resulted in the proposal of several approaches. These theoretical models either assume both simple and complex words to be represented individually with no need for any computation (e.g. Butterworth, 1983; Seidenberg & Gonnerman, 2000), or propose that morphological constituents are stored separately and complex words are first taken apart and their component parts activated in the mental lexicon before being recombined to result in the full meaning (e.g. Fruchter & Marantz, 2015; Stockall & Marantz, 2006; Taft & Forster, 1975).

There are also approaches which incorporate both whole-word storage and decomposition (e.g. Baayen et al., 1997; Clahsen et al., 2010; Pinker & Ullman, 2002). In models of this third type, which allow for either looking up a stored item or computing the morpho-logical structure to achieve lexical access, the preferred route at any given point is said to be affected by factors such as the regularity (i.e. whether the formation of a given form is regular or irregular, e.g. past tense formation in English: *walked* vs. *taught*), frequency and pro-ductivity (e.g. *–ness* vs. *–th* in English suffixation: *tidiness* vs. *growth*) of the processes involved. Thus, the last category of models, which falls somewhere in between, with both direct recognition and decomposi-tion operating during processing, suggests that words can be re-cognised by either route (e.g. Baayen et al., 1997; Caramazza et al., 1988; Frauenfelder & Schreuder, 1992) and these routes operate in parallel, one being prioritised over the other depending on the char-acteristics of the item in question (e.g. regular vs. irregular inflection; inflection vs. derivation; complexity) in a speaker's lexicon.

This question could also be asked specifically with regard to anto-nyms, as frequency is one of the key factors which determines whether a morphologically complex item is stored or assembled. Highly fre-quent items have been proposed to be stored for ease of access since they are needed so often that this is the more efficient approach. This division between storage and computation would suit those who support a categorical approach with canonical opposites being stored as a combination that can simply be retrieved while non-canonical pairs rely on conceptual evaluation to determine their opposite status (e.g. Gross et al., 1989), whereas others have advocated proposals based solely on semantic-conceptual evaluation (e.g. feature matching; Hutchison, 2003; Jeon et al., 2009). This notion of the storage of frequently used patterns is linked closely to the concept of entrench-ment introduced in the previous section, as frequent habitual usage of a pattern leads to conceptual entrenchment which, on the neurological level, is supported by very efficiently connected networks of cells. Thus, frequent antonymic construal of two particular concepts will lead to greater entrenchment and automaticity in activation, under-pinned by very easily and strongly activated attractor networks, and frequent co-occurrence will mirror this conceptual entrenchment at the lexical level. The strength of these entrenched links can vary and is not a stable property, and depending on the context or task, only relevant features may be activated (Kiefer & Pulvermüller, 2012). Continuous reinforcement is necessary to maintain strong links and thus concepts can be linked at the different levels to different degrees. The dis-creteness of the levels of representation and varying degrees en-trenchment of links between concepts at different levels forms the foundation of the following psycholinguistic model of opposition.

6.3.3 A psycholinguistic model of opposition

In Figure 6.1, *cat* was used to illustrate the levels of representation of a lexical entry and the consequences of such a division for processing. The same structure will be used to model the differences between opposite pairs in different parts of the canonicity continuum and illustrate how differences of antonymic strength can be explained in terms of the strength of links on different levels of representation. Three examples which have all been discussed in detail in the case studies will be used as examples: *small:big:little*, *giant:dwarf* and *mother:father*.

We will begin with two pairs which are unquestionably excellent opposites (Figure 6.2): *big:small* and *big:little*. They are gradable adjectives with an easily identifiable uni-dimensional scale which is the primary (only) feature of a very sparse conceptual category. They co-occur extremely frequently (in both pairings) and are also individually highly frequent (with *little* marginally less frequent than the other two items) with a broad (and often overlapping) semantic range. They are thus very strongly linked on the conceptual-semantic level as they fulfil all proposed criteria for good opposites. This is represented with bold bidirectional arrows between the semantic and conceptual nodes in Figure 6.2, indicating strong conceptual entrenchment.

As discussed in Case Study II, the size adjectives *small*, *little*, *big* and *large* are usually said to pattern in the following pairs according to native speaker intuition: *big:little* and *large:small*. However, neither the judgement task results nor the behavioural data reflect this generally fairly unified intuition. The results of a behavioural priming task show significantly faster reaction times for *big:small* (474 ms) than for *big:little* (624 ms). It seems that the presentation of *big* resulted in the automatic activation of *small* and thus, when *little* was presented, access to this entry was inhibited. When *little* or *small* were followed by *big*, reaction times were identical (508 ms for both pairings). This pattern of results can be explained by a difference in entrenchment on the lexical level: *big* has a very strongly entrenched lexical link to *small* and both *little* and *small* are lexically linked to *big*. However, while the lexical link between *big:small* is of a similar strength in both directions, in *big:little* the lexical link is much stronger in one direction (from *little* to *big*) as is represented by the direction of the arrows in Figure 6.2. The different degrees of entrenchment and thus automatic access explain the patterns found in the behavioural results.

Small is both more frequent and broader in semantic range than *little* and thus is both conceptually and lexically the better match

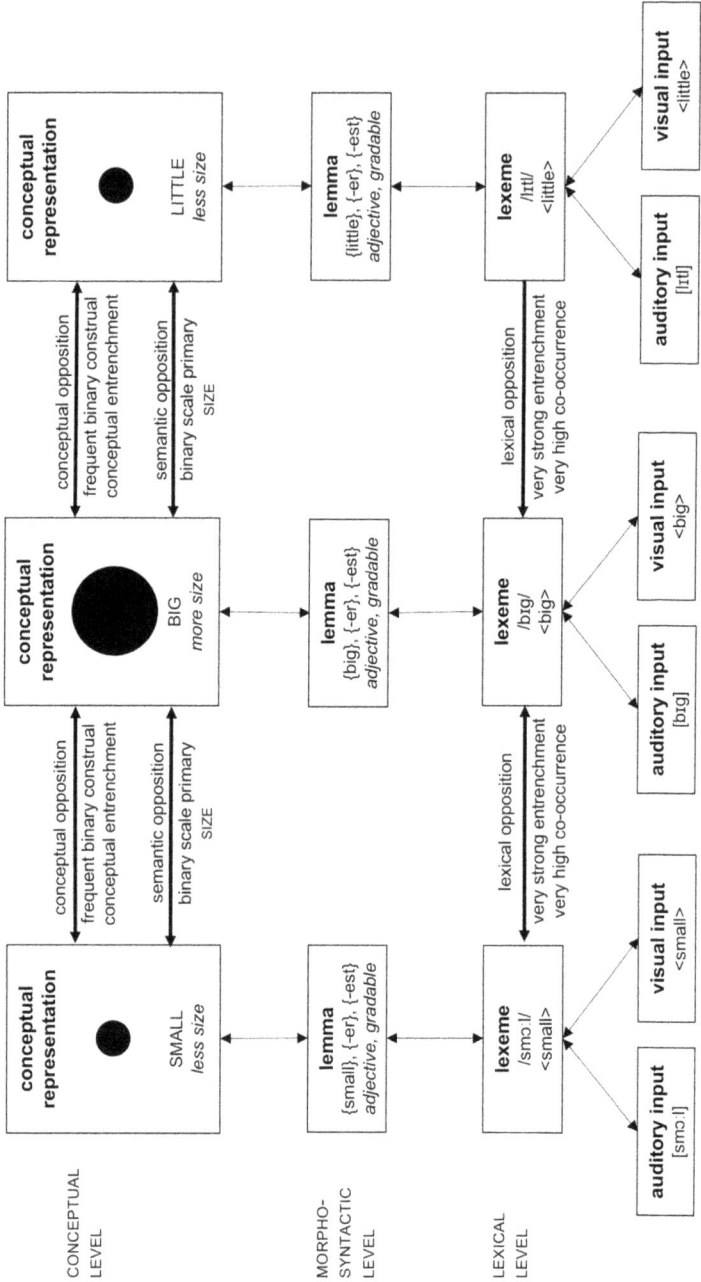

Figure 6.2 Representations for big:little and big:small.

for *big*. However, considered purely on the conceptual level, both pairs are very strongly opposed and neither of these pairings scored lower than 1.35/7 in the judgement task. This contrasts with the remaining pair, *large:little*, which is judged much lower in antonymic strength (2.05) and also resulted in longer reaction times, suggesting a decision on the basis of conceptual evaluation in the absence of a lexical link. Thus, the automatic co-activation on the lexical level does not, in the first instance, reflect the strong conceptual opposition but is guided by activation of the cell clusters representing word form rather than meaning.

Another pair which differs along the SIZE scale, *giant:dwarf*, is illustrated in Figure 6.3. Despite being a nominal pair, *giant:dwarf* is considered a good opposite pair in the judgement task and it also displays reasonably fast reaction times in both languages. However, the reaction times are not as fast as those for highly canonical opposites such as the size adjectives. Here, the distribution of links is somewhat different than in the previous case. The conceptual-semantic links are very strong because the conceptual opposition, that of size, is easily identifiable and, especially in a neutral context, primary. This conceptual opposition further strengthened by secondary contrasts, such as *clever:stupid,* which emerged in the attribute listing task (cf. section 3.4.7). On the lexical level, however, the link is not as strong and does not allow for the same level of automatic activation as in the case of the size adjectives. The opposite judgement is therefore reliant on a conceptual evaluation which necessitates the full activation of semantic-conceptual information before a decision can be made. Thus, in the previous example of *big:small*, links on all levels are very strong, which results in matching high scores in different measures despite different levels being of prime importance in each task. However, in the case of *giant:dwarf*, the links between the two items are stronger on the semantic-conceptual level than on the lexical level, resulting in longer reaction times.

The last example, *mother:father*, illustrates a different pattern again. As discussed in Case Study II, this pair was not judged to be very strongly antonymic in either language, but it was among the 'canonical' pairs in terms of reaction time. Figure 6.4 illustrates the underlying mechanisms which may be responsible for this discrepancy in scores.

Mother:father has very high reciprocal co-occurrence rates and thus has a very strong link on the lexical level as a result of entrenchment and conventionalisation, which accounts for the fast reaction times. However, while the two concepts are strongly linked

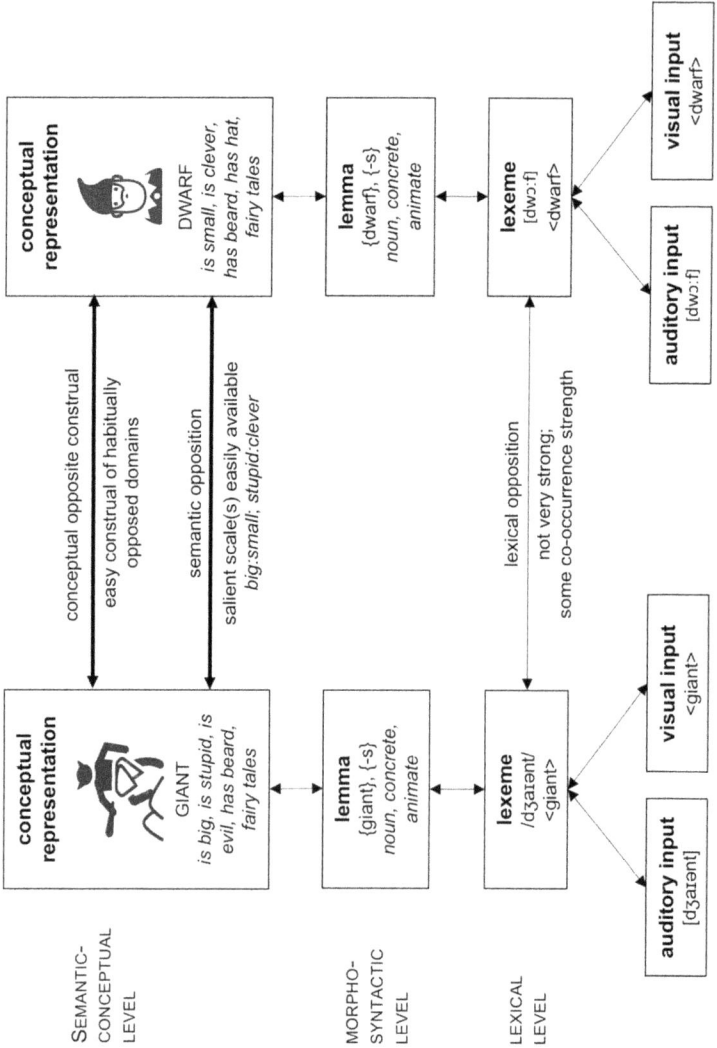

Figure 6.3 Representations for giant:dwarf

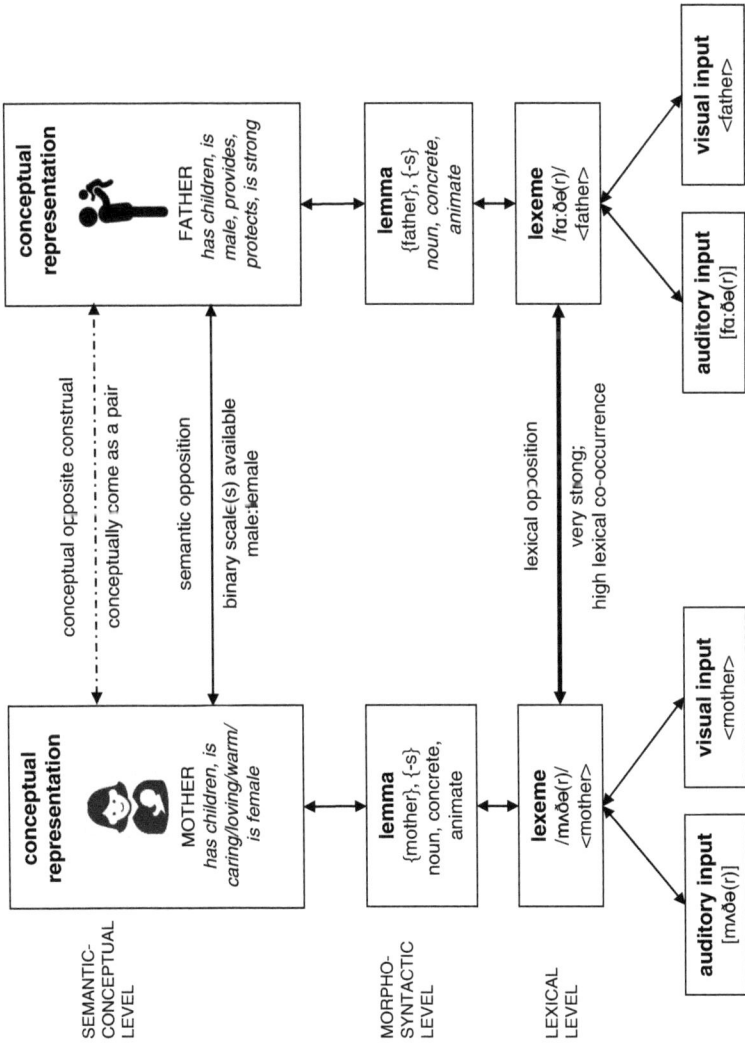

Figure 6.4 Representations for mother:father

on the semantic-conceptual level, the relation is not necessarily primarily one of opposition despite the availability of at least one dimension of opposition (*male:female*). The two concepts are frequently construed in opposition and occur in types of frames where they are conceptually opposed (*either mother or father*) but also in co-ordinated contexts (e.g. *both mother and father*). So, here we have a case where the lexical link between the concepts, which does not have to be based on antonymic use, can result in misleading patterns. It results in very fast co-activation of the two items, and as they are also antonymic in certain senses,[3] they are judged as opposites quickly. However, in a conceptual evaluation of the antonymic relation, the density of the conceptual category structure and the fact that the opposite dimension is not necessarily the most salient in a neutral context (and in other contexts may not be activated at all) diminish the strength of the opposition. This case is an example where the lexical and conceptual-semantic links pull in different directions, which a multi-method investigation is able to highlight but which may not be as easily interpretable in studies using only a single method.

The illustrations of the three pairs in the preceding section have shown how representations can be linked on different levels and how this affects their processing in terms of both the lexical and the conceptual level. The links proposed in the model here are not categorical but may be stronger, weaker or entirely absent (both conceptually, e.g. in ad hoc construal of opposites and lexically), and this may account for different degrees of perceived opposition as well as different response latencies in reaction time tasks. Thus, the best, most canonical opposites do not need to constitute a separate category, but they benefit from being very strongly entrenched on all levels and may display a ceiling effect while other, less canonical pairs pattern more evenly along the canonicity continuum depending on the degree of entrenchment and ease of online construal in the absence of any strongly entrenched patterns. The involvement of different types of relations in the spreading of activation in the lexicon is well attested and has also been examined in the context of antonymy.

In an investigation of the factors which underlie semantic priming, Hutchison (2003) proposes that, while both feature overlap and associative strength have an influence on semantic priming, in the case of both synonyms and antonyms an approach based on feature overlap is favoured. This is further supported by neurolinguistic evidence comparing the processing of synonyms and antonyms (Jeon et al., 2009). However, a purely conceptual approach to antonymy evidently fails to capture the privileged status of a small subset of highly canonical opposites which has been identified in much of the previous research and members of which speakers readily identify as good opposites (also sometimes called the 'clang phenomenon'; Charles & Miller, 1989; Muehleisen, 1997). A number of studies noted the different patterns observed for a select few members of the category of antonymy to which this online computation of conceptual similarity does not seem to apply. Earlier approaches, for example Gross et al. (1989), assumed a larger number of canonical opposites as they bisected the category of antonyms into direct and indirect opposites. Theirs is not a view which can be upheld in the light of recent investigations into antonymy which, on the whole, propose a continuum approach (e.g. Jones et al., 2012 among many others). However, it is clear that, in processing at least, certain opposite pairs elicit considerably faster reaction times and this can be attributed to the contribution of a lexical effect generated by their frequent association and co-activation.

The model introduced above distinguishes different levels of connections for those opposites which are purely (or largely) based on an evaluation of their conceptual properties and those where a strong link on the lexical level leads to automatic co-activation of the two members of the pair (which may not even necessitate activation of the full semantic-conceptual information). This lexical link, however, is secondary to the conceptual opposition and is generated by it, as it is the repeated conceptual antonymic construal of the two members of an opposite pair which leads not only to the entrenchment of the conceptual relation but also to the frequent use of the two words (which in turn allows for the lexical entrenchment). Factors such as the complexity of the conceptual category structure, salience of the underlying opposing dimension, symmetry, and semantic range all contribute to the degree of the conceptual entrenchment and, in the absence of strong entrenchment, to the online evaluation of the featural overlap.

The ordering preference shown by certain opposite pairs can also be accounted for here, because while this is usually based on certain conceptual (e.g. markedness) and lexical properties (e.g. phonology), it will also be reinforced by the use of pairs in a particular sequence, meaning that the entrenchment of the lexical link will be stronger in one direction than in the other, as seen with *big:little* and *little:big* above. The extent to which this plays a role in experimental results may well be dependent on the tasks and particular design as activation (especially on the lexical level) decreases relatively quickly, and therefore paradigms with little or no intervening time between items (such as the simultaneous presentation in this study) may show the strongest lexical effects. This may also explain certain patterns in the recent behavioural study by van der Weijer et al. (2012) as the lag time between their stimuli was relatively long even in the condition where the prime immediately preceded the target.

Another factor discussed throughout, morphological relatedness, is a particularly interesting case from a processing perspective, as morphologically complex opposite pairs, because if decomposition is assumed (e.g. Baayen et al., 1997; Fruchter & Marantz, 2015), morphologically complex opposite pairs are encoded by the same lexical entry. For instance, when *unhappy* is heard, it is divided into its constituent morphemes – *happy* and *un-* – which are retrieved separately from the lexicon and then recombined to determine the full meaning of *unhappy*. Thus in a behavioural task such as the one above, the evaluation of *happy:unhappy* is based on repeat access of the same lexical entry, and therefore very strong lexical activation, but these pairs may result in slightly slower reaction times as the recombination process requires added computation. They also do not benefit from the entrenched lexical opposition generated by frequent co-occurrence as this does not affect the activation level of the lexical entry.

Another phenomenon where the opposition requires only one lexical entry is that of antagonyms because their forms are identical and nevertheless, within the conceptual representation, encode opposing subsenses. However, these items are never considered good examples of opposition as their encoding in a single item without any distinction weakens the binarity of the opposition expressed by the subsenses. It seems that the particular encoding – in the same, morphologically related and completely unrelated items – does also contribute to the salience of the opposition on a conceptual level and, of course, in the case of antagonyms, prevents entrenchment through frequent use in discourse.

It is clear from the cognitive and psycholinguistic proposals put forward here that both conceptual and lexical factors play a role in the degree of perceived opposition of an antonym pair but that antonymy is in general a fundamentally conceptual relation which is dynamic in its construal and affected by a number of lexical and conceptual factors as well as linguistic, situational and cultural context. Frequent opposite construal of certain concepts leads to conventionalisation and subsequent entrenchment on the conceptual level which is underpinned by neurological patterns of activation (e.g. Schmid, 2020). Frequent co-construal, which leads to the repeated co-occurrence of the associated lexical items, subsequently leads to lexical entrenchment in certain cases, resulting in the continuous reinforcement= of this relationship.

Notes

1 There are other approaches which have argued for a further division between semantic and conceptual knowledge (e.g. Paradis, 2000; Pavlenko, 2000, 2009) as, for these scholars, semantic representations are already tied to certain lexical items and are thus language-dependent while conceptual representations are not.
2 There is no consensus as yet regarding the representation and processing of conceptual information from a neurolinguistics perspective (see Kiefer & Pulvermüller, 2012 for a review).
3 The nature of the task may also have had an effect here as the participants were asked to make an antonymy judgement.

7 Conclusions

7.1 What is *antonymy*?

Since the very first mention of *antonym* by C.J. Smith in 1867, the term has undergone many re-definitions. It originated as an alternative to *counterterm* and was defined simply as 'a term which is the opposite or antithesis of another, a counter-term' (OED; Simpson, 1989). In Lyons' (1977) and Cruse's (1986) definitions, *antonym* came to refer to only a subgroup of opposites defined by certain specific properties (adjectival, gradable opposite pairs). When the notion of antonymy began to be investigated from a cognitive perspective, the term was used to refer to the relationship between two antonyms and its lexical, semantic and conceptual properties.

The question, raised by Cruse (1986), of what qualifies as antonymy is one which has been raised repeatedly and does not only relate to, for instance, whether the category of converses should be considered part of lexical opposition but also whether any pairs beyond those central 'canonical' opposites are included in this category. Making this distinction, of course, already presupposes a categorical approach either to antonymy itself or to the degree of antonymy, in that is places a pair in one of two categories: canonical or non-canonical.

Earlier views which consider only those pairs which have become entrenched on the lexical level to constitute antonymy proper (e.g. Miller, 1990; Jones, 2002) have now made way for a more holistic consideration of phenomena of opposition within cognitive usage-based proposals in which any pair of words, when subjected to binary bounded construal, can be considered antonymous (e.g. Jones et al., 2012). This approach is supported by a wealth of evidence from a diverse range of studies which emphasises the conceptual nature, dynamic construal, context-sensitivity and wide range of use of antonymy in discourse.

DOI: 10.4324/9781003026969-7

The fundamentally conceptual nature of antonymy receives strong support from recent empirical studies, and the data presented in this book is no exception. The cross-linguistic analyses provide particularly convincing evidence that the locus of antonymy lies in the conceptual domain. The same pairs are judged to have very high antonymic strength in German and in English despite large differences in the comparison of co-occurrence data between the two languages with most of the 210 opposite pairs in the two languages differing by no more than 0.5 points on the seven-point rating scale. It seems unlikely that the lexical items encoding the same concepts in two different languages would form contrastive relationships of near-identical strength without some cognitive or conceptual trigger. The conceptual effects are also seen in the intralinguistic judgement ratings, which show considerably different patterns from those observed in the co-occurrence data in a significant number of cases. The successful and efficient construal of antonyms is determined by a number of factors, such as the salience of the opposing dimension, the semantic range of the two concepts involved and the distribution of the two concepts on a scale in the case of gradable properties. These cognitive factors affect the ease with which the antonymic relationship is construed and therefore how strongly antonymic certain pairs are perceived to be. Thus, results show a gradual decrease in antonymic strength from central, canonical opposites at one end of the continuum to pairs which are more (or sometimes entirely) dependent on contextual support (e.g. *tea:coffee, brother:sister*) and therefore a prototype structure for the category of antonymy.

However, the notion of a categorical distinction between canonical and non-canonical pairs still survives in many recent proposals (e.g. Paradis et al., 2009) where a small number of very highly canonical pairs are considered exceptional. This difference is usually attributed to an additional lexical relationship that comes as a result of frequent co-occurrence and has given rise to a very close connection, which has become conventionalised, between the two lexical items representing the opposing concepts. It therefore seems appropriate to define antonymy or lexical opposition as a cognitive relation of opposed concepts which are encoded by lexical items. In certain cases, the highly frequent antonymic construal of two concepts results in the additional entrenchment of the two associated lexemes as a pair and adds a lexical component to an essentially conceptual relation.

The proposal of the lexical representation of antonymy proposed in Chapter 6 includes this lexical component but without the need for a categorical division. Evidence for the existence and relevance of this lexical component comes from the behavioural data presented in Chapter 4, where the associative element influences participants' reactions to a greater degree than in the judgement task. The close association on the lexical level of representation which leads to very efficient automatic co-activation of the two members of a pair accounts for the extremely fast and consistent reaction times to these pairs as well as for the strong priming effects and stable elicitation results observed in other studies. However, this lexical link is not exclusive to antonymy, as it is simply a result of highly frequent co-occurrence which has led to lexical entrenchment. This can be seen by the comparable reaction time and elicitation data for *mother:father*, *man:woman* or *king:queen*, for instance, which are not considered good opposites and would also apply to collocations, such as *torrential rain* or any sequence of lexical items which is strongly conventionalised. Here and in previous research (e.g. Jones et al., 2012), this lexical association is considered a consequence of the conceptual entrenchment which leads to highly frequent co-occurrence and thus, in turn, to conventionalisation and entrenchment on the lexical level. This process of conventionalisation and entrenchment of certain patterns is a general cognitive and neural principle (see Schmid, 2020) which leads to the automatisation of certain processes, but it needs to be triggered by frequent repetition of the pattern – which, in the case of antonymy, comes about due to the strong opposition of these pairs as a result of their fulfilment of certain conceptual criteria.

This view of a fundamentally conceptual relation, with an additional lexical component for highly conventionalised pairs, could only be determined when the whole spectrum of antonyms along the canonicity continuum was considered using a number of different methods, since different strands of data contributed different pieces of information. As the psycholinguistic model indicates, each methodological approach prioritises different mechanisms, and it is therefore crucial to include several methods as each individual measure will only provide part of the story. Studies employing fewer empirical methods with a more restricted set of stimuli, while well suited to providing essential detail of particular phenomena, may result in a more one-dimensional interpretation.

7.2 Methodological considerations

The reason for adopting a multi-method approach here was the observation that while there are a large number of studies of antonymy using different methodologies, investigations making use of more than one method and cross-linguistic studies in particular have been lacking (notable exceptions being Paradis et al., 2009, 2015; Paradis & Willners, 2011 and further data presented in Jones et al., 2012). The question of what can be gained from the combination of several methods is relatively easily answered: a deeper and more thorough understanding of the phenomenon under investigation. The relation of antonymy had previously been considered from a number of different perspectives, ranging from highly theoretical and introspective classifications (Lyons, 1977; Cruse, 1986) to completely data-driven usage-based corpus studies (Jones 2002; Paradis et al., 2007); but bringing three sets of data together has provided useful anchor points for the investigation of antonym canonicity and the factors which influence speaker judgements, as well as the underlying mechanisms of storage and processing.

The strategy adopted here was one of using discrepancies in the data as starting points for closer investigation and building data-driven hypotheses regarding both the nature of opposition and the effects of individual factors which may affect the degree of antonymic strength. This has allowed for the corroboration of theoretical conceptual approaches proposed by others working in the field (e.g. Jones et al., 2012) as well as their extension into the psycholinguistic domain, resulting in the model presented in Chapter 6.

The different methods used in the study reflect the conceptual and lexical factors which affect antonym canonicity to different degrees, and it is only through a combination of the data sets that we can begin to understand the representations and processing mechanisms which underpin the conceptual evaluation of opposites. For instance, the judgement task showed much greater effects of the conceptual criteria as participants were asked to consciously evaluate the degree of opposition without any time constraints. In the reaction time study, the lexical effects surfaced more strongly and led to faster reaction times for pairs which were not strongly antonymic (e.g. *mother:father*) but also to inhibition of pairs which are generally considered canonical (e.g. *big:little*). This strong lexical association may well have an even greater effect in tasks which do not explicitly ask for an antonym judgement, such as standard lexical decision tasks where the judgement is simply one of lexicality (word vs. nonword). In the experiments presented here participants were still asked to provide a judgement of antonymy but the fast co-activation of two items with a strong lexical link leads to faster conceptual evaluation of the relation. However, in a lexical decision task, the effects may be different and could be more strongly guided by the lexical entrenchment as full conceptual activation is not necessary to provide a lexicality judgement.

Thus, methodological choices guide and constrain our interpretation of the data and combinations of different methods often result in a better understanding of the individual contribution of a number of effects. Some of these effects may be relatively small but it has recently been recognised that most psychological phenomena, with language processing no exception, are most probably the result of a combination of smaller individual effects (Götz et al., 2021): this may lead to greater appreciation of empirical studies which show comparatively small effects.

7.3 Further implications

It is clear from the recent increase in studies on antonymy that there is still much to be learned about this relation which is claimed to be fundamental to our cognition (Lyons, 1977; Lakoff & Johnson, 1980). Cognitive approaches have led to great strides in our understanding of the how the relation is construed on the conceptual level and which factors are crucial in facilitating this. The broader range of examples of opposition taken into account in research has also led to further elaboration of the discourse functions of antonymy (Section 2.3) and how concepts become associated as opposites in novel formations (e.g. Davies, 2012). One question which, to the best of my knowledge, has not yet been comprehensively addressed is whether the patterns of discourse function of antonymy affect the conceptual construal of an opposite pair. For instance, if *mother:-father* is used more in constructions which highlight their function as a unit rather than their opposition, can this lead to a weakening of the antonymic entrenchment on the conceptual level?

It is the corpus-linguistic approach which has so far attracted the most diverse range of studies in terms of the languages considered but in cognitive and especially psycholinguistic research the number of languages investigated is still very limited. As the cross-linguistic data in this study has proven to be of great interest, translating these (or similar) methods to other languages would allow for investigations of the effects of differences in linguistic structure and cultural influences on antonym construal and processing.

In order to address the more detailed points of the phenomena observed in the study, separate investigations with sets of stimuli which are carefully chosen to address one very specific question (e.g. processing of morphologically related vs. unrelated opposites) are necessary, and especially in the psycholinguistic and neurolinguistics domains much more evidence is needed to elaborate and verify the elements of the proposal put forward here. Thus far, only one ERP study (van de Weijer et al., 2014) examines neurotypical antonym processing and many more are needed to improve our understanding of the interaction and effects of lexical and conceptual components involved in processing.

For instance, as mentioned above, the structure of information in a lexical entry is controversial, and it remains an open question whether there is a distinct semantic level (e.g. Bierwisch & Schreuder, 1992; Pavlenko; 2000) on which lexical relations (such as synonymy and antonymy) are encoded or whether there is no need or empirical motivation for such a division (e.g. Roelofs, 2000; de Groot, 2000). The neurological underpinnings of semantic and conceptual processing are also not yet fully understood but proposals have been moving away from stable representations to approaches based on dynamic systems (e.g. Kiefer & Pulvermüller, 2012; Schmid, 2020). As the approach in this book has demonstrated, antonymy is certainly a relation which relies on dynamic construal which is influenced by a number of interrelated factors, some of which have additive effects. In context, even pairs of concepts with no inherent binary opposition can be successfully construed as opposites. Over time, any given pair of concepts can become conventionalised as a 'canonical' pair if repeated antonym construal leads to an entrenchment of the conceptual representation and, subsequently, to a corresponding entrenchment of the associated lexemes on the lexical level. However, while these links are mutually reinforcing while the relation remains stable, a change in use or meaning of particular lexemes and concepts may also result in the weakening of a previously entrenched opposition. While there are many further avenues to explore to determine the precise dynamics affecting entrenchment, it seems antonym canonicity is a matter of the degree of conceptual and lexical entrenchment with the most canonical opposites connected by very strong links on all levels of representation.

Appendix 1

English and German word pairs included in the judgement task

(glosses provided for pairs which are not translation equivalents)

English		German	
Word 1	*Word 2*	*Word 1*	*Word 2*
absent	present	abwesend	anwesend
actress	actor	Schauspielerin	Schauspieler
aloof	amiable	verschlossen 'locked'	unverschlossen 'unlocked'
animal	dog	Tier	Hund
answer	reply	Antwort	Entgegnung
apprentice	master	Lehrling	Meister
ask	answer	fragen	antworten
awake	asleep	wach	schlafend
away	home	weg	daheim
bad	satisfactory	schlecht	zufriedenstellend
bad	good	schlecht	gut
badly	well	kaufen 'buy'	verkaufen 'sell'
behind	in front	hinter	vor
big	tiny	groß	winzig
big	small	groß	klein
bland	hot	fad	scharf
blue	orange	blau	orange
book	page	Buch	Seite
brick	mortar	grau 'gray'	bunt 'colourful'
brief	long	Bein 'leg'	Fuß 'foot'
brother	sister	Bruder	Schwester
buy	spend	kaufen	ausgeben
buy	sell	kaufen	verkaufen
carrot	pea	Karotte	Erbse
child	parent	Kinder	Eltern
chilly	steaming	kühl	drückend
chilly	warm	frostig	warm

(*Continued*)

English		German	
Word 1	*Word 2*	*Word 1*	*Word 2*
clean	tidy	sauber	ordentlich
clever	bright	clever	helle
coffee	tea	Kaffee	Tee
cold	friendly	kalt	freundlich
cold	distant	kalt	fremd
cold	mild	kalt	mild
cold	hot	kalt	heiß
cold	sticky	kalt	klebrig
colossal	miniscule	kolossal	unscheinbar
contemporary	ancient	offen 'open'	verschlossen 'locked'
correct	mistaken	verlernen 'forget'	lernen 'learn'
cow	bull	Kuh	Bulle
credit	debit	Haben	Soll
crown	king	Krone	König
current	former	gegenwärtig	früher
dad	mum	Papa	Mama
damage	repair	beschädigen	reparieren
dark	light	dunkel	hell
daughter	mother	Tochter	Mutter
dead	fresh	tot	frisch
dead	gone	tot	weg
defend	attack	verteidigen	angreifen
dirty	clean	schmutzig	sauber
disorganised	organised	fest 'solid'	weich 'soft'
dog	cat	Hund	Katze
donate	steal	spenden	stehlen
double	single	doppelt	einfach
dry	sweet	trocken	süß
easy	uneasy	mild 'mild'	lau 'mild temperature'
easy	difficult	einfach	schwierig
egg	chicken	Ei	Huhn
employer	employee	Chef	Angestellter
escape	hunt	ausbrechen	jagen
even	uneven	gerade	ungerade
excellent	atrocious	exzellent	miserabel
excellent	bad	exzellent	schlecht
exclude	include	ausschließen	miteinbeziehen
fair	poor	angemessen	mangelhaft
false	true	falsch	wahr
far	near	weit	nah
fast	slow	schnell	langsam
father	mother	Vater	Mutter
father	daughter	Vater	Tochter

(*Continued*)

English		German	
Word 1	*Word 2*	*Word 1*	*Word 2*
figuratively	literally	einflusslos 'without influence'	einflussreich 'influential'
finger	hand	Finger	Hand
finish	continue	Hahn 'cockrel'	Henne 'hen'
fish	fowl	Fisch	Fleisch
fit	hot	Katze 'cat'	Maus 'mouse'
flammable	inflammable	einwilligen 'agree'	befolgen 'obey'
flee	chase	fliehen	jagen
freezing	boiling	eisig	tropisch
giant	dwarf	Riese	Zwerg
glove	hand	früh 'early'	spat 'late'
go	come	gehen	kommen
good	disobedient	brav	ungehorsam
good	mediocre	gut	mittelmäßig
good	evil	gut	böse
gracious	mean	satt 'satiated'	hungrig 'hungry'
happy	sad	glücklich	unglücklich
hard	easy	schwer	einfach
helpful	helpless	hilfreich	hilflos
helpless	helpful	hilflos	hilfreich
hot	cool	heiß	kühl
humid	hot	schmal 'slender, narrow'	dick 'thick, fat'
hungry	thirsty	hungrig	durstig
imprecise	exact	unpräzise	exakt
inaccurate	accurate	inakkurat	akkurat
incorrect	right	inkorrekt	richtig
indirectly	directly	indirekt	direkt
interested	disinterested	interessiert	uninteressiert
interested	uninterested	trostlos '	verzagt
keep	sell	behalten	verkaufen
king	queen	König	Königin
large	little	halb 'half'	ganz 'whole'
last	first	letztes	erstes
lease	let	lehren 'teach'	lernen 'learn'
legal	illegal	legal	illegal
lend	borrow	verleihen	ausleihen
less	more	weniger	mehr
life	death	Leben	Tod
light	heavy	leicht	schwer
little	gigantic	klein	riesig

(*Continued*)

English		German	
Word 1	*Word 2*	*Word 1*	*Word 2*
little	big	klein	groß
long	narrow	lang	schmal
loyal	disloyal	loyal	unloyal
lukewarm	tepid	Weib 'wench'	Mann 'man'
mad	angry	verrückt	wütend
male	female	männlich	weiblich
married	unmarried	verheiratet	unverheiratet
married	divorced	verheiratet	geschieden
masculine	feminine	maskulin	feminin
mediocre	brilliant	mittelmäßig	brilliant
mentor	protégé	Tasse 'cup'	Henkel 'handle'
miniature	gigantic	mini	riesig
misbehave	behave	unmoralisch 'immoral'	moralisch 'moral'
mobile	landline	Handy	Festnetz
mug	cup	Becher	Tasse
murderer	victim	Mörder	Opfer
nephew	niece	Neffe	Nichte
new	old	neu	alt
next to	opposite	neben	gegenüber
occupier	owner	Bewohner	Besitzer
odd	even	moralisch 'moral'	amoralisch 'amoral'
old	young	alt	jung
out	in	hinaus	hinein
over	under	über	unter
pack	unpack	packen	auspacken
pale	dark	blass	dunkel
patient	doctor	Patient	Doktor
possible	impossible	möglich	unmöglich
present	future	Gegenwart	Zukunft
present	past	Gegenwart	Vergangenheit
pupil	teacher	Schüler	Lehrer
quiet	still	ruhig	still
rain	wind	Regen	Wind
rational	irrational	rational	irrational
red	green	rot	grün
rent	let	mieten	vermieten
right	left	rechts	links
right	wrong	richtig	falsch
rose	flower	Rose	Blume
sad	unhappy	traurig	unglücklich
scorching	glacial	amoralisch 'amoral'	unmoralisch 'immoral'

(*Continued*)

English		German	
Word 1	*Word 2*	*Word 1*	*Word 2*
scream	kick	weich 'soft'	fest 'solid'
serious	trivial	scheußlich 'hideous'	verrucht 'wicked'
short	squat	bunt 'colourful'	einfarbig 'one colour'
short	polite	kurz	höflich
short	long	kurz	lang
sick	healthy	krank	gesund
similar	identical	ähnlich	identisch
similar	different	ähnlich	verschieden
sinful	virtuous	sündig	tugendhaft
single	married	single	verheiratet
small	huge	klein	gewaltig
small	tall	staatlich 'state-funded'	privat 'private'
small	large	Fee 'fairy'	Hexe 'witch'
small	large	schwach 'weak'	stark 'strong'
sober	drunk	nüchtern	betrunken
soft	easy	weich	einfach
soft	hard	weich	hart
sour	sweet	sauer	süß
spicy	mild	würzig	mild
square	long	viereckig	lang
still	sparkling	privat 'private'	dienstlich 'business'
succeed	fail	sommerlich 'summery'	frostig 'chilly'
suitable	wrong	passend	falsch
sweet	bitter	süß	bitter
sweltering	nippy	formal 'formal'	praktisch 'practical'
take	give	nehmen	geben
tall	short	schwierig 'difficult'	leicht 'light, easy'
teacher	student	Dozent	Student
tenant	landlord	Mieter	Vermieter
tiny	huge	winzig	riesig
tipsy	inebriated	irreal 'unreal'	real 'real'
tired	sick	Wasser 'water'	Feuer 'fire'
together	apart	zusammen	alleine
tomorrow	today	morgen	heute
top	bottom	oben	unten
town	country	Stadt	Land
trade	purchase	handeln	erwerben
traditional	trendy	traditionell	modisch
tutee	tutor	siezen 'to use Sie'	dozen 'to use Du'
uncle	aunt	Onkel	Tante

(Continued)

English		German	
Word 1	*Word 2*	*Word 1*	*Word 2*
undress	dress	ausziehen	anziehen
uneasy	easy	alt 'old'	grau 'grey'
unhappy	happy	unglücklich	glücklich
unhealthy	healthy	ungesund	gesund
unorganised	organised	erlauben 'allow'	verbieten 'forbid'
unsuitable	suitable	unpassend	passend
untidy	tidy	unordentlich	ordentlich
up	down	hoch	runter
valley	hill	Tal	Berg
walk	crawl	gehen	krabbeln
warm	cool	warm	kühl
white	coloured	weiß	farbig
wife	husband	Frau	Mann
wintry	sultry	real 'real'	unreal 'unreal'
woman	man	wohin 'where to'	woher 'where from'
work	play	Arbeit	Vergnügen
wrong	bad	falsch	schlecht
yell	call	brüllen	rufen
yellow	blue	gelb	blau

Appendix 2

Frequencies, t-scores and judgement ratings for all English pairs

Word 1	Freq	Word 2	Freq	Total FoC	T-score	QR 1-2	QR 2-1	QR overall
false	3584	true	17737	189	13.516	1.03	1	1.015
up	180792	down	91734	4017	50.309	1.08	1	1.04
soft	5869	hard	12834	82	8.639	1.03	1.1	1.065
right	74117	wrong	15505	664	23.540	1.08	1.1	1.09
fast	7352	slow	5724	85	8.991	1.1	1.13	1.115
top	22744	bottom	7304	474	21.390	1.1	1.13	1.115
cold	9328	hot	8733	421	20.319	1.08	1.18	1.13
new	124227	old	52486	1022	21.781	1.08	1.18	1.13
awake	1287	asleep	2252	27	5.168	1.15	1.13	1.14
last	71886	first	120825	802	13.000	1.2	1.08	1.14
exclude	1324	include	15148	7	2.267	1.2	1.1	1.15
dirty	2666	clean	6281	30	5.324	1.18	1.15	1.165
bad	14935	good	81100	856	27.189	1.2	1.15	1.175
dark	12653	light	19534	243	14.796	1.15	1.2	1.175
tall	4329	short	17792	62	7.385	1.13	1.23	1.18
inaccurate	458	accurate	2887	5	2.206	1.28	1.08	1.18
absent	1549	present	14691	31	5.363	1.33	1.05	1.19
far	36754	near	17048	126	8.436	1.2	1.18	1.19
unsuitable	691	suitable	6021	6	2.364	1.25	1.15	1.2
short	19660	long	50614	523	20.902	1.2	1.23	1.215
small	43118	large	34269	800	25.674	1.25	1.18	1.215
happy	11340	sad	3322	33	5.417	1.23	1.2	1.215
big	24853	small	43118	210	10.797	1.1	1.35	1.225
legal	12981	illegal	2392	31	5.289	1.38	1.1	1.24
little	29018	big	24853	128	8.129	1.18	1.3	1.24
out	149187	in	1843054	1659	-3.087	1.15	1.33	1.24
unhappy	1846	happy	11340	17	3.869	1.2	1.28	1.24
untidy	381	tidy	719	3	1.724	1.4	1.08	1.24
rational	2295	irrational	494	13	3.589	1.45	1.08	1.265
old	52486	young	32326	461	17.534	1.13	1.43	1.28
odd	4312	even	4146	18	4.104	1.2	1.4	1.3
disorganised	80	organised	767	0	0	1.33	1.28	1.305
easy	14414	difficult	21621	46	4.487	1.23	1.38	1.305
right	74117	left	13094	1211	33.406	1.23	1.38	1.305
succeed	2102	fail	3331	24	4.827	1.23	1.38	1.305
light	19534	heavy	9126	78	7.823	1.33	1.28	1.305
sick	4333	healthy	3527	9	2.745	1.38	1.25	1.315

(Continued)

Word 1	Freq	Word 2	Freq	Total FoC	T-score	QR 1-2	QR 2-1	QR overall
unhealthy	277	healthy	3527	4	1.975	1.35	1.3	1.325
possible	33656	impossible	6826	15	0.910	1.23	1.45	1.34
loyal	1330	disloyal	92	0	0	1.38	1.33	1.355
over	128305	under	60049	346	-2.087	1.38	1.35	1.365
less	34026	more	209697	4123	58.660	1.5	1.25	1.375
sober	595	drunk	2162	14	3.724	1.45	1.3	1.375
good	81100	evil	2773	271	15.779	1.38	1.4	1.39
interested	8787	uninterested	138	1	0.9394	1.43	1.4	1.415
misbehave	28	behave	1704	0	0	1.43	1.43	1.43
defend	2021	attack	1457	10	3.068	1.5	1.38	1.44
giant	958	dwarf	572	3	1.716	1.55	1.35	1.45
life	54993	death	19891	551	21.145	1.5	1.4	1.45
even	4146	uneven	664	0	0	1.28	1.63	1.455
take	69607	give	43976	235	5.356	1.53	1.45	1.49
tiny	5186	huge	7649	19	3.904	1.6	1.38	1.49
colossal	235	miniscule	21	0	0	1.58	1.43	1.505
pack	871	unpack	114	0	0	1.38	1.65	1.515
undress	144	dress	927	5	2.23	1.68	1.35	1.515
miniature	858	gigantic	400	0	0	1.6	1.45	1.525
hard	15291	easy	14414	28	3.211	1.43	1.68	1.555
together	29944	apart	3391	37	5.248	1.65	1.55	1.6
unorganised	32	organised	3911	1	0.993	1.65	1.58	1.615
indirectly	1038	directly	8607	366	19.107	1.55	1.75	1.65
behind	19098	in front	6950	62	7.032	1.45	1.9	1.675
buy	12293	sell	7539	205	13.994	1.93	1.43	1.68
go	85465	come	66694	702	15.749	1.9	1.65	1.775
masculine	620	feminine	728	80	8.941	1.58	2	1.79
imprecise	120	exact	2152	0	0	1.88	1.8	1.84
warm	6744	cool	3822	36	5.785	2.08	1.6	1.84
sinful	166	virtuous	175	0	0	1.78	2	1.89
married	9779	unmarried	584	18	4.175	2.13	1.8	1.965
figuratively	45	literally	1936	5	2.234	2.23	1.7	1.965
freezing	967	boiling	883	5	2.216	2.1	1.85	1.975
small	43118	huge	7649	24	1.536	2.05	1.95	2
male	7716	female	4980	1063	32.544	1.88	2.18	2.03
big	24853	tiny	5186	13	1.820	2.28	1.8	2.04
large	34269	little	62638	75	-3.719	2.15	1.95	2.05
interested	8787	disinterested	172	2	1.360	2.4	1.75	2.075
small	43118	large	34269	800	25.674	3.05	1.15	2.1
woman	22008	man	58165	946	28.678	2.18	2.03	2.105
excellent	6620	atrocious	118	0	0	2.05	2.23	2.14
credit	7297	debit	267	34	5.814	2.1	2.25	2.19
little	29018	gigantic	400	1	0.420	2.1	2.28	2.19
similar	18295	different	47604	131	7.644	2.28	2.1	2.19
brief	4327	long	33240	4	-1.846	2.58	1.83	2.205
chilly	336	warm	6082	2	1.342	2.45	2.08	2.265
badly	4187	well	108935	58	4.624	2.45	2.13	2.29
small	43118	tall	4329	21	2.548	1.38	3.23	2.305
serious	12093	trivial	873	10	2.995	2.45	2.2	2.325
correct	5812	mistaken	1099	0	0	2.73	1.95	2.34
incorrect	695	right	34396	0	0	2.08	2.6	2.34
valley	4613	hill	6881	71	3.738	2.55	2.15	2.35
damage	8301	repair	2276	100	9.905	2.75	1.98	2.365
lend	1254	borrow	1425	22	4.671	2.9	1.98	2.44
contemporary	4488	ancient	4910	9	2.633	2.78	2.15	2.465

(Continued)

Word 1	Freq	Word 2	Freq	Total FoC	T-score	QR 1-2	QR 2-1	QR overall
spicy	207	mild	1543	0	0	2.45	2.53	2.49
pale	3237	dark	9777	47	6.625	2.58	2.48	2.53
sweet	3177	bitter	2353	20	4.388	2.48	2.78	2.63
excellent	6620	bad	14935	4	-0.469	2.45	2.83	2.64
work	89441	play	21119	142	3.999	2.7	2.6	2.65
hot	8733	cool	3228	30	5.220	2.58	2.78	2.68
sour	622	sweet	3177	42	6.465	2.33	3.03	2.68
single	18074	married	9779	66	7.037	2.93	2.48	2.705
ask	18642	answer	14305	55	5.6201	2.9	2.55	2.725
away	47116	home	50539	801	24.099	2.63	2.88	2.755
present	17328	past	19097	601	23.841	2.43	3.13	2.78
employer	3002	employee	3108	109	10.395	2.93	2.75	2.84
scorching	122	glacial	269	0	0	3.35	2.75	3.05
married	9779	divorced	909	46	6.716	3	3.15	3.075
mentor	260	protégé	43	0	0	3.25	2.93	3.09
pupil	2307	teacher	8633	132	11.402	2.9	3.4	3.15
aloof	226	amiable	279	0	0	3.15	3.18	3.165
wife	16474	husband	10612	802	28.011	3.23	3.1	3.165
current	13292	former	16845	38	4.350	3.43	2.95	3.19
apprentice	500	master	5512	5	2.174	3.23	3.2	3.215
murderer	768	victim	3796	10	3.116	3.33	3.15	3.24
sweltering	56	nippy	43	0	0	2.95	3.6	3.275
good	77128	disobedient	72	0	0	3.05	3.7	3.375
patient	6820	doctor	9048	102	9.757	3.5	3.25	3.375
tutee	13	tutor	1081	0	0	3.33	3.45	3.39
brother	8277	sister	7150	310	17.438	3.33	3.5	3.415
gracious	423	mean	2493	0	0	3.35	3.53	3.44
flammable	75	inflammable	53	0	0	3.18	3.73	3.455
tenant	2570	landlord	2673	338	18.366	3.25	3.68	3.465
dad	6564	mum	8152	706	26.470	3.6	3.4	3.5
flee	445	chase	517	0	0	3.68	3.33	3.505
teacher	8633	student	7590	96	9.463	3.38	3.73	3.555
chilly	336	steaming	393	0	0	3.08	4.05	3.565
child	23669	parent	3707	254	15.662	4.05	3.1	3.575
mediocre	174	brilliant	3411	0	0	3.39	3.83	3.61
keep	26723	sell	7539	19	2.050	3.88	3.4	3.64
uneasy	923	easy	14414	0	0	3.75	3.6	3.675
town	17853	country	31416	511	21.366	3.18	4.25	3.715
traditional	9714	trendy	239	0	0	4.08	3.4	3.74
cow	1326	bull	1808	5	2.182	3.98	3.53	3.755
present	18538	future	22378	206	12.909	3.48	4.2	3.84
nephew	714	niece	455	13	3.601	3.83	4.03	3.93
mobile	182	landline	4	0	0	4.58	3.33	3.955
still	4903	sparkling	761	9	2.937	3.63	4.33	3.98
cold	9328	friendly	3951	1	-0.840	3.8	4.23	4.015
dead	10873	fresh	6614	4	0.204	3.85	4.18	4.015
donate	230	steal	869	0	0	4.18	4.1	4.14
suitable	6021	wrong	15505	0	0	4.33	4	4.165
helpful	3115	helpless	792	0	0	4.45	4.15	4.3
fair	8373	poor	14563	9	0.969	4.63	4.03	4.33
double	7070	single	18074	146	11.554	4.25	4.43	4.34
white	23427	coloured	2433	43	6.123	4.48	4.2	4.34
actress	1046	actor	2003	9	2.965	4.3	4.5	4.4
bad	14935	satisfactory	2161	0	0	4.58	4.25	4.415
finish	2824	continue	11641	3	0.784	4.23	4.75	4.49

(Continued)

Word 1	Freq	Word 2	Freq	Total FoC	T-score	QR 1-2	QR 2-1	QR overall
uncle	3350	aunt	2744	104	10.153	4.65	4.4	4.525
father	22744	mother	24201	954	29.996	4.48	4.63	4.555
wintry	124	sultry	119	0	0	4.88	4.25	4.565
helpless	792	helpful	3115	0	0	4.83	4.43	4.63
escape	4613	hunt	2601	0	0	4.73	4.8	4.765
king	15765	queen	7717	244	15.23	4.8	4.75	4.775
cold	9328	mild	1543	3	1.316	4.58	5.05	4.815
good	77128	mediocre	174	8	2.591	4.63	5	4.815
bland	608	hot	8733	0	0	4.58	5.13	4.855
dry	5273	sweet	3177	11	3.064	4.58	5.15	4.8675
tomorrow	8893	today	25855	245	14.918	4.93	4.83	4.88
occupier	382	owner	4957	21	4.561	5.08	4.78	4.93
dog	7814	cat	3847	113	10.488	4.73	5.38	5.055
red	14569	green	14199	435	20.361	5.25	4.88	5.065
daughter	9171	mother	24202	257	15.339	5.13	5.03	5.08
next to	2849	opposite	4890	4	1.652	5.2	5.18	5.19
trade	19841	purchase	4433	7	0.985	5.13	5.48	5.305
short	17792	polite	1092	1	0.029	4.9	5.8	5.35
father	22557	daughter	9171	119	9.961	5.28	5.55	5.415
hungry	1786	thirsty	271	18	4.236	5.4	5.43	5.415
blue	10059	orange	1790	28	5.121	5.45	5.65	5.55
buy	12293	spend	7323	10	1.740	5.15	6.05	5.6
rent	3440	let	24026	18	3.269	5.3	5.93	5.615
walk	10046	crawl	403	5	2.145	5.78	5.55	5.665
lease	2204	let	24026	6	1.369	5.4	6.25	5.825
answer	14305	reply	4225	3	-0.010	5.55	6.13	5.84
yellow	4366	blue	10059	204	14.129	6	5.73	5.865
egg	2436	chicken	2042	51	7.106	5.95	5.8	5.875
fish	10222	fowl	139	13	3.585	5.88	5.9	5.89
coffee	6286	tea	8030	467	21.493	5.7	6.1	5.9
similar	18295	identical	2148	66	7.882	6	6.15	6.075
brick	1803	mortar	603	5	2.211	6.08	6.15	6.115
clean	6281	tidy	719	78	8.806	6.03	6.2	6.115
lukewarm	169	tepid	81	1	0.999	5.88	6.55	6.215
long	33258	narrow	4711	175	12.637	6.2	6.35	6.275
glove	375	hand	32575	57	7.469	6.33	6.23	6.28
square	4012	long	50614	11	0.258	6.13	6.45	6.29
book	23916	page	10709	98	8.607	6.3	6.3	6.3
mug	685	cup	11913	6	2.283	6.3	6.33	6.315
yell	215	call	18778	0	0	6.1	6.55	6.325
rain	6253	wind	7357	217	14.574	6.45	6.28	6.365
tipsy	65	inebriated	31	0	0	6.38	6.35	6.365
carrot	377	pea	173	1	0.996	6.55	6.2	6.375
finger	3044	hand	32576	94	9.184	6.38	6.43	6.405
humid	208	hot	8733	35	5.900	6.4	6.63	6.515
soft	5869	easy	14414	18	3.246	6.33	6.7	6.515
fit	2942	hot	8733	0	0	6.5	6.55	6.525
short	19660	squat	273	8	2.733	6.3	6.78	6.54
cold	9328	distant	2772	23	4.526	6.38	6.75	6.565
cold	9328	sticky	809	1	0.623	6.6	6.6	6.6
wrong	15505	bad	14935	21	2.058	6.5	6.7	6.6
scream	952	kick	2269	5	2.187	6.5	6.73	6.615
quiet	5482	still	2323	9	2.721	6.68	6.58	6.63
tired	3852	sick	4333	68	8.145	6.48	6.78	6.63
dead	10873	gone	18474	53	5.901	6.55	6.73	6.64

(Continued)

Word 1	Freq	Word 2	Freq	Total FoC	T-score	QR 1-2	QR 2-1	QR overall
mad	2966	angry	4015	2	0.993	6.58	6.7	6.64
sad	3322	unhappy	1846	8	2.720	6.55	6.73	6.64
crown	5210	king	15765	40	5.675	6.75	6.73	6.74
rose	4963	flower	2126	13	3.459	6.85	6.65	6.75
animal	6611	dog	7814	21	4.0195	6.73	6.9	6.815
clever	2237	bright	5278	5	1.972	6.83	6.8	6.815
easy	14414	uneasy	923	0	0	3.33	3.2	3.265

Appendix 3

Frequencies, t-scores and judgement ratings for all German pairs

Word 1	Freq	Word 2	Freq	Total FoC	T-score	QR 1-2	QR 2-1	QR overall
unten	95453	oben	207252	15139	122.689	1.03	1.03	1.03
hell	19809	dunkel	32350	1138	33.692	1.05	1.03	1.04
alt	338295	neu	505688	3473	52.598	1.08	1.03	1.055
groß	346812	klein	195763	15599	123.709	1.08	1.08	1.08
heiß	53896	kalt	48404	954	30.702	1.08	1.08	1.08
jung	155435	alt	338295	39087	197.123	1.13	1.03	1.08
lang	423083	kurz	578171	6815	76.087	1.13	1.08	1.105
falsch	92620	richtig	342200	2852	52.109	1.08	1.15	1.115
langsam	120305	schnell	446308	1146	30.391	1.2	1.03	1.115
schwer	412910	leicht	314557	5251	68.552	1.13	1.13	1.13
hart	101564	weich	12530	596	24.299	1.13	1.19	1.16
stark	400220	schwach	41859	1127	32.481	1.05	1.3	1.175
ungerade	831	gerade	646331	173	13.063	1.15	1.23	1.19
leicht	314557	schwierig	90179	186	9.099	1.25	1.15	1.2
schwierig	90179	einfach	586074	559	18.765	1.23	1.18	1.205
illegal	27150	legal	10207	396	19.869	1.15	1.27	1.21
gut	1430211	schlecht	157271	6071	71.617	1.13	1.3	1.215
gesund	46397	krank	41996	653	25.387	1.23	1.21	1.22
sauber	34108	schmutzig	3503	38	6.122	1.23	1.23	1.23
weiblich	13540	männlich	11944	2663	51.597	1.28	1.18	1.23
böse	48416	gut	1430211	5008	68.632	1.38	1.15	1.265
erstes	97737	letztes	60296	215	13.785	1.15	1.38	1.265
glücklich	76882	unglücklich	24915	191	13.517	1.3	1.25	1.275
Zwerg	4903	Riese	7462	140	11.825	1.18	1.39	1.285
ordentlich	39576	unordentlich	397	7	2.632	1.25	1.33	1.29
unglücklich	24915	glücklich	76882	191	13.517	1.25	1.33	1.29
feminin	912	maskulin	316	39	6.244	1.35	1.24	1.295
Tod	225707	Leben	798017	12762	109.49	1.33	1.3	1.315
irrational	888	rational	2691	24	4.897	1.2	1.45	1.325

(Continued)

Word 1	Freq	Word 2	Freq	Total FoC	T-score	QR 1-2	QR 2-1	QR overall
einfach	586074	schwer	412910	1200	19.398	6.65	6.6	1.34
riesig	17167	winzig	2876	29	5.365	1.25	1.43	1.34
anwesend	31933	abwesend	3661	37	6.04	1.28	1.52	1.4
geben	729005	nehmen	478566	3433	45.599	1.58	1.23	1.405
moralisch	8193	unmoralisch	1686	22	4.683	1.33	1.48	1.405
hinein	56573	hinaus	256608	406	18.577	1.4	1.43	1.415
unmöglich	49085	möglich	581288	256	12.108	1.38	1.45	1.415
schlafend	1548	wach	20696	10	3.14	1.35	1.5	1.425
passend	24561	unpassend	2002	12	3.433	1.35	1.55	1.45
unloyal	22	loyal	2683	0	0	1.5	1.4	1.45
spät	104132	früh	178181	2454	48.72	1.48	1.45	1.465
wahr	54270	falsch	92620	379	18.904	1.53	1.42	1.475
betrunken	14281	nüchtern	13518	43	6.493	1.38	1.58	1.48
hungrig	5771	satt	15322	44	6.604	1.23	1.73	1.48
direkt	249382	indirekt	21595	3250	56.802	1.55	1.45	1.5
Mann	835267	Frau	844270	37543	185.818	2.95	2.63	1.5
anziehen	15962	ausziehen	6237	38	6.129	1.48	1.55	1.515
desinteressiert	874	interessiert	100522	3	1.621	1.4	1.64	1.52
vor	6365082	hinter	517920	14426	60.22	1.48	1.58	1.53
ungesund	2186	gesund	46397	64	7.972	1.5	1.58	1.54
verbieten	18367	erlauben	29237	70	8.226	1.6	1.48	1.54
uninteressiert	364	interessiert	100522	1	0.92	1.68	1.45	1.565
Berg	115945	Tal	54716	1049	31.96	1.4	1.79	1.595
verschlossen	12018	offen	257267	69	7.494	1.38	1.82	1.6
antworten	57656	fragen	405353	13965	117.742	1.65	1.63	1.64
runter	18644	hoch	325231	904	29.626	1.7	1.65	1.675
real	59008	irreal	614	27	5.18	1.48	1.88	1.68
dienstlich	2300	privat	63078	426	20.624	1.9	1.58	1.74
verkaufen	97557	kaufen	105307	1994	44.152	3.75	4.55	1.74
unter	3576918	über	5780459	52028	30.308	1.93	1.55	1.75
nah	41479	weit	438067	280	14.363	1.68	2.06	1.87
akkurat	2050	inakkurat	3	0	0	1.9	1.85	1.875
Feuer	144038	Wasser	351446	3327	55.765	2	1.75	1.875
kommen	917319	gehen	664390	6581	64.73	1.53	2.24	1.885
alleine	96405	zusammen	639483	401	13.307	1.93	1.95	1.94
miserabel	3444	exzellent	4831	0	0	1.83	2.05	1.94
unverheiratet	941	verheiratet	44182	20	4.451	1.93	1.97	1.95
angreifen	10928	verteidigen	42699	81	8.886	2.13	1.83	1.98
unverschlossen	578	verschlossen	12018	0	0	1.75	2.21	1.98
weich	12530	fest	664572	58	5.23	1.85	2.13	1.99
süß	12943	sauer	45217	350	18.64	2.13	1.88	2.005
einfarbig	566	bunt	36213	44	6.626	2.05	1.98	2.015
mehr	4011482	weniger	602034	68504	241.599	1.85	2.24	2.045
Soll	27880	Haben	46231	433	20.673	2.48	1.63	2.055

(*Continued*)

Word 1	Freq	Word 2	Freq	Total FoC	T-score	QR 1-2	QR 2-1	QR overall
ungehorsam	1678	brav	15829	3	1.698	1.78	2.38	2.08
miteinbeziehen	1088	ausschließen	17967	1	0.957	1.8	2.39	2.095
fest	443728	weich	12530	58	6.022	2.2	2.15	2.175
unreal	121	real	59008	3	1.723	2.5	1.94	2.22
einflussreich	411	einflusslos	41	0	0	2.33	2.12	2.225
privat	63078	staatlich	16988	119	10.694	2.3	2.21	2.255
duzen	900	siezen	245	50	7.07	2.4	2.28	2.34
exakt	42614	unpräzise	892	0	0	2.43	2.39	2.41
amoralisch	99	moralisch	8193	2	1.412	2.38	2.52	2.45
vermieten	6773	mieten	21597	39	6.193	2.6	2.3	2.45
tugendhaft	171	sündig	207	0	0	2.45	2.5	2.475
riesig	17167	klein	195763	48	5.869	2.28	2.73	2.505
Vermieter	20356	Mieter	48521	2380	48.741	2.68	2.35	2.515
Land	731001	Stadt	1336827	25911	147.722	2.45	2.61	2.53
Henne	3932	Hahn	86742	184	13.509	2.55	2.58	2.565
schlecht	157271	exzellent	4831	5	1.494	2.45	2.8	2.625
verschieden	13648	ähnlich	142149	67	7.668	2.85	2.53	2.69
richtig	342200	inkorrekt	145	4	1.945	2.38	3.03	2.705
mild	6008	würzig	1024	32	5.654	4.38	4.75	2.725
winzig	2876	groß	346812	25	4.564	2.48	2.97	2.725
gigantisch	3267	mini	9531	0	0	2.2	3.27	2.735
kühl	22800	warm	34646	178	13.212	2.48	3.03	2.755
reparieren	9775	beschädigen	3731	2	1.357	2.68	2.85	2.765
lernen	211052	lehren	16997	825	28.45	3.13	2.45	2.79
Mann	835267	Weib	4340	245	15.147	1.48	1.52	2.79
Vergangenheit	163546	Gegenwart	46635	5895	76.562	3.35	2.3	2.825
Opfer	254529	Mörder	28139	638	24.639	2.93	2.73	2.83
kochend	307	eisig	1830	0	0	2.63	3.08	2.855
Mama	32248	Papa	28595	4927	70.163	2.78	2.97	2.875
Lehrer	199088	Schüler	566654	28444	167.193	3.23	2.58	2.905
Schwester	84965	Bruder	150703	3054	54.757	2.8	3.03	2.915
Zukunft	518747	Gegenwart	46635	4044	62.762	2.98	2.85	2.915
Doktor	17981	Patient	31282	49	6.824	2.98	2.94	2.96
Meister	203124	Lehrling	12601	269	16.06	3.18	2.91	3.045
Angestellter	12746	Chef	198590	78	8.206	3.03	3.12	3.075
Vergnügen	38042	Arbeit	775269	801	26.028	3.35	2.88	3.115
Mutter	397872	Vater	310066	31909	177.123	3.43	2.93	3.18
daheim	51420	weg	180563	184	12.071	3.08	3.33	3.205
verheiratet	44182	single	13323	26	4.847	2.28	2.53	3.277
Bulle	4510	Kuh	18761	34	5.799	2.98	3.58	3.28
bitter	27780	süß	12943	251	15.793	3.18	3.39	3.285
warm	34646	frostig	2029	9	2.948	3.23	3.48	3.355
kühl	22800	heiß	53896	98	9.628	3.18	3.55	3.365
ganz	1378076	halb	49231	421	13.303	3.7	3.09	3.395

(Continued)

Word 1	Freq	Word 2	Freq	Total FoC	T-score	QR 1-2	QR 2-1	QR overall
Festnetz	10008	Handy	54734	379	19.406	3.6	3.21	3.405
früher	290291	gegenwärtig	37991	39	2.391	3.33	3.48	3.405
geschieden	8341	verheiratet	44182	250	15.76	3.15	3.7	3.425
jagen	13999	fliehen	12271	4	1.812	3.33	3.55	3.44
auspacken	2868	packen	22816	5	2.172	3.7	3.33	3.515
falsch	92620	passend	24561	4	-0.481	3.2	3.85	3.525
Student	23338	Dozent	9346	33	5.661	3.98	3.08	3.53
frostig	2029	sommerlich	2322	0	0	3.43	3.64	3.535
bunt	36213	unbunt	26	1	0.997	3.58	3.68	3.63
Katze	31395	Hund	87212	4042	63.482	4.4	2.88	3.64
woher	28444	wohin	47645	913	30.118	3.58	3.7	3.64
Eltern	525084	Kinder	1499055	66010	250.239	3.5	3.79	3.645
Königin	41606	König	138165	2169	46.303	4.08	3.23	3.655
Tante	21838	Onkel	25000	1050	32.366	4.1	3.33	3.715
einfach	586074	doppelt	61861	192	8.147	1.28	1.4	3.72
Nichte	5991	Neffe	5961	119	10.901	3.65	3.91	3.78
Maus	26994	Katze	31395	1816	42.571	3.98	3.65	3.815
dick	34756	schmal	6537	7	2.458	3.43	4.21	3.82
scharf	46067	fad	2931	3	1.561	3.53	4.18	3.855
lernen	211052	verlernen	568	23	4.741	3.45	4.3	3.875
modisch	3177	traditionell	46543	6	2.317	3.48	4.33	3.905
heute	1998661	morgen	485703	45963	204.509	4.65	3.55	4.1
ausleihen	6221	verleihen	24602	4	1.833	4.3	4	4.15
verkaufen	97557	behalten	64577	117	9.545	1.93	1.55	4.15
unscheinbar	2567	kolossal	480	0	0	4.15	4.25	4.2
farbig	5412	weiß	468495	68	7.575	4.38	4.03	4.205
Fleisch	54646	Fisch	34271	3185	56.363	4.45	4.15	4.3
Hexe	10892	Fee	5490	43	6.537	4.15	4.55	4.35
grün	65586	rot	77043	5491	73.952	4.43	4.28	4.355
zufriedenstellend	10261	schlecht	157271	17	3.269	4.2	4.7	4.45
Schauspielerin	37777	Schauspieler	93643	425	20.241	4.45	4.48	4.465
mild	6008	kalt	48404	39	6.143	2.55	2.9	4.565
dunkel	32350	blass	5677	4	1.799	4.4	4.76	4.58
durstig	1870	hungrig	5771	588	24.247	4.85	4.42	4.635
stehlen	12546	spenden	133234	3	-0.373	3.98	5.35	4.665
gegenüber	478057	neben	842634	921	1.385	4.33	5.03	4.68
Tee	25809	Kaffee	117728	4826	69.373	4.88	4.48	4.68
brütend	351	kühl	22800	1	0.982	4.73	4.68	4.705
mangelhaft	8470	angemessen	22233	0	0	4.78	4.7	4.74
freundlich	33820	kalt	48404	45	6.175	4.75	4.8	4.775
Mutter	397872	Tochter	236855	12546	110.173	4.75	4.88	4.815
brilliant	313	mittelmäßig	1378	0	0	4.98	4.75	4.865
akzeptabel	10381	furchtbar	8550	0	0	4.58	5.21	4.895
hilflos	15371	hilfreich	20831	3	1.328	4.05	5.58	4.94

(*Continued*)

Word 1	Freq	Word 2	Freq	Total FoC	T-score	QR 1-2	QR 2-1	QR overall
hilfreich	20831	hilflos	15371	3	1.328	5.3	4.58	4.94
krabbeln	3062	gehen	664390	35	5.165	5.03	5.28	5.155
Besitzer	85052	Bewohner	115822	86	6.955	5.08	5.4	5.24
praktisch	97602	formal	10358	18	3.722	5.05	5.43	5.24
frisch	79562	tot	60963	9	-0.527	5.33	5.48	5.405
Tochter	236855	Vater	310066	8898	92.63	5.7	5.15	5.425
orange	16996	blau	36757	802	28.271	5.38	5.55	5.465
süß	12943	trocken	39862	54	7.195	5.58	5.43	5.505
blau	36757	gelb	26569	3384	58.135	5.6	5.42	5.51
Huhn	9460	Ei	25423	290	16.998	5.73	5.3	5.515
mittelmäßig	1378	gut	1430211	90	9.033	5.6	5.64	5.62
jagen	13999	ausbrechen	5272	1	0.838	5.88	5.38	5.63
erwerben	38899	handeln	93991	16	2.005	5.6	5.78	5.69
schmal	6537	lang	423083	196	13.568	6.35	5.52	5.935
ausgeben	21255	kaufen	105307	35	5.09	6.08	5.91	5.995
unmoralisch	1686	amoralisch	99	5	2.235	6.15	5.91	6.03
rufen	52037	brüllen	3188	14	3.644	5.93	6.2	6.065
Seite	732578	Buch	250102	792	13.937	6.03	6.12	6.075
lau	6383	mild	6008	3	1.683	6.28	6	6.14
Entgegnung	750	Antwort	144522	2	1.246	6.23	6.1	6.165
Hand	354194	Finger	46930	1445	37.059	6.13	6.24	6.185
identisch	10270	ähnlich	142149	49	6.544	6.28	6.09	6.185
schlecht	157271	falsch	92620	293	15.26	6.3	6.12	6.21
befolgen	3299	einwilligen	510	0	0	6.08	6.39	6.235
Erbse	1911	Karotte	997	1	0.995	6.43	6.09	6.26
Fuß	118459	Bein	31334	199	13.532	6.35	6.21	6.28
Regen	105673	Wind	107424	3759	60.906	6.2	6.38	6.29
Tasse	9480	Becher	16705	27	5.129	6.23	6.36	6.295
lang	423083	viereckig	201	2	1.283	6.53	6.09	6.31
Henkel	15598	Tasse	9480	19	4.284	6.45	6.23	6.34
fremd	18165	kalt	48404	24	4.507	6.4	6.35	6.375
wütend	11316	verrückt	20363	4	1.748	6.35	6.45	6.4
ordentlich	39576	sauber	34108	364	18.924	6.55	6.33	6.44
helle	20478	clever	9949	0	0	6.55	6.58	6.452
höflich	8056	kurz	578171	38	4.515	6.2	6.82	6.51
verrucht	327	scheußlich	709	0	0	6.48	6.55	6.515
unglücklich	24915	traurig	32588	28	4.956	6.75	6.36	6.555
weg	180563	tot	60963	112	8.313	6.55	6.58	6.565
einfach	586074	weich	12530	75	6.81	3.83	3.61	6.625
still	37726	ruhig	64777	252	15.538	6.55	6.7	6.625
grau	19415	alt	338295	160	11.516	6.7	6.63	6.665
Blume	10657	Rose	36795	80	8.848	6.6	6.76	6.68
König	138165	Krone	64009	297	16.113	6.68	6.7	6.69
Hund	87212	Tier	79783	666	25.218	6.85	6.83	6.84
klebrig	544	kalt	48404	3	1.698	6.85	6.97	6.91

Appendix 4

Target stimuli for the antonym decision task

(only pairs which are not translation equivalents are glossed)

English		German	
soft	hard	weich	hart
cold	hot	kalt	heiß
new	old	neu	alt
young	old	jung	alt
right	wrong	richtig	falsch
big	small	groß	klein
large	little	schwierig 'difficult'	einfach 'easy'
little	big	schwer 'heavy, difficult'	leicht 'light, easy'
small	large	schwer 'heavy, difficult'	einfach 'easy'
long	tall	schwierig 'difficult'	leicht 'light, easy'
tall	short	stark 'strong'	schwach 'weak'
short	long	kurz	lang
happy	unhappy	glücklick	unglücklich
happy	sad	glücklich	traurig
even	odd	moralisch 'moral'	unmoralisch 'amoral'
even	uneven	gerade	ungerade
good	bad	gut	böse
right	left	rechts	links
even	uneven	duzen	siezen
married	single	verheiratet	single
organised	disorganised	verheiratet 'married'	unverheiratet 'unmarried'
organised	unorganised	anziehen 'dress'	ausziehen 'undress'
healthy	unhealthy	gesund	ungesund
healthy	sick	gesund	krank
pack	unpack	packen	auspacken
hard	easy	schwierig	einfach

(*Continued*)

English		German	
interested	uninterested	interessiert	uninteressiert
interested	disinterested	interessiert	desinteressiert
defend	attack	verteidigen	angreifen
more	less	mehr	weniger
give	take	geben	nehmen
giant	dwarf	Riese	Zwerg
colossal	miniscule	kolossal	mini
masculine	feminine	maskulin	feminine
male	female	männlich	weiblich
come	go	kommen	gehen
buy	sell	kaufen	verkaufen
warm	cool	warm	kühl
freezing	boiling	eisig	kochend
debit	credit	Soll	Haben
man	woman	Mann	Frau
big	tiny	groß	winzig
work	play	Arbeit	Vergnügen
pupil	teacher	Schüler	Lehrer
employer	employee	Arbeitgeber	Arbeitnehmer
wife	husband	Student 'student'	Dozent 'lecturer'
tenant	landlord	Mieter	Vermieter
brother	sister	Bruder	Schwester
patient	doctor	Patient	Doktor
dad	mum	Papa	Mama
flee	chase	fliehen	jagen
cow	bull	Kuh	Bulle
child	parent	Kinder	Eltern
actor	actress	Schauspieler	Schauspielerin
father	mother	Vater	Mutter
cold	mild	kalt	mild
king	queen	König	Königin
occupier	owner	Bewohner	Besitzer
hungry	thirsty	hungrig	durstig
coffee	tea	Kaffee	Tee
sweet	bitter	süß	bitter
sweet	sour	süß	sauer

Bibliography

Corpora and databases

Korpora des Instituts für Deutsche Sprache, (COSMAS – II$_{web}$) (2008). https://cosmas2.ids-mannheim.de/cosmas2-web/.Mannheim. [last accessed January 2010]

The British National Corpus, version 2 (BNC World) (2001). Distributed by Oxford University Computing Services on behalf of the BNC Consortium. http://www.natcorp.ox.ac.uk. [last accessed April 2009]

Wilson, M.D. (1988). The MRC psycholinguistic database: Machine readable dictionary (Version 2). *Behavioural Research Methods, Instruments and Computers* 20 (1), 6–11. [last accessed March 2009]

Dictionaries

Hornby, A. S. (Ed.) (2005). *Oxford Advanced Learner's Dictionary of Current English* (7th ed.). Oxford University Press.

Kluge, F. (Ed.) (2002). *Etymologisches Wörterbuch der deutschen Sprache* (24th ed. by E. Seebold). Walter de Gruyter.

Langenscheidt (Ed.) (2007). *Pocket Dictionary German*. Langenscheidt KG.

Simpson, J. (Ed.) (1989). *The Oxford English Dictionary*. Oxford University Press. [also OED online: www.oed.com - last accessed May 2021]

References

Aitchison, J. (2012). *Words in the mind. An introduction to the mental lexicon*. Wiley-Blackwell.

Aristotle (4th century BC). (1984). *De Interpretatione* and *Prior Analytics*. In J. Barnes (Ed.), *The complete works of Aristotle*. Princeton University Press.

Baayen, R. H., Dijkstra, T., & Schreuder, R. (1997). Singulars and plurals in Dutch: Evidence for a parallel dual route model. *Journal of Memory and Language*, *37*, 94–117.

Bierwisch, M. & Schreuder, R. (1992). From concepts to lexical items. *Cognition*, *42*, 23–60.

Bock, K. & Levelt, W. (1994) Language production. Grammatical encoding. In M. A. Gernsbacher (Ed.), *Handbook of psycholinguistics* (pp. 965–984). Academic Press.

Butterworth, B. (1983). Lexical representation. In B. Butterworth (Ed.), *Language production* (Vol. 2, pp. 257–294). Academic Press.

Caramazza, A., Laudanna, A., & Romani, C. (1988). Lexical access and inflectional morphology. *Cognition*, *28*, 297–332.

Chaffin, R., & Herrmann, D. J. (1984). The similarity and diversity of semantic relations. *Memory and Cognition*, *12*, 134–151.

Charles, W. G., Reed, M. A., & Derryberry, D. (1994). Conceptual and associative processing of antonymy and synonymy. *Applied Psycholinguistics*, *15*, 329–354.

Charles, W. G., & Miller, G. A. (1989). Contexts of antonymous adjectives. *Applied Psychology*, *10*, 357–375.

Clahsen, H., Felser, C., Neubauer, K., Sato, M., & Silva, R. (2010). Morphological structure in native and non-native language processing. *Language Learning*, *60*, 21–43.

Clark, E. V. (1972). On the child's acquisition of antonyms in two semantic fields. *Journal of Verbal Learning and Verbal Behaviour*, *11*, 750–758.

Collins, A. M., & Loftus, E. F. (1975). A spreading-activation theory of semantic processing. *Psychological Review*, *82*(6), 407–428.

Croft, W., & Cruse, D. A. (2004). *Cognitive linguistics*. Cambridge University Press.

Cruse, D. A. (1976). Three classes of antonym in English. *Lingua*, *38*, 281–292.

Cruse, D. A. (1986). *Lexical semantics*. Cambridge University Press.

Cruse, D. A. (1990). Prototype theory and lexical semantics. In S. L. Tsohatzidis (Ed.), *Meanings and Prototypes* (pp. 382–402). Routledge.

Cruse, D. A. (1992). Antonymy revisited: Some thoughts on the relationship between words and concepts. In A. Lehrer & E. Kittay (Eds.), *Frames, fields and contrasts* (pp. 289–306). Lawrence Erlbaum.

Cruse, D. A. (1994). Prototype theory and lexical relations. *Rivista di Linguistica*, *6*, 167–188.

Cruse, D. A. (2000). *Meaning in language. An introduction to semantics and pragmatics*. Oxford University Press.

Cruse, D. A., & Togia, P. (1995). Towards a cognitive model of antonymy. *Lexicology*, *1*, 113–141.

Cutler, A. (1981). The reliability of speech error data. *Linguistics*, *19*, 561–582.

Cutler, A. (2012). *Native listening. Language experience and the recognition of spoken words*. MIT Press.

Davies, M. (2012). A new approach to oppositions in discourse: The role of syntactic frames in the triggering of noncanonical oppositions. *Journal of English Linguistics*, *40*(1), 41–73.

de Groot, A. M. B. (2000). On the source and nature of semantic and conceptual knowledge. *Bilingualism, Language and Cognition*, *3*(1), 7–9.

Deese, J. (1964). The associative structure of some common English adjectives. *Journal of Verbal Learning and Verbal Behaviour*, *3*, 347–357.

Deese, J. (1965). *The structure of associations in language and thought*. The Johns Hopkins Press.

Fellbaum, C. (1995). Co-occurrence and antonymy. *International Journal of Lexicography*, *8*, 281–303.

Frauenfelder, U. H., & Schreuder, R. (1992). Constraining psycholinguistic models of morphological processing and representation: The role of productivity. In G. E. Booij & J. van Marle (Eds.), *Yearbook of morphology 1991* (pp. 165–183). Kluwer.

Fromkin, V. A. (1973). *Speech errors as linguistic evidence*. Mouton.

Fruchter, J., & Marantz, A. (2015). Decomposition, lookup, and recombination: MEG evidence for the full decomposition model of complex visual word recognition. *Brain and Language*, *143*, 81–96.

Götz, F. M., Gosling, S. D., & Rentfrow, J. (2021). Small effects: The indispensable foundation for a cumulative psychological science. Perspectives on Psychological Science, 1–11. 10.31234/osf.io/hzrxf

Grandy, R. E. (1992). Semantic fields, prototypes, and the lexicon. In A. Lehrer & E. Kittay (Eds.), *Frames, fields and contrasts* (pp. 103–122). Lawrence Erlbaum.

Gross, D., & Miller, K. (1990). Adjectives in WordNet. *International Journal of Lexicography*, *3*, 265–277.

Gross, D., Fischer, U., & Miller, G. A. (1988). Antonymy and the representation of adjectival meanings. *Cognitive science laboratory report*, *13*. Princeton University.

Gross, D., Fischer, U., & Miller, G. A. (1989). The organization of adjectival meanings. *Journal of Memory and Language*, *28*, 92–106.

Harley, T. (2013). *The psychology of language. From data to theory*. Psychology Press.

Hartsuiker, R. J., & Moors, A. (2017). On the automaticity of language processing. In H.-J. Schmid (Ed.), *Entrenchment and the psychology of language learning: How we reorganize and adapt linguistic knowledge* (pp. 201–225). APA and Walter de Gruyter.

Hassanein, H. (2018). Discourse functions of opposition in Classical Arabic: The case in Hadith Genre. *Lingua*, *201*, 18–44.

Herrmann, D. J., Chaffin, R., Conti, G., Peters, D., & Robbins, P. H. (1979). Comprehension of antonymy and the generality of categorization models. *Journal of Experimental Psychology: Human Learning and Memory*, *5*, 585–597.

Herrmann, D. J., Chaffin, R., Daniel, M. P., & Wool, R. S. (1986). The role of elements of relation definition in antonym and synonym comprehension. *Zeitschrift für Psychologie*, *194*, 133–153.

Herrmann, D. J., & Chaffin, R. (1986). Comprehension of semantic relations as a function of the definitions of relations. In F. Klix & H. Hagendorf (Eds.), *Human Memory and Cognitive Capabilities*. (pp. 311–319). Elsevier.

Horn, L. (1989). *A natural history of negation*. The University of Chicago Press.

Hsu, C.-C. (2015). A syntagmatic analysis of antonym co-occurrences in Chinese: Contrastive constructions and co-occurrence sequences. *Corpora*, *10*(1), 47–82.

Hsu, C.-C. (2017). A corpus-based study on the functional distribution of the different morphostructurual antonyms in Chinese. *Language Sciences*, *59*, 36–45.

Huettig, F. & McQueen, J. M. (2007). The tug of war between phonological, semantic and shape information in language-mediated visual search. *Journal of Memory and Language*, *57*(4), 460–482.

Hutchison, K. A. (2003). Is semantic priming due to association strength or feature overlap? A *micro*analytic review. *Psychonomic Bulletin & Review*, *10*(4), 785–813.

Izutsu, M. N. (2008). Contrast, concessive, and corrective: Toward a comprehensive study of opposition relations. *Journal of Pragmatics*, *40*(4). 646–675.

Jeon, H., Lee, K., Kim, Y., & Cho, Z. (2009). Neural substrates of semantic relationships: Common and distinct left-frontal activities for generation of synonyms vs. antonyms. *Neuroimage*, *48*, 449–457.

Jones, S. (2002). *Antonymy. A corpus-based approach*. Routledge.

Jones S. & Murphy, M. L. (2005). Using corpora to investigate antonym acquisition. *International Journal of Corpus Linguistics*, *10*(3), 401–422.

Jones, S. (2006). A lexico-syntactic analysis of antonym co-occurrence in spoken English. *Text and Talk*, *26*(2), 191–216.

Jones, S. (2007). Opposites in discourse: A comparison of antonym use across four domains. *Journal of Pragmatics*, *39*, 1105–1119.

Jones, S., Murphy, M.L., Paradis, C., & Willners, C. (2012). *Antonyms in English: Construals, constructions and canonicity*. Cambridge University Press.

Justeson, J., & Katz, S. (1991). Co-occurrences of antonymous adjectives and their contexts. *Computational Linguistics*, *17*, 1–19.

Justeson, J., & Katz, S. (1992). Redefining antonymy: The textual structure of a semantic relation. *Literary and Linguistic Computing*, *7*, 176–184.

Kiefer, M., & Pulvermüller, F. (2012). Conceptual representations in mind and brain: Theoretical developments, current evidence and future directions. *Cortex*, *48*(7), 805–825.

Kjellmer, G. (2005). Negated adjectives in modern English. A corpus based study. *Studia Neophilologica*, *77*, 156–170.

Kneale, W. & Kneale, M. (1962). *The development of logic*. Oxford University Press.

176   *Bibliography*

Kostić, N. (2011). Antonymous frameworks in Serbian written discourse: Phrasal contexts of antonym co-occurrence in text. *Poznań Studies in Contemporary Linguistics, 47*(3), 509–537.

Kostić, N., (2015a). Antonym sequence in written discourse: A corpus-based study. *Language Sciences, 47*, 18–31.

Kostić, N. (2015b). The textual profile of antonyms: A corpus-based study. *Linguistics, 53*(4), 649–675.

Kutas, M., & Federmeier, K. D. (2011). Thirty years and counting: Finding meaning in the N400 component of the event-related brain potential. *Annual Review of Psychology, 62*, 621–647.

Lakoff, G. (1987). *Women, fire and dangerous things. What categories reveal about the mind.* University of Chicago Press.

Lakoff, G. & Johnson, M. (1980). *Metaphors we live by.* University of Chicago Press.

Langacker, R. W. (2008). *Cognitive grammar: A basic introduction.* Oxford University Press.

Lehrer, A. (1985). Markedness and antonymy. *Linguistics, 21*, 397–429.

Lehrer, A. (1990). Prototype theory and its implications for lexical analysis. In S. L. Tsohatzidis (Ed.), *Meanings and Prototypes* (pp. 368–381). Routledge.

Lehrer, A. (2002). Gradable antonymy and complementarity. In D. A. Cruse, F. Hundsnurscher, M. Job, & P. Lutzeier (Eds.), *Handbook of Lexicology* (pp. 498–506). De Gruyter.

Lehrer, A., & Lehrer, K. (1982). Antonymy. *Linguistics and Philosophy, 5*, 483–501.

Lehrer, A., & Kittay, E. (Eds.) (1992). *Frames, fields and contrasts.* Lawrence Erlbaum.

Levelt, W. J. M. (1989) *Speaking: From intention to articulation.* MIT Press.

Levelt, W. J. M., Roloefs, A., & Meyer A. (1999). A theory of lexical access in speech production. *Behavioural and Brain Sciences, 22*, 1–75.

Lobanova, A., van der Kleij, T., & Spenader, J. (2010). Defining antonymy: A corpus-based study of opposites by lexico-syntactic patterns. *International Journal of Lexicography, 23*, 19–53.

Lutzeier, P. (1997). Gegensinn als besondere Form lexikalischer Ambiguität. *Linguistische Berichte, 171*, 381–395.

Lutzeier, P. (2001). Polysemie mit spezieller Berücksichtigung des Gegensinns. *Lexicographica, 17*, 69–91.

Lyons, J. (1977). *Semantics.* Cambridge University Press.

Lyons, J. (1995). *Linguistic semantics: An introduction.* Cambridge University Press.

MacGregor, L. J., Pulvermüller, F., van Casteren, M., & Shtyrov, Y. (2012). Ultra-rapid access to words in the brain. *Nature Communications, 3*, 2–7.

MacWhinney, B. (2017). Entrenchment in Second-Language Learning. In H.-J. Schmid (Ed.), *Entrenchment and the psychology of language learning: How we reorganize and adapt linguistic knowledge* (pp. 343–366). APA and Walter de Gruyter.

Marslen-Wilson, W., Tyler, L. K., Waksler, R., & Older, L. (1994). Morphology and meaning in the English mental lexicon. *Psychological Review, 101*(1), 3–33.

McClelland, J. L., & Rumelhardt, D. E. (1981). An interactive activation model of context effects in letter perception: Part 1. An account of the basic findings. *Psychological Review, 88,* 375–407.

McClelland, J. L., & Elman, J. L. (1986). The TRACE model of speech perception. *Journal of Cognitive Psychology, 18,* 1–86.

McNamara, T. P. (1992). Theories of priming: I. Associative distance and lag. *Journal of Experimental Psychology: Learning, Memory and Cognition, 18,* 1173–1190.

McNamara, T. P. (1994). Theories of priming: II. Types of prime. *Journal of Experimental Psychology: Learning, Memory, and Cognition, 20,* 507–520.

McNamara, T. P., & Altarriba, J. (1988). Depth of spreading activation revisited: Semantic mediated priming occurs in lexical decisions. *Journal of Memory and Language, 27,* 545–559.

Mettinger, A. (1994). *Aspects of semantic opposition in English.* Oxford University Press.

Miller, G. (1990). WordNet: An on-line lexical database. *International Journal of Lexicography, 3,* 235–312.

Miller, K. J. (1998). Modifiers in WordNet. In C. Fellbaum (Ed.), *WordNet: An electronic lexical database* (pp. 47–68). The MIT Press.

Miller, G. A., & Fellbaum, E. (1991). Semantic networks of English. *Cognition, 41,* 197–229.

Mohammad, S., Dorr, B., & Hirst, G. (2008). Computing Word-Pair antonymy. *Proceedings of the 2008 conference on empirical methods in natural language processing* (pp. 982–991).

Muehleisen, V. (1997). *Antonymy and Semantic Range in English.* [unpublished doctoral dissertation]. Northwestern University.

Muehleisen, V., & Isono, M. (2009). Antonymous adjectives in Japanese discourse. *Journal of Pragmatics, 41*(11), 2185–2203.

Murphy, G. L. & Andrew, J. M. (1993). The conceptual basis of antonymy and synonymy in adjectives. *Journal of Memory and Language, 32,* 301–319.

Murphy, M. L. (2003). *Semantic relations and the lexicon.* Cambridge University Press.

Murphy, M. L. (2006). Antonyms as lexical constructions: Or, why paradigmatic construction isn't an oxymoron. In Schönefeld, D. (Ed.), *Constructions all over: Case studies and theoretical implications.* Special volume of Constructions, SV1-8/2006. http://www.constructions-online.de/.

Murphy, M. L., & Jones, S. (2008). *Antonyms in children's and child-directed speech. First Language, 28,* 403–430.

Murphy, M. L., Paradis, C., Willners, C. & Jones, S. (2009). Discourse functions of antonymy: A cross-linguistic investigation. *Journal of Pragmatics, 41*(11), 2159–2184.

Needham, R. (1987). *Counterpoints.* University of California Press.

Nelson, K. (1977). The syntagmatic-paradigmatic shift revisited: A review of research and theory. *Psychological Bulletin, 84,* 93–116.

Norris, D., Cutler, A., McQueen, J. M., & Butterfield, S. (2006). Phonological and conceptual activation in speech comprehension. *Cognitive Psychology, 53,* 146–193.

Ogden, C. K. (1967). *Opposition: A linguistic and psychological analysis.* Indiana University Press [originally published in 1932].

Osgood, C., Suci, G. J., & Tannenbaum, P. H. (1957). *The measurement of meaning.* University of Illinois Press.

Paradis, M. (2000). Cerebral representations of bilingual concepts. *Bilingualism, Language and Cognition, 3*(1), 22–24.

Paradis, C. (2004). Where does metonymy stop? Senses, facets, and active zones. *Metaphor and Symbol, 19,* 245–265.

Paradis, C. (2005). Ontologies and construals in lexial semantics. *Axiomathes, 15,* 541–573.

Paradis, C., & Willners, C. (2007). Antonyms in dictionary entries: Methodological aspects. *Studia Linguistica, 61*(3), 261–277.

Paradis, C., Willners, C., Murphy, M.L., & Jones, S. (2007). Googling for opposites: A web-based study of antonym canonicity. *Corpora, 2*(2), 129–155.

Paradis, C., Willners, C., & Jones, S. (2009). Good and bad opposites. Using textual and experimental techniques to measure antonym canonicity. *The Mental Lexicon, 4*(3), 380–429.

Paradis, C., & Willners, C. (2011). Antonymy: From convention to meaning-making. *Review of Cognitive Linguistics, 9*(2), 367–391.

Paradis, C., Löhndorf, S., Van de Weijer, J., & Willners, C. (2015). Semantic profiles of antonymic adjectives in discourse. *Linguistics, 53*(1), 153–19.

Pavlenko, A. (1997). *Bilingualism and cognition.* [unpublished Ph.D. dissertation]. Cornell University.

Pavlenko, A. (2000). New Approaches to concepts in bilingual memory. *Bilingualism: Language and Cognition, 3*(1), 1–4.

Pavlenko, A. (2009). Conceptual representation in bilingual and second language vocabulary learning. In A. Pavlenko (Ed.), *The bilingual mental lexicon: interdisciplinary approaches* (pp. 125–160). Multilingual Matters.

Pinker, S. & Ullman, M. T. (2002). The past and future of the past tense. *Trends in Cognitive Science, 6,* 456–463.

Pulvermüller, F. (1999). Words in the brain's language. *Behavioural and Brain Sciences, 22,* 253–279.

Pulvermüller, F. (2013). How neurons make meaning: Brain mechanisms for embodied and abstract-symbolic semantics. *Trends in Cognitive Science, 17*(9), 458–470.

Roelofs, A. (2000). Word meanings and concepts: What do the findings from aphasia and language specificity really say? *Bilingualism: Language and Cognition, 3*(1), 25–27

Rosch, E. (1973). On the internal structure of perceptual and semantic categories. In T. E. Moore (Ed.), *Cognitive development and the acquisition of language* (pp. 111–144). Academic Press.

Rosch, E. (1975). Cognitive representation of semantic categories. *Journal of Experimental Psychology*, *104*(3), 193–233.

Rosch, E. (1978). Principles of categorization. In E. Rosch & B. B. Lloyd (Eds.), *Cognition and Categorization* (pp. 27–48). Lawrence Erlbaum.

Rosch, E. & Mervis, C. (1975). Family resemblances: Studies in the internal structure of categories. *Cognitive Psychology*, *7*(4), 573–605.

Sabourin, L. & Libben, G. (2000). Lexical processing of synonymy and antonymy: An exploration of task and word form differences. *Papers in Experimental and Theoretical Linguistics. University of Alberta working papers*, *5*, 114–136.

Sapir, E. (1944). Grading. *Philosophy of Science*, *11*, 83–116.

Saussure, F. (1916). *Cours de linguistique générale*. Published by C. Bally, A. Sechehaye & A. Riedlinger (1965). Bayot.

Schmid, H.-J. 2010. Does frequency in text really instantiate entrenchment in the cognitive system? In D. Glynn & K. Fischer (Eds.), *Quantitative methods in cognitive semantics: Corpus-driven approaches* (pp. 101–133). Walter de Gruyter.

Schmid, H.-J. (2020). *The dynamics of the linguistic system: Usage, conventionalization and entrenchment*. Oxford University Press.

Seidenberg, M. S., & Gonnerman, L. M. (2000). Explaining derivational morphology as the convergence of codes. *Trends in Cognitive Science*, *4*, 353–361.

Smith, C. J. (1967). *Synonyms and antonyms*. Bell & Daldy.

Stockall, L., & Marantz, A. (2006). A single route, full decomposition model of morphological complexity. *Mental Lexicon*, *1*, 1871–1340.

Storjohann, P. (2015). Deutsche Antonyme aus korpuslinguistischer Sicht: Muster und Funktionen. *Online Publizierte Arbeiten zur Linguistik*. Institut für Deutsche Sprache. 10.14618/opal_03–2015.

Taft, M., & Forster, K. (1975). Lexical storage and retrieval of prefixed words. *Journal of Verbal Learning and Verbal Behaviour*, *14*, 638–647.

Taylor, J. R. (1989). *Linguistic categorization: Prototypes in linguistic theory*. Clarendon Press.

Taylor, J. R. (1990). Schemas, prototypes, and models. In *Tsohatzidis* (1990, pp. 521–534).

Traxler, M. (2012). *Introduction to psycholinguistics. Understanding language science*. Wiley-Blackwell.

Tsohatzidis. S. L. (Ed.) (1990). *Meanings and prototypes*. Routledge.

Ullman, M. T. (2004). Contributions of memory circuits to language: The declarative/procedural model. *Cognition*, *92*, 231–270.

Ungerer, F. & Schmid, H.-J. (2006). *An introduction to cognitive linguistics*. Longman/Pearson Education.

van de Weijer, J., Paradis, C., Willners, C., & Lindgren, M. (2012). As lexical as it gets: The role of co-occurrence of antonyms in a visual lexical decision experiment. In D. Divjak & S. Gries (Eds.), *Frequency effects in language representation* (pp. 255–279). Mouton de Gruyter.

van de Weijer, J., Paradis, C., Willners, C., & Lindgren, M. (2014). Antonym canonicitiy: Temporal and contextual manipulations. *Brain and Language*, *128*, 1–8.

Vandeloise, C. (1990). Representation, prototypes and centrality. In S.L. Tsohatzidis (Ed.), *Meaning and prototypes*. (pp. 403–446). Routledge.

Wilbur, R. (2000). *Opposites, more opposites and a few differences*. Harcourt.

Wilbur, R. (2004). *Collected poems 1943-2004*. Harcourt.

Willners, C. (2001). Antonyms in context. A corpus-based semantic analysis of Swedish descriptive adjective. *Travaux de l'Institut de Linguistique de Lund*, 40. Lund University.

Willners, C., & Paradis, C. (2010). Swedish opposites: A multi-method approach to 'goodness of antonymy'. In Storjohann, P. (Ed.), *Lexical-semantic relations: Theoretical and practical perspectives* (pp. 15–48). John Benjamins.

Wu, S. (2017). Iconicity and viewpoint: Antonym order in Chinese four-character patterns. *Language Sciences*, *59*, 117–134.

Zimmer, K. (1964). *Affixal negation in English and other languages: An investigation of restricted productivity*. Linguistic Circle of New York.

Index

Note: **Bold** page numbers refer to tables.

adjectival word pairs 12, 15, 17, 27,
    85, 86, 90, 106, 107, 121, 126, 129
Andrew, J. M. 22
antagonyms 93, 119, 146
antipodals 12
antonym canonicity 19, 22, 26, 28, 29,
    43, 51, 91, 117–126
antonym decision task 70–92,
    170–171
antonymic dimension 43, 121,
    129, 130
antonymic strength 6–8, 35, 39,
    41–43, 45, 55, 59, 62, 67, 68, 70,
    75–78, 81, 104, 122, 125, 128, 129
antonym order 20–21, 55–58
antonym selection 35–36
antonym sequence 81–82
antonym type 58–62, 86–89
Aristotle 3
associative strength 7, 35, 36, 40,
    43–45, 61, 68, 71, 72, 78, 91, 100,
    104, 124–126
asymmetrical pairs 49, 51, 103, 123

binary opposition 3, 11, 12, **14**
brain 26–29, 133–146

canonical antonyms 4, 12, 21–22, 28,
    29, 35, 36, 49, 51, 59, 68, 79, 82,
    122, 127, 129, 149, 153;
    see also antonym canonicity
case studies 93–114

category structure 67, 68, 103, 109,
    110, 112, 121, 128–131; complexity
    128–130
cognition 152
cognitive antonym research 28–29
cognitive construal 126–133
cognitive-pragmatic approach 23–24
cognitive proposals 24–25
cognitive structuring principle 11
common opposite pairs 45
conceptual categories 7, 29, 61, 121,
    128, 129; structure 62–67
conceptual construal 127–133
conceptual entrenchment 131–133
conceptual opposition 23, 52, 99, 104,
    112, 119, 124, 131, 141, 145
conceptual relation 21, 25, 26, 29, 90,
    103, 128, 145, 146, 149, 150
conceptual representations 90, 134,
    136, 146, 153
context effects 130–131
control items 40
control words 73
conventionalisation 5
converse pairs 59, 78, 80, 86, 87,
    90, 96
co-occurrence patterns/rates 17–18,
    27, 29, 40–41, 45, 52, 61, 74, 89,
    100, 103
corpus data: analysis procedure 41;
    corpora 40–41; frequency of co-
    occurrence (FoC) 40

corpus perspectives 16–17
corpus research 21
corpus studies 5, 11, 16, 17, 19, 40,
    81, 123
counterparts 12
Croft, W. 4, 24
cross-linguistic differences 36, 93
Cruse, D. A. 4, 12–16, 18, 22, 24, 25,
    49, 61, 123, 148

data cleaning 74
design, opposite pairs 71–72
directional opposition 12–14
discourse 16–21

empirical evidence 4
empirical techniques 5
encyclopaedic knowledge 126, 131
English converse pairs 78, 87
English word pairs 36, 42, 49, 82, 96,
    97, 103, 104, 106, 154–159;
    frequencies, t-scores and
    judgement ratings 160–164

Fellbaum, C. 17
frequencies, English pairs 160–164
frequency of co-occurrence (FoC) 40,
    78–81, 124–126

gender pairs 67, 106, 121, 124
German word pairs 4, 7, 154–159;
    frequencies, t-scores and
    judgement ratings 165–169
good antonyms 10, 16, 29–32, 112,
    124, 141
gradable opposites 49–53, 78, 96, 148
Gross, D. 97, 137

Hutchison, K. A. 71, 144

Jeon, H. 28
Johnson, M. 3
Jones, S. 17, 19, 20, 23–25, 91, 123
judgement ratings 160–164
judgement task analysis 39–43, 55,
    67, 75–78, 82, 86, 87, 90, 103, 104,
    125, 141

Kostić, N. 20

Lakoff, G. 3
language comprehension 26, 90,
    133, 136
language processing 121, 126, 133,
    137, 152
lexical decision tasks 11, 71, 151
lexical effects 4–5, 7, 8, 10–11, 27, 49,
    68, 91, 104, 133–137, 145, 146, 148,
    149, 151
lexical factors 5, 8, 23, 70, 146, 151
lexical or conceptual relation 21–23
lexical semantics 6
linguistic perspective 3
Lyons, J. 12–15, 30, 119, 148

markedness 11, 20, 145
medium categories 78–80, 106
medium pairs 78, 80
mental lexicon 133–137
methodological considerations
    150–152
Mettinger, A. 126
Miller, K. J. 97, 137
mind 21–25, 126–133
minimal difference 118–119
morphological relatedness 30, 39, 43,
    45–49, **50**, 84–85, 89, 106, 119–121
Muehleisen, V. 19, 97
Murphy, G. L. 22
Murphy, M. L. 23, 118

neurolinguistic evidence 28
nominal converses 61–62
nominal pairs 65–67, 85–87, 89, 97,
    103, 104, 107, 109, 124, 125
Norris, D. 136

opposite pairs 6, 20, 26, 29, 30, 36,
    70–92, 118, 127, 128, 137, 145
opposition entrenchment 126–133
orthogonal opposition 12

Paradis, C. 17, 18, 24, 26–27, 123, 128
participants, opposite pairs 74
predictor, antonymic strength 43–45
previous perspectives,
    antonymy 9–32
prototype category 126–127
psycholinguistic experiments 11

psycholinguistic model 26–32, 117–147; antonym canonicity 117–126
psycholinguistics 6
purity 62–67, 121–122

rationale, opposite pairs 71–72
reversives 12
rhetorical tool 11

salience 121–122, 130–131
Sapir, E. 12
Schmid, H.-J 132
semantic generality 53–55, 123–124
semantic range 53–55, 123–124; and non-propositional meaning 18–19
shared semantic range 48, 54, 55, 97, 99, 112
Smith, C. J. 10, 148
spatial opposites 39, 58
stimuli 73
structuralist account, opposition 11–12; classifications 12–15; 'good' opposites, criteria 15–16
symmetrical pairs 51, 84, 100, 122
symmetry 122–123; and conceptual

distance 49–53; of distribution 82–84
synonym 10
syntactic frames 17–18

task design 73
textual functions 19–20
Togia, P. 24
t-scores 74, 90, 160–164
type of antonymic relation 36–39

unrelated pairs 28, 39, 48

van de Weijer, J. 27, 28, 146
verbal converses 36, 45, 59–61, 86, 87, 93
verbal pairs 65, 86, 87, 121, 130

Wilbur, R. 3, 130
Willners, C. 26–27
word classes 4–5, 39–40, 62, 65, 73, 85–86, 90, 129, 134
word forms 22, 134, 141
WordNet 21, 22
word pairs 5, 6, 10, 42, 73, 74, 81, 112
Wu, S. 20

Milton Keynes UK
Ingram Content Group UK Ltd.
UKHW050144260424
441726UK00013B/62

9 781032 149592